# Spanish American Images of the United States

## 1790-1960

# Spanish American Images of the United States

## 1790-1960

JOHN T. REID

A University of Florida Book

The University Presses of Florida

Gainesville / 1977

Library of Congress Cataloging in Publication Data

Reid, John Turner, 1908–
  Spanish American images of the United States, 1790–
1960.

    Bibliography:   p.
    Includes index.
    1.   United States—Foreign opinion, Latin American.
2.  Public opinion—Latin America.  3.  United States—
Relations (general) with Latin America.  4.  Latin
America—Relations (general) with the United States.
I.  Title.
F1418.R395      301.15′43′973      77–3621
ISBN 0–8130–0547–7

TYPOGRAPHY BY MODERN TYPOGRAPHERS, INCORPORATED
CLEARWATER, FLORIDA

PRINTED BY MIAMI BOOK MANUFACTURING COMPANY, INCORPORATED
MIAMI, FLORIDA

*To Marian*

*whose endless patience I appreciate*

# Preface

Nearly every American who is interested in Latin America feels the urge to describe the image or opinion of the United States held by the other Americans of the hemisphere. It is a favorite, although often masochistic, conversational piece. Such descriptions may be based on casual personal experiences and desultory reading, or occasionally on a broad and scholarly knowledge of Latin America. There is lacking, however, a comprehensive, documented study of Latin American attitudes toward the United States and their historical development, although some very illuminating preliminary work in this field has been done by José de Onís, and pertinent material may be found in several informative volumes by Harry Bernstein.[1]

The purpose of this study is to make a further and modest contribution toward the clarification of the tangled question concerning the nature and extent of the vision of the United States in the minds of educated Spanish Americans over a period of nearly two centuries.

Stated in this way, the task seems overly ambitious indeed, and some explanation of the limitations of this survey is called for. First, there is the crucial question of sources. Ideally, a historical examination of attitudes would be based on a thorough content analysis of newspapers and periodicals published in Spanish Amer-

1. Onís, *The United States as Seen by Spanish American Writers* (an excellent study to which I am greatly indebted for guidance in preparing the first six chapters of this book); Bernstein, *Origins of Inter-American Interest: 1700–1812*. A doctoral dissertation by Elizabeth Rezner Daniel, "Spanish American Travelers in the United States before 1900," was also substantially helpful.

ica during the period and on the utilization of such private manuscript material and books written by prominent and representative
citizens as may be available. The study of modern and contemporary attitudes would ideally include, in addition to data from
published writings, the results of many carefully designed public
opinion surveys and an estimate of the influence of the mass media
on the formation of images of the United States.

For many reasons, some obvious, this study does not pretend to
have utilized the whole gamut of theoretically desirable sources.
For the most part, its sources are printed material, mostly in the
form of books written by prominent or representative Spanish
Americans. Most of these writers could be called "intellectuals,"
to use a very elastic term which may include men and women of
quite diverse callings. For the modern period the results of the
few available opinion surveys and of one newspaper content analysis have been considered as supplementary evidence.

How were the sources on which the study is based selected? The
first criterion was the generally recognized reputation and stature
of the author, not only in his homeland but in Spanish America
as a whole. Clearly, the opinions of such men and women as Francisco de Miranda, Simón Bolívar, José María Heredia, Domingo
Sarmiento, José Martí, Rubén Darío, José Enrique Rodó, and Gabriela Mistral are significant, not only for their intrinsic worth,
but also for the probable influence of their attitudes on their fellow citizens.

A second criterion was the fact that the writer had visited the
United States. This circumstance, we assume, would lessen the
probability that the writer's image of the United States would be
a mere stereotype based on hearsay and conventional wisdom.
This criterion explains the use of testimony from a few relatively
obscure visitors whose writings may have had a certain impact as
the impressions of eye-witnesses.

Furthermore, some attempt has been made to cite material that
gives a balanced geographic spread, especially in the modern period. This attempt has not been entirely successful, and opinion
from such countries as the Dominican Republic, Paraguay, Bolivia,
and some other countries is lamentably scant. No attention has
been paid to balancing opinions favorable to the United States
against those generally inimical to the Colossus of the North. As
it turns out, the source material exhibits a wide variety of opinions,
ranging from fairly rosy views of the *yanqui* and his civilization
to consistently critical attitudes. But, as will be evident, the images

of the United States in the minds of the majority of the witnesses typically show an ambivalent mixture of favorable and unfavorable impressions. They are complicated and multiple and, for the most part, do not constitute a single, logically consistent "super-image."

Still another limitation imposed by the author on his survey has been its restriction to that part of Latin America where Spanish is the official language. In their colonial heritage and in the circumstances of their births as independent republics, the Spanish-speaking countries had a unity of experience and thought patterns not shared by Brazil or Haiti. Even today there exists in Spanish America a loose cultural community, based on language and common traditions, which often tends to exclude other parts of Latin America. That community shares many common attitudes toward the United States that are somewhat different in their nature and historical roots from those developed in Brazil.

It may be superfluous to note that the images of the North American and his culture analyzed in this study are not necessarily the pictures in the mind of the Spanish American man-in-the-street. They are not, in other words, pure stereotypes. It is doubtless true that the authors cited formed their images partly on stereotypes and preconceptions current in their home society. Generally, however, the underlying pictures were retouched and refined by direct experience with North American life or by some degree of sophisticated reflection. It is doubtful that there is any accurate or dependable way of uncovering the stereotypes held by the average Latin American. One may honestly question whether he has, by and large, anything more than the most blurred and simplified picture of Americans and their civilization. Such opinion surveys as are available indicate that he possesses a limited knowledge of or interest in the world beyond his immediate habitat. A tentative formulation of some popular stereotypes is presented in Appendix 1.

In structuring the material of this survey it has seemed useful to disregard national boundaries and to treat the opinions collected as originating in Spanish America as an undifferentiated area. Sound objections to such a procedure may well be raised in view of the considerable diversity in national development and political experience with the United States among the eighteen Spanish-speaking republics. One might expect, for example, that a Mexican's view of his neighbor would differ markedly from that of an Argentine. To a limited extent this is true, but in the total mosaic of images of the United States resulting from the source material collected here one discerns a surprising uniformity of judgment, which generally transcends national lines. This unexpected uniformity is probably due to the fact, observable particularly in the twentieth century, that there is a real international community of intellectuals in Spanish America in which lines of communication are fairly numerous through periodicals, personal correspondence, travel, and international conferences. Whenever it has seemed pertinent, peculiarly national views have been noted.[2]

The analysis of the source material has been divided into three chronological segments: 1790–1825, 1826–90, and 1891–1960. I have resisted the temptation to include more recent material. To do so would bring in complications arising from important changes in the North American life pattern, and the task would, in fact, be a separate study. It will be apparent in this survey that the burden of interest and emphasis falls on the last segment, partly because the preceding periods have been the subject of previous studies, and partly because less source material has been available for them. Consequently the treatment of the images developed before 1890 is summary and in the nature of useful background, rather than as detailed as the presentation accorded to the more contemporary period. The value of historical perspective in surveying the modern images needs to be stressed. Generally speaking, twentieth-century opinions of the United States were not invented in this century and usually have their roots in the formative years of the New World republics.

The chapters covering each chronological period are prefaced by a brief description of the principal channels of information through which material for image formation may have become available, and by a discussion of certain background factors which influenced trends of opinion toward the United States.

A NOTE ON TERMS

Everyone who has dealt with inter-American questions has run into the minor but exasperating problem of how to refer to citizens

2. Even though it may be too sweeping, Frank Tannenbaum's judgment on this point is pertinent: "Latin America may be divided into twenty separate nations, but intellectually it is very much one community. . . . There is a community of public opinion which is as wide as the land that includes all of the nations south of the American border . . . and to no small degree this is the work of the intellectuals" ("Toward an Appreciation of Latin America," p. 57).

of the United States of America. One soon detects that in some Latin American quarters there is, quite naturally, some sensitivity about those citizens arrogating to themselves the name "Americans," a term Latin Americans frequently employ to identify themselves. *Estadounidense*, sometimes used in Spanish, is awkward even in that language and is untranslatable to English. *Norteamericano* in Spanish or in English translation leaves the careful scholar with the uneasy feeling that his Canadian and even his Mexican neighbors are being dealt with unjustly. There is really no good solution to the problem, and in this study I have simply taken the easiest way out by using more or less indiscriminately "North American," "American," "*yanqui*," and a variety of circumlocutions to identify the inhabitants of the United States. Sensitivities aside, I have considerable justification for not forsaking our own favorite term "American," since a surprising number of my Spanish American witnesses, from Bolívar to contemporary writers, are satisfied to let *americano* stand as descriptive of the United States citizen. *Yanqui* I have used frequently, especially in the third part of the study, leaving it in its Spanish form in order to avoid the Yankee–New Englander–Northerner concept. *Yanqui* refers to Americans in general and often has a pejorative connotation, ranging from downright dislike to faint disdain. I have usually avoided "gringo," so current in Mexico and Central America, because farther south the word is customarily applied to foreigners in general and European immigrants in particular.

In these pages the word "image" is used fairly frequently, although with some reluctance. It is a favorite catch-word in the advertising and public relations business and often seems to imply a vague connotation of falsity or manipulation. I have tried to employ the term without any such connotation and in a reasonably exact sense which may be explained as "a descriptive summation of percepts—what people see—and attitudes—how they feel about it" (Herbert Passin and John W. Bennett, "The American-Educated Japanese," *Annals of the American Academy of Political and Social Sciences* 295:83). Rémond, in his excellent study of French attitudes toward the United States, accepts "image" as a useful term, but would prefer "representation collective." "Attitude," "concepts," "conception," "view," and "opinion" all express one part of the meaning of "image" as I use the word, while "picture" (or "picture in the mind," as Lippman put it), as well as "vision," covers the other part.

"Stereotype," although similar in meaning to "image," has a

more negative connotation. A stereotype is an image which is highly standardized, rigid, widely held, oversimplified, relatively stable, and slow to change. (See a discussion of the meaning of "stereotype" in William Buchanan, "How Others See Us," p. 2.) In this survey, it often refers to the image said to be held by the "common man" in contrast to that described by visitors and relatively sophisticated commentators.

# Acknowledgments

I am grateful to the following publishers and individuals for granting me permission to use excerpts from the works indicated:

Dr. Harold E. Davis (*Latin American Social Thought*)

Dodd, Mead and Co. (Adams, *Latin America: Evolution or Explosion?*)

National Planning Association (May and Plaza, *The United Fruit Company in Latin America*)

Harcourt Brace Jovanovich, Inc. (Inman, *Latin America: Its Place in World Life*)

Harvard University Press (Crawford, *A Century of Latin American Thought*)

Dr. José de Onís (*The United States as Seen by Spanish American Writers*)

Princeton University Press (Joseph, *As Others See Us*; Bunkley, *A Sarmiento Anthology*)

Charles Scribner's Sons (Duggan, *The Two Americas*)

University of California Press (Torres-Ríoseco, *The Epic of Latin American Literature*)

University of Chicago Press (Gamio and Vasconcelos, *Aspects of Mexican Civilization*)

University Presses of Florida (Bernstein, *Making an Inter-American Mind;* Dozer, *Are We Good Neighbors?*; Merrill, *Gringo*)

University of North Carolina Press (González, *José Martí*)

University of Oklahoma Press (Zea, *The Latin American Mind*)

University of Pennsylvania Press (Burr and Hussey, *Documents on Inter-American Cooperation*)

University of Texas Press (Ramos, *Profile of Man and Culture in Mexico*)

Unless otherwise indicated, translations of quotations used in this study are mine.

Part of the research for this study was made possible by an Executive Fellowship from the Brookings Institution and a leave of absence with pay granted by the United States Information Agency.

# Contents

Contents

# Part One

# 1790-1825

# 1

# Underlying Factors and Channels
# of Information

When we consider how relatively limited was the direct acquaintance of Spanish Americans with the United States during this period, we may properly wonder if they had any picture at all of the northern republic. To most of them it must have seemed remote and legendary. Nevertheless, there was in the minds of at least many of the leaders of the struggle for independence a vision of the United States, however vague, shadowy, and distorted by abstract preconceptions. Before attempting to exhibit the nature of that picture, it will be worthwhile to review several factors in the Spanish American social and intellectual background which influenced the development of the image, and to identify the principal channels through which these leaders derived their meager information.

## ORIENTATION TOWARD EUROPE

Twentieth-century concepts of hemispheric solidarity, sometimes based on economic or political realities and not infrequently on wishful thinking, tend to obscure the fact that the intellectual orientation of the Spanish colonies achieving independence and later that of the new republics was toward Europe, and specifically toward France and Spain, rather than toward the United States. Even the documents of North American independence, which were a powerful stimulus to the early Spanish American patriots, often reached the colonists in revolt through French channels.[1] The first

1. According to the Chilean historian Barros Arana, some *criollos* in Chile had French translations of the Declaration of Independence; see H. C. Evans, *Chile and its Relations with the United States*, p. 12.

3

translations of the writings of Benjamin Franklin in Spanish America were made from French versions.[2] While a few brave souls, such as Camilo Henríquez, the Chilean patriot, and Hipólito Unánue, a Peruvian scientist and patriot, undertook to learn English, the ability to read English was uncommon. On the other hand, some knowledge of French was apparently usual among educated persons. Inventories of personal libraries of the time abound in French titles, and even those books about the United States consulted by Spanish Americans appear to have been for the most part the works of Frenchmen. Books in English by North Americans were in little evidence.

Even in the realm of revolutionary inspiration and the choice of models for political institutions, French influence was strong and evident. The United States provided an admirable working example of a free republic, and its political documents were considered worthy of imitation as structural plans; but the basic political and social theory of liberty as expressed by the French *philosophes* was particularly congenial to the Spanish American mind.[3] To a lesser extent British influence was operative, especially in the realm of economic theory.

THE CONCEPT OF A WESTERN HEMISPHERE

To a limited degree, the development during this period of what Whitaker has called "the Western Hemisphere idea"[4] influenced the attitude of Spanish Americans toward the United States. During colonial days, in both North and South America, a kind of incipient nationalism began to germinate, slowly and often unconsciously. Men of the New World, dealing with a different natural environment with its distinctive problems, ceased to regard themselves entirely as transplanted Europeans. At first their sentiments embraced only their particular corner of the New World, but at a later stage the embryonic national consciousness was expanded among a few thoughtful people to include, at least in an abstract sense, the whole of the Western Hemisphere. This process was stimulated by certain intellectual currents in Europe itself.

2. John E. Englekirk, "Franklin en el mundo hispánico," p. 325.

3. See Arthur P. Whitaker, ed., *Latin America and the Enlightenment*, pp. 47–50; Nicolas García Samudio, *La independencia de Hispanoamérica*, p. 58; and Charles C. Griffin, *The United States and the Disruption of the Spanish Empire*, p. 56.

4. Whitaker's *The Western Hemisphere Idea* is a detailed account of the development of this concept.

The eighteenth-century Enlightenment guided the minds of a number of educated men in Spanish and English America to dreams of reform and universal progress. The men who were influenced by the ideology of the Enlightenment were internationally minded, and sometimes the curiosity of Spanish American amateurs of science or social philosophers was awakened by what their confreres in the North were thinking or doing. Some feeling of kinship developed as among men who were striving to create, within the Enlightenment dream, a Utopia in the Western Hemisphere.

This relationship was evident among a small group of scientists in both parts of the hemisphere. In a series of documented studies, Harry Bernstein has shown that, however limited and fragmentary they were, scientific relations between Spanish America and the United States existed in the late colonial and early republican days.[5] There is no question that the rudimentary scientific speculation in the Americas depended heavily on European developments, but inter-American communication was by no means lacking. Benjamin Franklin's scientific experiments were an important link; as early as 1764, a Jesuit professor in Córdoba, Argentina, was ranking Franklin along with Newton and Descartes, and it appears that his electrical experiments and theory of the nature of electricity were known to professors in Buenos Aires and Caracas in the period 1780–1800.[6] Some of his scientific letters were published in the *Gaceta de Literatura de México* in 1789–90,[7] and Hipólito Unánue knew of Franklin's work and had a high opinion of him.

In other ways Unánue was a notable example of the way in which the ideals of the Enlightenment drew selected men of the Americas together. Reacting vigorously against the theory, publicized by the Comte de Buffon and Abbé Raynal, that the Americas produced immature and inferior types of animals and men, Unánue wrote his well-known *Observaciones sobre el clima de Lima*. Here he denied with considerable erudition and point by point the allegations of the European writers and made a more or less plausible case for the admirable qualities of man in the New World. It is significant to record that the Peruvian scientist was

5. See especially Bernstein, *Origins; Making an Inter-American Mind*; and "Las primeras relaciones entre New England y el mundo hispánico."
6. Guillermo Furlong, "The Influence of Benjamin Franklin in the River Plate Area before 1810."
7. Englekirk, "Franklin," pp. 324–25.

acquainted with and quoted from Thomas Jefferson's *Notes on Virginia*, which was also in part a defense against the anti-American speculations of Buffon and Raynal.[8]

In a less specialized sense, the idea that the peoples of the Western Hemisphere had a common destiny to pursue and defend against European pretensions had some currency among statesmen of the newly independent republics of the New World. In the United States, Henry Clay was not only the eloquent proponent of recognition of the new Spanish American republics, but also the defender of the great potentiality of Spanish Americans as citizens of the New World. He made clear his conviction of the essential unity of the Western Hemisphere republics when he said, "There cannot be a doubt that Spanish America, once independent, whatever may be the government established in its several parts, these governments will be animated by an American feeling, and guided by an American policy. They will obey the laws of the system of the New World, of which they compose a part, in contradistinction to that of Europe."[9] Jefferson was Clay's predecessor in believing in the uniqueness of a New World political mystique, and they represented a respectable body of opinion in the United States. Dr. William Thornton, a visionary soul and a great friend of Spanish America, went further than the mere recognition of a community of interests in the Western Hemisphere and drew up a detailed plan for an all-American federation of all the New World republics.[10]

In Spanish America the idea of a federation of American states was fairly common among the leaders and thinkers of the independence movement. Although ordinarily such an idea did not envisage the inclusion of the United States, a few of the more enthusiastic admirers of the northern republic carried the Western Hemisphere idea to its logical conclusion and referred to the possibility of a federation of all the American republics. Camilo Henríquez in Chile wrote a poem to celebrate on July 4, 1812, the independence of the United States. It read in part, "The illustrious New World is joined—In an eternal Confederation."[11] In a similar

8. A full account of this controversy is presented in Antonello Gerbi's *La disputa del Nuevo Mundo: historia de una polémica, 1750–1900*; see also Whitaker, *The Western Hemisphere Idea*, pp. 18–19, and Leopoldo Zea, *América como conciencia*, pp. 111–20.

9. Clay, *Works*, 6:145–46.

10. See Andrew N. Cleven, "Thornton's Outline of a Constitution for United North and South Columbia."

11. C. L. Chandler, *Inter-American Acquaintances*, p. 76.

lyrical vein, a writer in *El Satélite del Peruano* (March 1, 1812) exclaimed, "The whole vast extension of both Americas is what we conceive of as our fatherland. . . . All of us who inhabit the New World are brothers . . . worthy of constituting a nation."[12] Manuel Torres, Colombia's first diplomatic representative in the United States, had ideas of hemispheric unity which closely resembled those of Henry Clay and his followers.

Generally speaking, however, the plans and statements issued by the Spanish American founding fathers regarding a continental federation were limited clearly or implicitly to the new Spanish-speaking states. Bolívar, although he admired the United States in many ways, was opposed to any attempt to include the northern republic in his proposed federation.

In summary, we can say that the Western Hemisphere concept created among a few idealists in both North and South America a vague and abstract feeling of brotherhood, of being united in theory against a hostile or scornful Europe, and of sharing certain political ideals and destinies believed to be peculiar to the New World. Insofar as this concept was current among Spanish Americans, it directed their attention to the United States and helped to mold an attitude of respect and admiration.

### INVOLVEMENT OF THE IMAGES IN HOME AFFAIRS

A third background consideration of importance in an image study during this period, or indeed at any time, is a basic and obvious fact: rarely do concepts of the character of other nations and peoples exist apart from or unrelated to the problems and ideals of the society in which the observer and image-maker lives. Occasionally one reads the impressions of a relatively detached and objective commentator, such as Francisco de Miranda, the Venezuelan precursor of independence. But particularly in the impassioned days of the Spanish American Wars of Independence, concepts about the United States were usually woven very closely into the patterns of political and even personal controversy at home. These patterns inevitably dictated the fields of interest of the observer, swayed his selection of significant topics, and entered into his judgments of North American institutions, customs, and character. In other words, the views of Spanish Americans about the

12. Quoted in Luis Monguío, "Nationalism and Social Discontent in Literature," p. 65; J. B. Lockey refers to other statements of a similar nature in periodicals (*Orígenes del panamericanismo*, pp. 329–30).

United States are often data more important for the history of the nascent Spanish-speaking republics than for an estimate of their image of the United States.

Three controversies in Spanish America particularly involved the image of the United States, all of them relating to fundamental questions of the nature of the new states. The most important was the widespread debate between the proponents of a unitary government and those who believed in a federal system; in practically all parts of the Spanish New World there were often bitter engagements between the two schools of thought which continued throughout most of the century. A second controversy, less widespread but nevertheless significant, was that involving the monarchical ideal, usually constitutional on the British model, versus the republican system. The last debate, which from time to time inflamed the architects of the new governments, concerned the question of religious toleration in the constitutions of these governments. Since Spanish America was predominantly Catholic, this dispute was frequently acrimonious to an extreme.

## CHANNELS OF INFORMATION

The avenues of communication between Europe and both Anglo-America and Spanish America were far more numerous and open than between the Americas themselves. Language and tradition presented important barriers, and the isolation which the Spanish monarchy so frequently sought to impose on its American colonies did not encourage intercourse with the restless English colonies to the North or later with the United States. Even as the Spanish Americans gained their independence, means of exchanging information remained haphazard and scanty.

*Books and other publications.*—Toward the end of the eighteenth century and particularly as Europe became interested and aroused by the founding of the United States, a few books from Europe about the new republic to the North began to filter into the Spanish colonies. Among them was a *Diccionario geográfico-histórico de las Indias Occidentales o América*, compiled by an Ecuadorian scientist, Antonio de Alcedo y Bexarano, and published in Madrid in 1788–89. The *Diccionario* not only supplied a good deal of factual information about the geography and economic life of the new nation, but also gave a fairly full account of the former English colonies' struggle for independence. Probably because of the latter material, the edition was eventually suppressed in Spain, but there is reason to believe that this work became relatively well known in Spanish America and helped to form the image of the United States.[13]

A sampling of the few inventories we have of private libraries of the time reveals exceedingly few other titles which would give any information about the history of North America, not to mention contemporary conditions. In spite of the Spanish government's proscriptive measures, both Raynal's *Histoire philosophique* and William Robertson's *History of America* (in French or Spanish translations) were to be found on the shelves of some educated men; such information about the English colonies as these volumes offered must have provided a somewhat limited and not always dependable background for studious Spanish Americans. For example, in the inventory of one of the largest private book collections of the period discovered to date, the 394 titles, covering an exceptionally diverse range of subjects, include only Alcedo's *Diccionario* and Raynal's *Histoire* to enlighten the Mexican owner concerning his neighbors to the north.[14]

It may be that at least a few Spanish Americans read some of the considerable number of accounts of the North American experiment in forming a new nation written by Frenchmen who had visited or sojourned in the United States. Bolívar had a copy of the Chevalier Félix de Beaujour's *Apercus des Etats Unis au commencement du XIXᵉ siècle*.[15] In a controversy that raged in Venezuela in 1811–12, concerning religious toleration in the United States,[16] Juan Nepomuceno Quintana of the University of Caracas footnoted his fulminations against religious liberty in the United States with numerous writings of French observers.[17] It seems

13. Onís, *United States*, pp. 40–41. Onís gives the titles of six other volumes published in Spain between 1778 and 1812 that included at least fragmentary data about the United States. It is probable that some use was made of Jedediah Morse's pioneering *American Gazetteer*, perhaps in an Italian or Spanish translation; Manuel de Salas mentioned it as a source of agricultural information (*Escritos de Don Manuel de Salas*, 1:184).

14. Harry Bernstein, "A Provincial Library in Colonial Mexico, 1802."

15. Víctor Andrés Belaúnde, *Bolivar and the Political Thought of the Spanish American Revolution*, chap. 10, appendix.

16. This controversy will be discussed in some detail later.

17. Among them: D'Auberteuil, *Essais historiques et politiques sur les Anglo-Américains*; La Rochefoucault-Liancourt, *Voyage dans les Etats-Unis de l'Amérique*; Abbé Mably, *Observations sur le gouvernement et les loix des Etats d'Amérique*; Philip Mazzei, *Recherches historiques et politiques sur les Etats Unis*; Carlos F. Cardot, *La libertad de cultos*, pp. 364–75.

more than probable that the prolific journalistic productions of Abbé de Pradt (widely read in Spanish America) also provided, if not information, at least a variety of opinion about the United States, its political future, and its relations to the new Spanish American republics.[18]

The writings by North Americans which were most readily available and familiar to Spanish Americans were overwhelmingly political in nature. There is abundant evidence that many if not most of the early patriots had read the Federal Constitution of the United States, the Declaration of Independence, some of the works of Thomas Paine,[19] and the more famous early presidential addresses. Some of these were translated in books and periodicals published in South America; others were published in the United States in Spanish translation by Spanish Americans temporarily resident there, usually agents of the revolutionary cause. It is probable that some North American merchants and whalers visiting ports in South America carried with them copies of the basic documents and state papers of their homeland. There is no doubt that this literature not only fanned the flames of revolt and provided models for the new Spanish American political structures, but also, as we shall see, contributed to the formation of the dominant image of the United States in Spanish America.[20]

Other works by North Americans apparently were rarely encountered in Spanish America. Although the name of Benjamin Franklin and his reputation were well known, there is no evidence that his writings, except for a few scientific articles, were read by educated Spanish Americans. A translation of the *Autobiography*, which was to attain considerable popularity later in the century, was published in Madrid in 1798, but the generation of the Wars of Independence does not seem to have been generally familiar with it.[21] We have mentioned that Unánue knew Jefferson's *Notes*

18. Arthur P. Whitaker, *The United States and the Independence of Latin America*, pp. 102–7.

19. See Alfred Aldridge, "Camilo Henríquez and the Fame of Thomas Paine and Benjamin Franklin in Chile."

20. William S. Robertson, *Hispanic American Relations with the United States*, chap. 3, and Onís, *United States*, pp. 63–85, contain detailed information on this literature; Robertson presents a good survey of North American influence on early Spanish American constitutions. See Appendix 2 of this study for a condensed listing of several important translations.

21. Englekirk, "Franklin," pp. 339–42; Miranda read the *Autobiography*, apparently in French. A copy of *Poor Richard's Almanac* (translated as *Miscelánea*) was found in the library of the Peruvian patriot Luna Pizarro (ibid., p. 340). Furlong notes examples of Franklin's works in English found in Caracas and Buenos Aires during the late colonial years.

*on Virginia*; a few other kindred souls were acquainted with it also, doubtless in the French translation.[22]

Manuel García de Sena's translation (Philadelphia, 1812) of John M. M'Culloch's *Concise History of the United States* apparently had considerable influence in building an image of the United States. Henry Brackenridge, an American statesman and diplomat, writing from Buenos Aires, stated that it was read "by nearly all who can read."[23]

In short, with the exception of certain political documents, published material concerning the United States was a narrow channel through which flowed only trickles of information to Spanish America.

*Personal contacts.*—Opportunities for personal acquaintanceship between North and South Americans, which were almost nonexistent during colonial times, increased considerably in the years when Spanish America was achieving independence. Even then, however, they were limited and fleeting, largely determined by the events related to the Wars of Independence.

A small number of Spanish Americans visited the United States during this period (1810–25).[24] Most of them were official agents of the colonies in revolt who came to seek North American aid or to use the United States as a point of origin for their propaganda in favor of the revolution. Only a very few, such as José Felipe Flores, the scientist from Guatemala, or José María Heredia, the Cuban poet, came with no specific political motive in mind.

The others, from the nature of their missions, tended to be somewhat biased observers of the North American scene, who, for the sake of their efforts to spur the independence movement at home, viewed the new northern republic in a flattering and largely political light. Even though the picture presented by these visitors was clouded by abstractions associated with their theories concerning political institutions, it was undoubtedly influential in determining the kind of image held by Spanish Americans of the United States. They spread ideas about the United States by word of mouth on their return, often using the example of the new republic as a point of argument in their deliberations and conversations with their compatriots. Some of them wrote letters to their family and friends, and a good number wrote books, most of which

22. Robertson, p. 83, and Irving Leonard, "A Frontier Library, 1799."
23. Pedro Grases and Alberto Harkness, *Manuel García de Sena y la independencia de Hispanoamérica.*
24. See Appendix 3 for a list of Spanish American visitors and their writings.

were avowedly propagandist publications but in some instances included a respectable amount of information about the United States.

North Americans likewise found their way to the new Spanish American republics. Long before the United States recognized them in 1832, special agents and occasionally consuls were officially sent to Latin America. Usually they were charged with reporting on political developments in the rebellious colonies, but some interpreted their often ambiguous orders as authorization to foment and aid the insurgent cause, in spite of the neutral policy of the United States. Among those who were actively sympathetic to the ideal of Spanish American independence were Joel Poinsett (1810–14, Argentina and Chile), William Shaler (1810, Cuba), and Henry M. Brackenridge (1817, Argentina).

These and other agents were well-educated and cultivated men eager to know the culture of their host countries; they occasionally acted as informal cultural emissaries. Several used their talents to write books about Spanish America. Because of their often high calibre and their sympathy for Spanish American problems, it is likely that many of them contributed to the formation of a positive image of their native land.[25]

Less is known about the citizens of the United States who took part in the Spanish American Wars for Independence. During the whole period from the first rumblings of separatist action to 1822, hundreds of individuals from the North participated in a struggle for freedom in which they either believed deeply on ideological grounds, or which seemed profitable or adventuresome to support. Considerable numbers of North Americans were engaged in military activities organized by Francisco de Miranda in Venezuela, Xavier de Mina in Mexico, and José Miguel Carrera in Chile, to mention only a few examples. There is little evidence to tell us what sort of picture of their homeland these warriors left behind; we know that certain individual volunteers aroused admiration and perhaps affection, and it may be, as Robertson says, that "those citizens of the United States who joined the insurrectionary armies made the republic of the North seem like a living example to some Spanish Americans."[26]

25. See J. Fred Rippy, *Joel R. Poinsett, Versatile American*; Roy F. Nichols, "William Shaler, New England Apostle of National Liberty"; Eugenio Pereira Salas, *Henry Hill, comerciante, vice-cónsul y misionero*, and *Jeremías Robinson, agente norteamericano en Chile, 1818–1823*.
26. Robertson, p. 64.

In spite of legal restrictions imposed by Spain, ships from the English colonies and later from the United States made their way to Spanish American ports, especially in the Caribbean. Even in the seventeenth century there was some commerce between Boston and Yucatán, and by the end of the eighteenth century United States vessels were stopping in the Río de la Plata, Valparaíso, and Callao; some were whaling ships and others traders on their way to China and India.[27]

Sailors and merchants on some of these ships were carriers of North American political ideas. A royalist Chilean churchman complained, "The clandestine trade and permission to fish for whales introduces traders and adventurers from the United States into all the coast, islands, and other Spanish possessions, giving them the opportunity to convince the Spanish colonists of the flourishing state and advantageous situation of their own country, decrying the Spanish colonial government and subjection to the mother country in Europe as ignominious slavery . . . they have adopted and put into practice the most powerful means to undermine and destroy the political and religious edifice of the Spanish colonies. . . ."[28] Liberal propaganda was introduced in the form of copies of the Declaration of Independence, books, newspapers, conversation, and allegorical charms and medals.

Thus, these North Americans helped to form in the Spanish American mind an image of the United States as a significant and progressive example of freedom. What other impressions they left during their short visits it is difficult to estimate. Many were relatively well educated New Englanders endowed with intellectual curiosity, and it is possible that some were considered representative of a literate, cultured young nation. On the other hand, the cocky, boastful nationalism of others and their self-righteous intolerance of Catholicism undoubtedly created a distasteful picture of their native land, especially among the more conservative Spanish Americans.

Aside from transient seamen and merchants, a few other citizens of the United States made their home in Spanish America, temporarily or for long periods of time. Most of them were engaged in some kind of business and were concentrated chiefly in Mexico City, Havana, Buenos Aires, and Santiago de Chile. We know that some of them, like David Curtis de Forest in Buenos Aires, Henry

27. See Bernstein, *Origins*, chap. 3.
28. Quoted in Onís, p. 31; see also Bernard Moses, *The Intellectual Background of the Revolution in South America*, pp. 39–41.

Hill in Chile, William Davis Robinson in Caracas, and Stephen F. Austin in Mexico, were sympathetic to the Spanish American struggle for independence and lent their substantial aid. On the whole, these expatriates probably furthered respectful and friendly relations between North and South America.

# 2

# Early Images of the United States

The most universal Spanish American vision of the United States was seen through the lens of hero worship for George Washington. To summarize abstractions in the person of a hero is a common habit, and in Spanish America, hero worship has been a particularly eloquent mode of political thought. Regardless of the political complexion of the commentator or his opinions of the United States, writers were practically unanimous in their praise of and reverence for Washington. In this respect, they may well have been imitating a similar cult in France.[1] And, of course, every observer was aware that in the United States itself Washington became almost deified.

Even those who regarded the United States as a nefarious example for their new republics paid homage to the first North American President. Dr. Antonio Gómez of the University of Caracas, while prophesying eventual ruin for the North American republic because of its federative system and its religious tolerance, piously evoked Washington's emphasis on religion and morality as bases for political action.[2]

Among unconditional admirers of the United States like the crusading patriots Vicente Rocafuerte (Ecuador) and Miguel de Pombo (Colombia), the Washington cult took on almost religious tones. Rocafuerte referred to "the delicate plant of freedom which may only be found in the shade of the laurels and cypresses which

1. René Rémond, *Les Etats-Unis devant l'opinion française, 1815–1852*, 2:558–60.
2. Cardot, *La Libertad*, p. 244.

cover the tomb of the immortal Washington."[3] He described Washington as "the glory of the human race, the hero of all centuries, the true great hero of impartial history: he was prudent as Fabius, as active as Marcellus, as unselfish as Cincinnatus, more sublime than Caesar. . . ."[4] Pombo waxed equally rhetorical when he wrote, "illustrious geniuses of Washington and Franklin, you who have so justly deserved the title of legislators for the New World and who with your wisdom and virtues illumined the spirits and molded the hearts of your fellow-countrymen so that they should not falter in the struggle for independence: We Americans of the South call upon you in similar circumstances! Come in our midst, teach us to love moderation, frugality, disinterest, the spirit of union and the other virtues which are the bases of republics. . . ."[5]

The patriots whose general view of the United States was moderate also paid high tribute to Washington. Manuel Belgrano, one of the sturdiest of the Argentine insurgents, translated and published the "Farewell Address" and referred, in the preface, to Washington as "that hero worthy of admiration and loyal patriotism" (Onís, p. 82). It is said that Belgrano carried this document with him on his military campaigns.[6]

Another Argentine, Mariano Moreno, even though he was doubtful of the value of the North American federative system in Spanish America, looked upon Washington with almost religious devotion: "Your principles and your system would be sufficient to guide us:—lend us your genius so that we may accomplish the results which we have contemplated."[7]

Simón Bolívar professed great admiration for Washington, with whom he was often paired in the pantheon of heroes, and on occasion he spoke of him in praiseful terms. When his friend, the Abbé de Pradt, compared him with Washington, he replied, "The parallel which you have drawn between Whasington [sic], Napoleon, and myself is more daring than exact. Washington surpassed me in moral and religious virtues, as he also surpassed all men in modesty and patriotism."[8] In Bolívar's time of troubles toward the end

3. *Ideas necesarias a todo pueblo que quiere ser libre*, p. 10. Future references to this book will be found in the text.

4. *Ensayo político*, quoted in Onís, *United States*, pp. 74–75. Future references to Onís will be found in the text.

5. Quoted in García Samudio, *La independencia*, pp. 102–3. Future references will be found in the text.

6. Quoted in Chandler, *Inter-American Acquaintances*, p. 58.

7. Quoted in Robertson, *Relations*, p. 83.

8. Quoted in M. Aguirre Elorriaga, *El Abate Pradt en la emancipación hispanoamericana*, p. 329.

of his life, he said, "If my heart does not deceive me, I shall follow in the footsteps of Washington and shall prefer a death like his to being Monarch of all the earth."[9] In 1826, George Washington Custis and Lafayette presented the Liberator with a medallion bearing a miniature portrait of George Washington by Gilbert Stuart. Writing to thank Lafayette, he referred to Washington as "the Great Citizen, the First-Born Son of the New World . . . the noble protector of social reforms."[10]

It is probable that some of the qualities attributed to Washington were also believed to characterize North American society in general. Considering the general view of North Americans at the time, it would appear that at least Washington's moderation, frugality, and moral virtues were thought to be shared by his compatriots.

To a somewhat lesser extent, the memory of Benjamin Franklin was venerated in Spanish America. We have noted that his reputation as a scientist was well established, but that less was known of his role as Founding Father. Nevertheless, he was often referred to in the panegyrical terms used in the case of Washington. Miranda mentioned "the sublime and universal genius of the wise Franklin . . . this great friend of society."[11] When the Colombian Antonio Nariño was arrested and tried for spreading seditious ideas, the Spanish authorities found a portrait of Franklin in his study, and during his trial he is said to have declared, "Oh country of the Franklins, of the Washingtons, of the Hancocks and of the Adamses, who is not glad that they lived both for themselves and for us!" (Onís, p. 64). Francisco José de Caldas, another Colombian patriot, wrote, "There are still kept in Auditor Alba's strongbox the portraits of Franklin and Washington, those guiding geniuses of America, which the Auditor had seized from Nariño's house in the year 94 to be used as evidence in the trial." Indignantly, he continued, "Are not the busts of these heroes reproduced and scattered throughout Europe and the whole world? Any literary man, any politician, any man of taste—did they not have at that time the image of those illustrious Americans as the best adornment of their studies and parlors?" (García Samudio, pp. 63–64).

The story is told that when in 1811 the Argentine envoys, Belgrano and Echeverría, came to say goodbye after parleying with

9. Quoted in W. R. Shepherd, "Bolivar and the United States," p. 275.
10. Quoted ibid., p. 276; see also Onís, p. 70.
11. Quoted in Englekirk, "Franklin," p. 328.

the Paraguayan dictator, Dr. José G. R. Francia, he offered them a steel engraving of Franklin hanging in his office, and said, "This is the first democrat in the world and the model we should imitate."[12]

Although full admiration for Franklin did not develop in Latin America until the middle of the nineteenth century, he seems to have symbolized even for the early patriots the wise and humanitarian aspects of the North American character. They, of course, were not alone in their worship of Franklin; in France and in Europe generally he was regarded as a legendary symbol of many qualities frequently considered typical of the United States.[13]

POLITICAL INSTITUTIONS: THE UNITED STATES AS A MODEL

Some of the more enthusiastic Spanish American patriots held the United States as a perfect example to imitate, first as a people who had broken away from European domination, and later as a political model to follow as closely as possible. As early as 1785, a London journalist said, "The flame which was kindled in North America, as was foreseen, has made its way into the American dominions of Spain. The example of North America is the great subject of discourse and the grand object of emulation."[14] One of the earliest of the revolutionary documents, a letter written in London in 1792(?) by Father Juan Pablo Viscardo y Guzmán and circulated by the insurgent leaders in Buenos Aires and by Miranda, stated, "The bravery with which the English colonies of America have fought for the liberty which they now so gloriously enjoy covers our indolence with shame. We yield to them the palm with which they, the first people of the New World, have been crowned with independent sovereignty" (García Samudio, p. 25). Even Bolívar, who had reservations about the North American political system, said, "The United States, the sons of England, were the first to point out to us the path of independence."[15]

The more radical patriots declared in rhapsodic tones that the United States provided the ideal pattern to emulate in building new institutions. Rocafuerte, making an impassioned defense of the republican form of government as opposed to monarchical, exclaimed, "the most perfect government is the [North] American,

12. Chandler, p. 67.
13. See Rémond, 2:570–91.
14. Quoted in J. Fred Rippy, *Latin America in World Politics*, p. 27.
15. Letter to the United States Chargé d'Affaires, 1826; quoted in García Samudio, p. 9.

the only one where man enjoys the greatest advantages of society with the least possible bondage." He acclaimed the United States as "the only hope of oppressed peoples . . . the only beacon which guides man in the course of his happiness" (*Ideas*, pp. 5, 11). Miguel de Pombo made the same point explicitly: "Which is the people we should imitate and whose political constitution must serve as a model for the one we are going to make for ourselves? That people is in our same continent, the people of the United States, that people made up of philosophers to whom was reserved the glory of communicating to South America the principles of its representative governments and the kind of wise confederation adopted in all its republics" (García Samudio, p. 102). It is true, as Robertson has demonstrated,[16] that a good many of the early Spanish American constitutions were modeled, to varying degrees, on that of the United States.

## THE DISSENTERS

But by no means were all of the revolutionary leaders unreservedly committed to imitating even the basic principles of the political structure of the United States. Some of the more thoughtful were aware of the enormous differences in background and temperament between Spanish and Anglo-America. Simón Rodríguez, the tutor of Bolívar, said, "Spanish America cannot imitate the United States, for they are unlike except that they both have a form of government with the same name: republic. . . . Our America should imitate . . . neither Europe, which has no practical skill in politics and is corrupt in its customs . . . nor the United States, whose circumstances are entirely different."[17] Bolívar expressed similar sentiments: "I must say that it has never for a moment entered my mind to compare the position and character of two states as dissimilar as the English American and the Spanish American."[18] The Colombian statesman José Manuel Restrepo was even more forthright: "There is as much difference between the sons of the Spaniards and their colonies, and the former English colonies, as there is between day and night."[19] Both Bolívar and Bernardo Monteagudo of Argentina recognized that the United States, before

16. Robertson, chap. 3.
17. Quoted in Leopoldo Zea, *The Latin American Mind*, p. 95.
18. Address at Second Angostura Congress, 1819; in Harold E. Davis, *Latin American Social Thought*, pp. 21–22.
19. Letter to Jared Sparks; in H. B. Adams, *Jared Sparks*, 2:328–29.

independence, "was educated in the school of liberty," as Monteagudo said, and was heir to many of the political institutions
of Britain.[20]

The greatest stumbling block in using North American institutions as a model was, for a respectable group of the early Spanish
American nation-makers, the federative principle. While men like
Rocafuerte, Pombo, and a great many others insisted that federal-
ism was the key to future prosperity and happiness, the two great
liberators of South America, San Martín and Bolívar, were firmly
opposed to the federal scheme, and they had their followers. San
Martín remarked that even in a relatively stable country like the
United States the federal system had shown its weakness in the
War of 1812 and that South America was certainly not ready for
such a system.[21] Bolívar admitted the theoretical virtues of North
American federalism, but rejected it as a workable structure for
the new republics of the South: "The more I admire the excellence
of the federal Constitution of Venezuela [modeled on that of the
United States], the more I am convinced of the impossibility of
its application to our state." "It is a marvel," he added, "that its
prototype in North America endures so successfully and has not
been overthrown at the first sign of adversity or danger."[22] Although Bolívar on several occasions expressed high regard and
admiration for the character and virtues of North Americans, he
was suspicious, not only of federalism, but of their basic political
system: "Until our compatriots acquire the political virtues and
talents of our brothers of the North, systems which are entirely
popular, far from being favorable for us, may, I fear, become our
ruination."[23] Writing to a British friend, Colonel Belford Wilson,
in 1829, he repeated his doubts: "It is unfortunate that we cannot
achieve the happiness of Colombia with the laws and customs of
the North Americans. You know that this cannot be; it is even less
probable than for Spain to be like England."[24]

In the minds of many of these men there was a real fear of
excessively democratic institutions, where power was placed in

20. Quoted in Moses, *Intellectual Background*, p. 155. Bolívar said that
the United States was "cradled in liberty, reared on freedom" (Davis, p. 21).
21. Robertson, pp. 86–87.
22. Davis, p. 21; similar doubts about the durability of the federal system
were expressed by Monteagudo (Moses, p. 155).
23. In the so-called Letter from Jamaica, in John E. Englekirk, et al., *An
Anthology of Spanish American Literature*, p. 101.
24. In *Selected Writings of Bolivar*, ed. Harold A. Bierck, 2:729; for further views of Bolívar on this subject see his "Memorial" of December 15,
1812, cited in Moses, p. 283.

the hands of the people and not with a properly prepared elite. Such a fear was explicit in Miranda's mind as he observed the republican processes at work during his trip through the United States. A great admirer of English institutions (as was Bolívar), "he was occasionally startled at the extremes to which he thought the spirit of democracy had carried the people."[25] In Boston, Miranda wrote, "On various occasions I attended the meeting of the General Assembly of the legislative body of the State, where I was able to see in a most marked manner the defects and inconveniences of placing the legislative power in the hands of entirely ignorant persons." He then cited the example of one legislator who recited silly verses and another who could not keep track of the question at issue. Innkeepers, blacksmiths, etc., they lacked the education and status to do their job properly. When Miranda met Samuel Adams, one of the political questions he raised was "in a democracy whose very basis was 'virtue' should not a proper place be given to this quality? Particularly as the exact contrary was the case, and all distinction and power is given to Property, which is really the poison in a Republic such as this." In what was perhaps the first Spanish American criticism of materialism in the United States, Miranda complained that young Bostonians were wasting their substance on imported finery and observed, "commerce will always be the principal ruination of Democratic virtue. . . . So this is the simplicity and equality of peoples!"[26]

## THE LAND OF HUMAN RIGHTS AND RELIGIOUS TOLERATION

High among the North American virtues admired by Spanish Americans was the prevalence of political freedom. José María Heredia, the Cuban poet, even though homesick, suffering from the unfamiliar cold, and bewildered by a "barbaric tongue," hailed the United States as "the land of liberty, in which an immense asylum is opened up to all the oppressed of the world," where they would be protected by just laws.[27] Rocafuerte referred to Philadelphia as the "asylum of the oppressed, the center of rights, the bulwark of liberty," and Camilo Henríquez praised "that love of liberty, that zeal for social rights, that undying hatred of servitude

25. *The Diary of Francisco de Miranda*, ed. William S. Robertson, 2:237–38.
26. J. H. Stabler, *Fragments from an Eighteenth-Century Diary*, pp. 59, 61. Future references will be in the text.
27. Heredia, *Revisiones literarias*, p. 131. Future references will be in the text.

and oppression which inspired those regions and which brings to them daily so many immigrants from all parts of the world. There great souls have found an inviolable refuge."[28]

The working of the judicial system in the United States aroused praiseful comment from some observers. José Bernardo Gutiérrez de Lara, a Mexican patriot, in connection with his visit to the prison in Philadelphia, marveled at the course of even-handed justice and quoted a prisoner as being in entire agreement with the sentence dealt out to him.[29] Miranda wrote, "During this period, I went many times to the Court of Justice; I really cannot express my pleasure and satisfaction at seeing the admirable system of the British Constitution in practice—Great Heavens! What a contrast to the Spanish system of Government!" (Stabler, pp. 35–36).

Of all the freedoms attributed to political life in the United States, none aroused such discussion as the toleration of multiple religions and sects. Opinion on this issue ranged from Rocafuerte's assertion that religious toleration "has strengthened the social bonds among the whole population"[30] to the strident insistence of a Venezuelan conservative that the North American concept of man being individually answerable only to his God was "heretical, impious and detestable, an infamously authorized pretext for committing without punishment all kinds of crime and evil. . . ."[31]

Vicente Pazos, the Bolivian Indian advocate of independence, wrote, "But the history of the United States teaches the consoling truth, that civil and religious liberty has transformed her trackless forest . . . into the garden of the world; where cities have sprung up; manufacturing, art, sciences, and commerce flourish; and where a system of legislation has been established which Solon and Lycurgus never imagined. . . ." More specifically he claimed that "the practical lesson afforded by the United States leaves no doubt that religious liberty and the rivalry of different sects is the best means of maintaining in their purity the morals of the people" (Onís, pp. 80–81).

In a similar vein, the Irish propagandist for Spanish American independence, William Burke, published in 1811 in the *Gaceta de Caracas* a strong defence of religious toleration and alluded to the

28. Quoted in M. L. Amunátegui, *Camilo Henríquez*, 1:62.
29. Gutiérrez de Lara in his diary, p. 290. Future references will be in the text.
30. Rocafuerte, *Cartas de un americano*, no. 7. Future references will be in the text.
31. Cardot, p. 364.

experience of the United States: "In spite of this liberty, there certainly is in no country a group of clergymen more pious, nor a people more religious, moral, and orderly than the North Americans." He claimed especially that the superiority of Pennsylvania in commerce, the arts, and science, as well as its prosperity, was proof of the beneficial results of religious toleration.[32]

Following the publication of this article, an explosion of rebuttal burst forth from the brethren of the Church and other advocates of the status quo. Dr. Antonio Gómez, a professor at the University of Caracas, warned that the United States, because of its federative system and its tolerance of heretical sects, was headed for catastrophe. It would be a shame, he says, echoing popular hero worship, "that the venerable ashes of Franklin should be whirled about among the ruins of North American independence."[33] Juan Nepomuceno Quintana, also of the University of Caracas, attacked from a different angle. Quoting French sources, he claimed that the English colonies before independence and the United States afterward were in reality terribly intolerant, and cited the persecution of Catholics and Quakers. Actually, he said, the much-vaunted tolerance in North America is simply indifference: "The government of the United States of America is in a certain sense a government without God and without religious law." He painted an apocalyptic picture of the result: "the mass of the North American people presents the image of a great Free-Mason lodge in which men, drawn together from all climes and countries, with all languages and beliefs, by a monstrosity without precedent in human history, strive only to build and to plant, live as if they would never die, die as if they had never sinned—heaven is a farce, eternity a dream, and death only the end of life's miseries." Quoting at length from Abbé Mably about the probable sad fate of the United States, the Venezuelan professor concluded that "the Anglo-American system, as far as religion is concerned, cannot serve as a model for any nation."[34]

Although there was a definite anti-clerical trend among some of the Spanish American revolutionaries, there is little doubt that such statements must have left a profound impression among the more pious and conservative citizens of the new republics. We do not know to what extent such ideas were circulated, but as late in this period as 1823, the United States agent in Buenos Aires

32. Ibid., pp. 197–98.
33. Ibid., p. 244.
34. Ibid., pp. 369, 371–75.

reported that the Buenos Aires press was printing aspersions "not only on the character of our government, but on the total want of religion and honor among North Americans."[35]

There existed among some Spanish Americans, incidentally, considerable curiosity and interest regarding several Christian sects in the United States. Miranda was amused and sometimes annoyed by odd religious practices during his North American sojourn; adult baptism, the public confession of sins, and the puritanical Sabbath struck him as peculiar. In South Carolina he was reprimanded for playing his flute on Sunday and said, "all countries on earth, even the most civilized, have their stupid superstitions" (Stabler, p. 31). He believed that the Unitarians had gone too far in their denial of the reality of the Trinity. He was, however, often favorably impressed by North American religious toleration: "Each person praises God in the language and manner dictated by his own conscience. There is no dominant religion or sect,— all are good and equal." But, by the same token, he objected to churchmen influencing legislation in New Hampshire, and to several state constitutional requirements that legislators be Christians.[36] Miranda visited a Quaker meeting and praised the Friends, even though he found the simplicity of their meetinghouse very dull.[37] Another traveler, Gutiérrez de Lara, attended a Methodist revival meeting in New Orleans and gave an interested, sympathetic account of the emotional spectacle.[38] Minister Joaquín Campino of Chile was amazed that in Philadelphia every man had to go to some church, and that there were ninety-seven churches in the city.[39]

William Duane, a North American journalist visiting the Venezuelan town of Mérida in 1822, found the people there very inquisitive about the United States; they expressed great surprise on learning that so many sects live together harmoniously, that the clergy wore no gowns, and that Congress had chaplains of various sects. "Some of the citizens who were present," Duane said, "expressed their admiration of the institutions which produced so much concord . . . and some of the clergymen concurred."[40]

35. Griffin, *The United States and the Disruption of the Spanish Empire*, p. 260.
36. Robertson, *The Diary of Francisco de Miranda*, pp. 50, 118, 134.
37. Stabler, pp. 42–43; José Manuel Restrepo also found the Quakers admirable (*Autobiografía*, p. 135).
38. Robertson, *Diary*, p. 294.
39. Letter in Salas, *Escritos*, 2:257. Future references will be found in text.
40. Duane, *A Visit to Colombia in the Years 1822 and 1823*, p. 301.

## THE COLOSSUS OF THE NORTH

Although it was not a dominant note, the idea of an imperialistic United States threatening the integrity of the new nations—a concept which later in the century became so persistent—was occasionally voiced. A Cuban, Francisco Arango y Parreño, in a communication to the Cortes of Cádiz in 1811, referred to the potential future power of the United States and said, "in the North, there is growing a colossus composed of all castes and languages that threatens to swallow, if not all of our America, at least the northern part of it. . . . The only escape is to grow along with that giant, sharing with him his very breath of life" (Onís, p. 48). Although it is open to various interpretations, some have seen in a statement of Bolívar's made in 1820 a hint that he foresaw imperialistic designs on the part of the United States: "North America, pursuing its arithmetical round of business, will avail itself of the opportunity to gain the Floridas, our friendship, and a great hold of commerce."[41]

There is no doubt that Luis de Onís, Spain's diplomatic representative in the United States from 1809 to 1819, did all in his power to cultivate and propagate the fear of North American expansionism. In his *Memoria sobre las negociaciones entre España y los Estados Unidos de América . . .* , published first in Spain in 1820, he warned the emerging Spanish American nations: "The [North] Americans at present think themselves superior to all the nations of Europe; and believe that their dominion is destined to extend now to the Isthmus of Panama and hereafter over all the regions of the new world."[42] The *Memoria* was republished in Mexico in 1826 by the British Minister during his campaign to discredit the United States, and perhaps was in the mind of the first Mexican Minister to the United States, Manuel Zozaya, when he wrote in 1822, "The haughtiness of these republicans will not allow them to look upon us as equals but merely as inferiors, and in my judgment their vanity goes so far as to believe that their capital will be that of all the Americas."[43] Onís' book is said to have received wide distribution, and the Chilean Minister Campino

---

41. Quoted in Shepherd, "Bolivar and the United States."
42. Quoted in William R. Manning, *Early Diplomatic Relations between the United States and Mexico*, p. 279; see J. Fred Rippy, "Introduction" to Manuel Ugarte's *Destiny of a Continent*, p. xi, and Onís, *United States*, pp. 48–49.
43. Quoted in Rippy, "Introduction," p. viii.

sent it to his friend Salas, stating, "Its idea of the physiognomy of the country, its customs, its manners, and its policies is entirely accurate" (Salas, 3:258). Onís also wrote to leaders in Spanish America stressing the imperialistic plans of the United States, and some of the letters were published in journals in Buenos Aires and Chile (Onís, p. 48). British agents at the Congress of Panama tried to use his ideas to create fear of the United States. Although there was some reflection of Onís' propaganda in Mexican periodicals,[44] it is not apparent that it was very convincing to many outside of Mexico. Possibly the position and nationality of Onís subtracted from his credibility.

Obviously, it is impossible to point to or describe any single opinion of political institutions in the United States held by Spanish Americans. There were many of them, and they depended to a great extent on the political and religious persuasion of the person in question. If one can make a loose generalization, it seems certain that a large number considered those institutions as nearly ideal, even when not applicable to their own lands; a minority thought they might be dangerous from several points of view and were doubtful of their ability to endure. Manuel de Salas, a Chilean scientist and educator, probably represented the middle-of-the-road view of a substantial number of thinking citizens: "If our republics would limit themselves to proposing an imitation of what is solid and useful [in the United States], in place of imitating precisely the wrong things, then we might come near to being what they are like" (Salas, 3:85).

### THE CHARACTER OF NORTH AMERICAN SOCIETY

*Social institutions.*—In Spanish America, most observers of the United States were so preoccupied with the political contours of the northern republic and implications for their own countries that very few of them examined in any detail the social characteristics of North American life. Among the ardent proponents of the United States political system, it became almost commonplace to state that the prosperity, social well-being, and the generally desirable state of society in the United States were direct products of the political structure and would follow in any nation adopting that structure.[45] This attitude indicates a certain shallowness in their understanding of the early North American scene, which

44. Griffin, p. 68.
45. Restrepo's conclusions are a good example (*Autobiografía*, p. 148).

often is apparent in the little they have to say about social institutions in the North.

*Social equality.*—Closely related to the Spanish Americans' vision of political equality as characteristic of the North American system was the fact, surprising to most of them, that social equality, or at least a free-and-easy mingling of social classes, prevailed in the United States. Miranda was not too pleased to note during his travels that lowly servants and the boy who took care of the carriage horses ate at the same table as the gentry, and he related that he had real trouble in getting separate meals for his own servant. In North Carolina he went to a barbecue where a keg of rum melted class distinctions: "the first magistrates and gentlemen of the region ate and drank promiscuously with the most untutored and lowly kind of people, shaking hands and drinking from the same glass; it is impossible to conceive of a more democratic sort of gathering."[46] Even in those days, however, the degraded situation of the Negro did not go unnoticed. After describing in fairly favorable terms the House of Correction in Baltimore, Minister Campino remarked that most of the inmates were Negroes who were picked up, jailed, and fined if they walked on the streets at night. This, he noted, would be "something which would scandalize your Bill-of-Rights enthusiasts" (Salas, 3:253).

*A land of little ceremony.*—Even more striking to the Spanish Americans was the lack of ceremony and formality, particularly among the leaders of the nation. Rocafuerte argued that a republic, as exemplified in the United States, was much better and cheaper than a monarchy since the President received a modest salary and was not surrounded by obsequious courtiers (*Ideas*, p. 9). Simón Rodríguez, after describing the propitious soil in which democracy had thrived in the United States, claimed that citizens there spoke without affectation, and that they considered public office a patriotic responsibility and not a means of gaining and displaying their prestige and power. "In the United States (and this comes to them from the English)," he said, "the President, the cabinet ministers, and all the magistrates are called by their names, and not, as in South America, by fancy titles."[47] The difference in this regard between his own country and the United States also was noted by Pazos who remarked on the general lack of pretension in North American society and on the absence of ceremony in the treatment of the President (Onís, p. 81).

46. Robertson, *Diary*, pp. 6, 82–83.
47. Quoted in Zea, *The Latin American Mind*, p. 8.

*Education and reading.*—With their faith in progress through education, born of the Enlightenment, it was inevitable that the Spanish American patriots should have been impressed by the attention given by North Americans to schools. Camilo Henríquez, whose information was second-hand, placed this regard for education high in his catalogue of virtues in the northern republic: "Education, this great principle of public prosperity, the guarantee of constitutional liberty, has not been forgotten [in the United States]. In almost all the states public schools have been established so that the poorest man does not have to endure the sorrow of seeing his children raised in ignorance."[48] Vicente Pazos also stressed the importance of popular education in the United States as a preparation for widespread newspaper reading and successful independent government (Onís, p. 81).

Rocafuerte, after noting the prodigious increase in schools and colleges in the United States of his time, added that literary and other periodicals had grown correspondingly in number and circulation (*Cartas*, no. 7). Echoing a European observer who claimed in 1791 that "all ranks and degrees now read," Henríquez painted a truly idyllic picture: "In every house, even the poorest, you find books and periodicals. Everybody reads, thinks, and speaks with freedom. The industrious man, coming home from his work, reads, improves his mind and compares his happy state with that of people who are weeping under an oriental despotism."[49]

As for higher education, Gutiérrez de Lara remarked on his tour of Philadelphia that the College of Philadelphia (i.e., the University of Pennsylvania) was an admirable institution (p. 290), but Miranda was harsher in his judgment of Harvard, which he visited in 1784. The dormitories were "comfortable, but without any decoration or taste"; the library was clean and well enough organized, but the Museum of Natural History had a meagre and badly exhibited collection. In summary, Miranda concluded, "this institution is better calculated to turn out clergymen than able and well-informed citizens . . . it is an extraordinary thing that there is not one chair of modern languages and that theology is the principal subject in this college. The manner of dressing, of comporting oneself and behaving in Society are matters to which not the slightest attention is paid, and therefore the appearance of the students is the most ill favored of any students of this kind which

48. Amunátegui, 1:62.
49. Quoted in Russel B. Nye, *The Cultural Life of the New Nation, 1776–1830*, p. 250; Amunátegui, 1:62.

I have ever seen" (Stabler, pp. 63–64). It might be recalled, of course, that Miranda was known as something of a dandy and man-about-town, extremely fond of society.

*The general welfare.*—Progress in other social institutions that impressed Spanish Americans, although not to the degree true later in the century, related to penal institutions, hospitals, and in general to the care given to the social well-being of the citizens. Miranda made a sweeping assertion: "in all my observations and travels through this Country . . . never did I find one individual who appeared to be naked, hungry, ill, or unemployed."[50] Even Heredia, who certainly was no sociologist, was surprised at the absence of beggars or signs of poverty; everybody seemed to be busy (p. 38). Doubtless Bolívar had an abstract concept of social welfare in mind when he referred to the United States as "a beneficent government that, with an able, active, and powerful hand, ever and everywhere, guides all its springs of action toward social perfection, which is the sole end of human institutions."[51]

It is interesting and perhaps significant, in view of subsequent developments in the Spanish American republics, to note that at least one commentator was convinced that the North American system of small, individually owned plots of agricultural land was a clue to prosperity. Miguel de Pombo, in an address to the Supreme Junta in Bogotá, 1810, said, "Let us imitate then the procedure of the Anglo-Americans and, like them, divide up the land insofar as possible in as many plots as we have citizens" (García Samudio, p. 103).

On a still more specific plane, Gutiérrez de Lara, when he visited Philadelphia, was amazed by and filled with admiration for the treatment of inmates in the prison, the cleanliness and order of the hospital (particularly the kitchen), and the organization of the almshouse (p. 292). Later in the century, incidentally, prison reform, and especially the Philadelphia experiment, commanded the curiosity and study of both Spanish Americans and Europeans.[52] The Chilean Joaquín de Campino, no unconditional admirer of the United States, wrote to his friend Manuel Salas a detailed account of the methods used in the House of Correction in Baltimore. Salas replied that he found the account as useful as

50. Robertson, *Diary*, p. 49.
51. Address at Angostura quoted in Shepherd, pp. 279–80.
52. Vicente Castro (Cuba) and Manuel Payno (Mexico) visited the United States on this account in mid-century (Onís, p. 110); for French interest in prisons see Rémond, 2:562–65.

would be advice from Franklin and that he intended to initiate similar reforms in Chile (Salas, 3:81).

*The position of women.*—North American women, in addition to stimulating some flattering comment on their physical beauty (Heredia, Miranda, Gutiérrez de Lara), also aroused surprise and interest because of their social status. Gutiérrez de Lara noted in passing that in Kentucky wives worked incessantly, but it was Miranda who made the most complete exploration into the status of women in the new republic. Through his chain of letters of introduction, Miranda met a great many women in society in various cities, and his reaction to North American women varied slightly depending on the city and probably on the way they received him. Although he observed that unmarried girls had freedom to go about as they wished without social criticism, he judged them vain, bashful, and deficient in elegance and the social graces because their social life was restricted to their own tea parties.[53] Married women, on the other hand, "keep a monastic seclusion, and such a submission to their husbands as I have never before seen!" They spend their lives devoted to their husbands and their houses (Stabler, pp. 29–30). These observations, we may suppose, can be interpreted either as a tribute to a high moral code or as an attribution of stupidity.

*Arts and literature in a republic.*—The status of the arts in the United States was the subject of relatively little comment among Spanish Americans. Camilo Henríquez, who was positive about the progress of farming, manufacturing, and social welfare in the northern republic, was of the opinion that its inhabitants "lag behind in painting and sculpture."[54] A traveler like Miranda, on the other hand, was greatly impressed by Charles Willson Peale's collection of a hundred portraits "of considerable merit" in Philadelphia. He not only found them pleasing to a cultivated foreigner like himself, but also a stimulus to virtue and patriotism among the young. "Certainly it makes an example to be followed by other nations which appreciate virtue and good taste" (Stabler, p. 37). Both Gutiérrez de Lara (p. 284) and Heredia (p. 44) were interested in Peale's museum, but apparently it was the skeleton of a mammoth exhibited there that attracted their attention. About the only good thing Miranda had to describe at Harvard was the Hall of Philosophy, which was "well-proportioned and spacious" and

53. Stabler, pp. 30, 58; these observations were exactly those of the Frenchman St. Mery (Nye, p. 138).
54. Quoted in Evans, *Chile*, p. 12.

displayed some portraits and engravings by John Singleton Copley (Stabler, pp. 36–37).

The youthful Heredia was charmed, as were most Spanish American visitors, by the beauty of Philadelphia as a city. Its regularity, the square city blocks, the wide streets aroused his admiration. But Heredia's tribute to early American architecture was unique. Among the public buildings that he described, the Bank of the United States took first place. This structure, "of the simplest and purest Grecian taste," was, he said, "the most beautiful I have seen on the face of the earth" (p. 42).

With the exception of Heredia, the Spanish American visitors appear to have paid no attention to the faltering efforts of the United States in the field of belles lettres. While they eagerly acquainted themselves with the political literature, they gave no indication that they were aware of the early quest for a national literature as exemplified in the works of Bryant, Irving, and Cooper. Heredia, the exception, lived in the United States from 1823 to 1825. In addition to publishing the first edition of his poems in New York in 1825, he apparently familiarized himself with North American literary life and, several years later in Mexico, published appreciative reviews of Irving's *Life of Columbus* and of Cooper's novels.[55]

While the embryonic artistic development of the United States was far overshadowed in the Spanish American mind by the political picture, it was not lost sight of by all observers.

*Characteristic traits of North Americans.*—If, as we have seen, the Spanish Americans' vision of social life and institutions in the United States was fragmentary and imprecise, their picture of the typical traits of character among their hemispheric neighbors and their concept of how the latter differed from themselves or from Europeans were even more generalized, abstract, and frequently meaningless. This fact is understandable in view of the usually fleeting nature of their actual contact with North Americans, and particularly because stereotypes of the American character among Europeans, and even among North Americans themselves, were as yet only in the formative stage. It would not be until much later in the nineteenth century that the hard-riding cowboy, the cigar-chewing businessman, the slave of the machine, the naïve, virtuous country lad, and other crystalized national character images would emerge to provide what seems to be an indispensable framework

55. See Manuel Pedro González, "Two Great Pioneers of Inter-American Cultural Relations."

within which foreigners think about the characteristics of other foreigners. Moreover, as in the case of the social structure of the United States, the Spanish Americans were more absorbed in the blueprints for political construction produced in the North than in the character of the people who produced them.

It is true that some of the finer minds of the nascent republics were aware that political institutions arise from the character of the people. Bolívar accused the framers of the first Venezuelan Constitution of "believing that the blessings they [the North Americans] enjoy result exclusively from their form of government, rather than from the character and customs of the citizens." The Liberator did not, however, outline in any detail the nature of that character except to refer briefly to the North American people as "a singular model of political virtue and moral rectitude"—a rhetorical phrase at the best.[56]

Rocafuerte included in one of his *Cartas de un americano* (no. 7) a list of traits which were supposed to characterize the inhabitants of the various states and territories of the republic. For the most part, they are trivial, complimentary, and extremely general, and the principal recurring trait is the addiction to strong drink in so many parts. Since this listing was part of Rocafuerte's series of statistical tables which he had obviously lifted from available sources, it is not likely that they represented any personal opinions or impressions on his part, and it is doubtful that this mishmash of almanac material created any clear images in the minds of his readers.

To judge from the meagre primary sources used in this chapter, the principal character traits which symbolized the people of the United States in Spanish American eyes may be reduced to three: industriousness, cleanliness, and a sense of order.

We have seen that the prosperity of the new republic was attributed typically to the excellence of its political institutions, but direct observers of the North American scene also noted that the citizens worked hard to create the well-being and abundance which often dazzled them. A passage in Miranda's *Diary* probably gives as representative a view of the industrious North American as any. In New England he observed that the land is poor; "nevertheless, such is the industry and spirit which liberty inspires in these people that from a small plot of land they take enough to maintain their large families, pay heavy taxes, and live with comfort and

---

56. Address at Angostura, in Davis, p. 23.

pleasure, a thousand times happier than the proprietors of the rich mines and fertile lands of Mexico, Peru, etc."[57]

The travelers' accounts are filled with happy references to the clean conditions in which North Americans lived. Even though Gutiérrez de Lara suffered some squalid, frontier experiences on his trek from the Mississippi to Washington, he remarked on the general elegance and neatness of the homes at which he stayed, and in Baltimore he was impressed by the clean fashion of dress. Heredia was fascinated with the waterworks in Philadelphia that supplied the city abundantly with clean water for domestic and public use (p. 44). Miranda, as he traveled from North Carolina to Boston, was constantly amazed and pleased by the comfortable, clean lodgings in which he stayed. In describing Philadelphia, which he considered "the largest and most beautiful in all this Continent," he stressed, like Heredia, the clean water supply available in public wooden pumps and the neat, spotless homes of the city (Stabler, pp. 36–37).

Philadelphia was also the showplace and symbol for the orderliness which came to be associated with the North American character. The inhabitants' civic sense of responsibility was everywhere manifest, the visitors thought, in the straight streets, the brick sidewalks, the street lights, the efficient orderly work of the fire companies, the tranquility imposed by organized watchmen and police, the good management of the hospital, and even the uniform height of the brick dwellings.

Whether or not this North American trait of trying to organize daily life in a neat fashion produced an entirely favorable view of the American character is open to question. Heredia, for example (p. 46), found the climate of the United States unbearably cold and missed the human noise of Havana, but also, he confessed, found the orderly regularity of Philadelphia tiresome. "Call me a fool if you will, but that is the truth. I like better the brilliant disorder of New York."[58]

## THE LIMITATIONS OF THE IMAGES

It has been obvious in this survey of Spanish Americans' attitudes toward the United States during this period that their concept of the North American republic was woefully incomplete. This situation may be due in some measure to the absence or unavailability

57. Roberston, *Diary*, p. 129.
58. See, for example, Restrepo's comment, p. 128.

of pertinent data for the present-day investigator, and it is possible that a thorough examination of family papers, obscure periodical files, American sea-captains' documents, and the like would reveal a wider spectrum of knowledge and opinion concerning the complex life of the United States at the beginning of the nineteenth century.

But even in the light of more abundant data it is likely that Spanish Americans would appear to be truly uninformed about large segments of the civilization, values, and problems of the United States. The significance of the movement toward the West, the growing gap between the Eastern seaboard and the frontier, the proud and desperate search for a national identity with its resulting boastfulness, the germs of fratricide latent in slavery, the practical problems involved in making a new political system work—all these and many other broad aspects of North American life were largely ignored by those Spanish Americans who were attentive to the North American experiment.

They were likewise unaware of or uninterested for the most part in the myriad of little social habits and attitudes which were beginning to characterize the inhabitants of the United States as non-Europeans. If they sensed imperfections in the tumultuous model republic, they either garnered them for debates on home-grown questions, or—more often—swept them under the rug of an ideal vision to be imitated.

In short, they were behaving as the members of most human societies do when they are confronted with an alien culture. They were generally not concerned with it except insofar as selected and partial images of it could be meaningfully fitted into the pattern of their own problems.

# Part Two

## 1826-1890

# Climates of Opinion and Points
# of Contact

$A$s the southern republics began to acquire distinctive identities, the factors which influenced their views of the United States became more varied and complex than in the period of independence. While opportunities for communication between the two halves of the hemisphere increased, conditions within the new republics and events on the international scene changed the outlines of the images of the United States held by Spanish Americans. We will take a summary look at some of the forces working in the background and the means by which knowledge about the United States was acquired.

## PROBLEMS OF NATIONAL GROWTH

For the first four decades at least after the victory of the wars for independence, the Spanish American republics were to a large extent isolated from the United States. Their attention was perforce centered on the grievous problems of trying to devise for themselves viable governments and economies. In the majority of the newly independent states, the ideals of the founding fathers were not being realized in anything approaching a satisfactory manner. With some exceptions, such as Chile, anarchy alternated with tight personal dictatorships; constitutions were made and unmade with unseemly frequency; revolutions and civil strife were the rule, not the exception; the economic life of the new nations suffered and often floundered badly. For these reasons and others the shining northern model of political perfection to which the early patriots had looked with such hope now seemed far away and often chimerical. Two factors, however, served to keep the United States in their minds.

One was the fact that political exiles, not only from caudillo-ridden republics but particularly from Cuba, often found their way to the United States. In New York, a Spanish American traveler was always sure of finding a sizeable group of exiles who spoke his tongue. Benjamín Vicuña Mackenna, a Chilean statesman, for example, was delighted in 1856 to meet there Generals Paez and Mosquera, at one time so prominent in the politics of Venezuela and Colombia, as well as José Antonio Irizarri, the roving Guatemalan statesman.[1] Literary exiles were very common, José Eusebio Caro and Gustavo Arboleda of Colombia and Juan Clemente Zenea of Cuba being notable examples. It is said that at one time some 125 periodicals were published in the United States by Cuban exiles (Onís, p. 17). These émigrés not only formed images of their temporary home, but influenced the education of other Spanish Americans as to the nature of the strange northern republic.

The persistence of the image of the United States as a political model was maintained throughout most of the period by the fact that the great debate between partisans of a unitary form of government and those of a federal solution continued in many of the new republics. As Domingo Sarmiento said, "Half of the republics —Mexico, Central America, Colombia, the Republic of Argentina— have involved themselves in revolutions in order to become federalist states like the United States" (Onís, p. 185). The originally unitary ideal of Sarmiento himself was modified to include federalist elements as a result of his experience in the United States. Many of the proponents of the federal system were disciples of North American political theory, and those who advocated a centralized political structure, like Lucas Alamán and his cohorts in Mexico, were frequently in opposition to North American ways.

The question of religious toleration, which so exercised the earlier patriots, also persisted as a live issue, and the example of the United States lingered in the minds of liberals as a kind of paragon. Men like Vicente Rocafuerte and Francisco Bilbao were stalwart champions of shearing the political power of the Catholic Church, and they still looked to the United States for their inspiration.

1. Benjamín Vicuña Mackenna, *Páginas de mi diario*, p. 91. Future references will be in the text.

Toward the middle of the century a change began to be evident in the intellectual climate of most Spanish American states. By then it was becoming apparent to many thinkers and statesmen that the political solutions adopted so eagerly at the time of independence were hardly an adequate prescription for the health of new republics with a Hispanic background. Seeing the smooth working of democratic institutions seriously hampered by endemic anarchy and despotism and aware that Spanish America was lagging far behind the rest of the Western world in material and social progress, many lost the facile optimism of the revolutionary period. Influenced by British empiricists and utilitarians and by Comte's positivism,[2] they tried to be realistic and practical and to search out the reasons for the retarded state of their republics. The liberally minded thought that their emancipation from Spain was only half complete. As they reasoned, it was also necessary to free their minds from the Hispanic tradition, to substitute modern education for scholasticism, scientific attitudes for mysticism and fatalism, railways for convents, fresh immigration for the indolent criollo strain. While theoretical inspiration for these advocates of scientism came from France and England, many of them saw in the United States a pattern of progress in which health and energy, directed toward practical, orderly goals, had brought within a democratic framework railroads, factories, steamships, and increasing material amenities. For men like Domingo Sarmiento, Francisco Bilbao, José Victorino Lastarria, and, to a certain extent, Juan Bautista Alberdi, one of the important problems was to discover the practical secret of North America's saga of progress and success. Consequently, their images of the United States often included some definition of that secret. The material progress of some of the republics from 1870 to 1890 (Argentina, Chile, and Mexico particularly) may have been in part a consequence of the pragmatic and imitative approach of these and other planners.

## THE IDEAL OF CONTINENTAL UNITY

While the desire to emulate the material advances of the United States was a significant element in the ideology of many liberals, there coexisted a growing apprehension of the northern republic

2. See Zea, *América como conciencia*, chap. 7, for a good account of positivism in Spanish America.

as a threat to their national integrities. This fear, coupled with uneasiness in the face of occasional acts of European aggression, led many Spanish American leaders to recall the old ideal of Spanish American unity, so cherished by some of the founding fathers. There was a good deal of eloquent talk about the need for some kind of a federation or defensive alliance among the Latin republics, and periodically congresses were convened to consider this and other mutual problems. The results of these meetings were not substantial; never were all the republics represented, and the agreements reached were seldom implemented. Nevertheless, they served to accentuate a factor that was increasingly to influence the nature of the Spanish American image of the United States: the cultural abyss which was believed to separate the nations of the Latin tradition from the United States with its Anglo-Saxon background.

Although a minority opinion in these debates favored an invitation to the United States to join the proposed federation of American states,[3] it was generally made clear that the basic aim of the efforts toward unity was to consolidate spiritual and physical power against an alien danger. Especially at the conferences called in Lima (1847–48) and in Santiago de Chile (1856), fear of the Colossus of the North was rampant, and concerted defense was advocated. Alberdi, admirer as he was of some North American political institutions, saw no reason to include the United States in the federative design. "I consider frivolous," he wrote in 1844, "our pretensions to form a common family with the English republicans of North America. If their political principles are what calls us to community, then, why not the Swiss? . . . Certainly the North Americans have never refused us toasts and written compliments, but I do not recall that they have fired a cannon shot in our defense."[4]

Juan Manuel Carrasco Albano of Chile not only rejected in 1855 any idea of including the United States in the continental confederation, but defined as the union's objective "to impede successive usurpations by the North American colossus." Guided by the concept of inevitable conflict between the Germanic and Latin "races," which was to gain wide acceptance later in the century, he foresaw that the tension between the two parts of the hemisphere was a far-flung battle between the "poetry, enthusiasm, and abnega-

3. For example, Francisco Paula González Vigil of Peru in 1856; R. N. Burr and Roland Hussey, *Documents on Inter-American Cooperation*, 1:119–28.
4. Quoted ibid., 1:93–94.

tion" of the Latin race and the material force and "ominous influence of self-interest" of the Germanic race.[5]

José María Samper of Colombia also saw in 1859 a conflict between "the degenerate and spurious democracy in the oldest of the republics" and "the Colombian race," which he defined in terms of cultural and moral unity rather than physical characteristics. The proposed union of Spanish American nations in Samper's vision would oppose slavery, intervention, filibustering, the government of oligarchies, lynch law, and commercialism; he left little doubt about the identity of the enemy of the Spanish American federation.[6]

These two seemingly incompatible currents of thought—the fascination with North American material progress and the urge toward unity in the face of a threat from the north—are of particular significance for the theme of this study because they help to explain the ambivalent attitudes in the Spanish American mind toward the United States as will be evident in later discussion.

### THE UNITED STATES AND SPANISH AMERICA

For its part, the United States during most of this period paid relatively little attention to Latin America. This negligence was part of its isolationist preoccupation with internal development and domestic problems. Building new cities, canals, railways, and fleets of ships, exploring and settling the expanding western frontier, to say nothing of wrestling with the gigantic problems of slavery, were tasks enough to keep even the *yanqui* occupied. During the earlier decades of the period the mystique of Manifest Destiny germinated and developed, and, as a result there arose the only major involvement with Spanish America—the annexation of Texas and the Mexican War, with its sequel of territories added to the Union.

Indirectly arising from the acquisition of California were the filibustering expeditions of William Walker in Central America, episodes that we count as minor in our histories of the United States, but which galled the Spanish Americans as much as, or even more than, the Mexican War. Walker, a Tennessee-born advocate of slavery and Manifest Destiny, believed that the route across

5. Quoted ibid., 1:110–12.
6. Samper, in Sociedad de la Unión Americana, *Colección de ensayos y documentos relativos a la unión y confederación de los pueblos hispanoamericanos*, pp. 344–69.

Nicaragua to the California goldfields, established by Commodore Vanderbilt, should logically be American territory. Therefore, in 1856, taking advantage of the invitation of a dissident Nicaraguan political faction, he and fifty-six fellow adventurers sailed to Nicaragua, seized power, and set up a Walker-managed government that was recognized by the United States. Assailed by forces from other parts of Central America, he surrendered to a United States navy vessel in 1857, filibustered again in Honduras, and was finally captured and shot by Central Americans in 1860.

The Mexican War, a central episode in the expansionism of Manifest Destiny, and the Walker affair, seemingly peripheral incidents in the national life of the United States, were powerful determinants of the attitudes taken by Spanish Americans toward their northern neighbor, especially before the Civil War. That bloody struggle changed our relations with Spanish America to some extent. Lincoln and the North felt the need of foreign support and consciously wooed the other American republics, using as talking points the crusade against slavery, the preservation of democratic principles, and the allegation that the former imperialistic aspirations of the United States were in reality the result of southern Confederate doctrine, and that Walker's adventure was a pro-slavery proposition. Whether because of the Union's propaganda or because of sincere sympathy for the Union cause and increasing fear of European aggression, the fact is that liberal attitudes toward the United States during the Civil War were relevantly benevolent and sympathetic; it was, as one scholar says, "an episode of unparalleled friendship."[7] Salvador Camacho Roldán, a Colombian economist, some years after the war, still held the conviction that the North fought for noble ideals in a way which inspired high admiration. "The war-cry," he wrote, "was no longer one of fury, vengeance, and extermination; it was a cry of tenderness the like of which I have not seen in the history of any other war, except possibly that for the freedom of Greece."[8]

After the Civil War, the intense industrialization of the United States and the rising tendency among very vocal publicists and politicians in the United States to raise the sights of Manifest Destiny toward the Caribbean and Panama disquieted and frightened many Spanish Americans. While, as we shall see, there was eager

7. Nathan L. Ferris, "The Relation of the United States with South America during the Civil War."

8. Camacho Roldán, *Notas de viaje*, p. 886. Future references will be in the text.

contemplation of the wonders which post-war industrialism was bringing to the wealthy colossus, there was also renewed fear of the power there represented, and perhaps a bit of irascible envy.

## FACING TOWARD EUROPE

Lest what has been said imply that Spanish Americans of this period were deeply and exclusively engrossed in watching, fearing, and imitating the United States, the well-known fact of their continued dependence on Europe for ideas, cultural trends, and even fashions should be repeated and emphasized. As a matter of fact, both Americas looked to the Old World for inspiration for their intellectual life and often learned about each other from a European source. While Henry Clay and others were reading Humboldt as an authority on Spanish America, the books of French and English travelers in the United States were often the source of the Spanish Americans' images of that country. Tocqueville in particular was widely known to them and was not infrequently cited as an authority on the northern republic. Lastarria referred to "the powerful voice of the immortal Tocqueville" and admitted, "He revealed the existence of a mighty republic where democracy is a reality."[9] The French writer's glorification of the Puritan origins of the United States was frequently reflected in the chronicles that are the source material of this study. The views of other European travelers or pundits were often cited, either in agreement or rebuttal. Alberdi, in his introduction to the life of William Wheelwright, quoted Herbert Spencer at length to prove that all was not perfect in North American life,[10] and Lastarria copied pages of Macaulay adverse to the United States only to refute the Britisher's gloomy view (pp. 36–37). Sarmiento seemed continually to have in the back of his mind his reading of European authors and conversations with Europeans about the United States, mostly to contradict them. With reference to North American culture, he wrote, "I have not spoken with a Frenchman or an Englishman who has not ridiculed the knowledge of the North Americans, limited according to them to reading, writing, and the few notions they pick up from their newspapers" (Onís, p. 107). José Milla (Guatemala) told a satirical anecdote about a boardinghouse in

9. José Victorino Lastarria, *Obras completas*, 7:96–97. Future references will be in the text.
10. Alberdi, *La vida y los trabajos industriales de William Wheelwright*, pp. 28–30.

New York frequented by various nationalities, all critical of the United States. The French made fun of Central Park, American food, and *yanqui* manners; the Italians scorned American musical tastes; the Germans ridiculed the lack of philosophy in the United States; and the Hispanic Americans all claimed their own countries were more advanced than the *yanqui* republic.[11]

In this connection, it is a significant fact that many of the Spanish translations of American literature that were read in Spanish America were made from French translations of the originals. This was natural since French was the preferred second language of the educated classes, and not a few of them were educated in France. In their own literary production, although attempts were made to give national content and spirit to the novels and poetry, the literary fashions of England and Europe found automatic echoes in Spanish America.

Thomas McGann, discussing Argentina in the 1880s, describes the Argentines as money-mad, but at the same time yearning to be civilized. "And Europe was civilization to these Argentines. Europe's inventions and gimcracks were imported and her fads and ideas transmitted by the newspapers to the hungry *porteño* public." The United States, in contrast, received scant attention in the press. "North American coal production and railroad construction or the water system of New York City were matters which the pragmatic *porteño* occasionally found instructive, but his interest ended there."[12] Even though this state of mind may have been particularly notable in Argentina at that time, to some degree it was common to the elite of most Spanish American countries during a good part of the century.

In spite of the occasional fits of fear and anger at European infringement of their sovereignty, the average Spanish American intellectual of the last century admired Europe and looked to it for cultural and intellectual sustenance. The United States, its material progress, and its cultural life were constantly compared with European norms. This triangular base of allegiance—the homeland, Europe, and the United States—was responsible, I believe, for many of the slippery ambiguities that may be detected in their views about the northern republic.

11. Milla, *Un viaje al otro mundo*, p. 147. Future references will be in the text.
12. McGann, *Argentina, the United States, and the Inter-American System*, p. 38.

### YANKEE SEAFARERS

Probably the most direct contact with the United States experienced by Spanish Americans during most of this period resulted from the visits of American ships. This was true at least until the Civil War. The money value of North American trade with Latin America increased considerably during the entire period under discussion, climbing from a total (imports and exports) of $25 million in 1830 to $241 million in 1890.[13] As far as personal contact is concerned, however, this startling increase is deceptive. In the early years of the century, the bulk of this trade was carried in American vessels manned predominantly with American officers and crews. Even as late as 1860, two-thirds of the total foreign trade of the United States was in American bottoms. But after the Civil War, due partly to depradations during the war and partly to the absorption of Americans in internal development, fewer American ships were evident on the seas; in 1900 only 9.3 per cent of our foreign trade was transported in United States vessels.[14] For example, in 1885, the American Consul in Buenos Aires reported that during the year, 1,153 British ships and 1,126 French vessels had arrived and departed, but not a single ship flying the American flag.[15] Furthermore, in the few American ships on the seas the percentage of American crew members declined progressively.[16]

In the heyday of American shipping, however, American ships and sailors were a common sight in Havana, La Guaira, Montevideo, Buenos Aires, Valparaiso, Callao, and Panama. American-built vessels, especially the legendary clipper ships, were famous in Spanish America. Sarmiento said, "The Yankee ship is the best, cheapest, and largest in the world . . . the king of the universe."[17] Whaling ships also put in occasionally to Spanish American ports, providing some opportunity to get acquainted with North Americans. With the lack of easily available data, it is difficult to say what kind of impression American sailors made in the ports where they appeared. It is possible that they generally reinforced the

13. Robertson, *Hispanic American Relations with the United States*, Appendix.
14. J. E. Otterson, *Foreign Trade and Shipping*, chap. 8.
15. McGann, p. 91.
16. Samuel Eliot Morison, *The Maritime History of Massachusetts*, pp. 352–55.
17. *A Sarmiento Anthology*, pp. 224–25. Future references will be in the text.

image of the *yanqui* as a domineering, haughty person. Vicuña Mackenna described the American seafarer as a typical, tough North American conquistador, whose "noblest pleasure is to gaze from the masthead on the grandeur of the sea which they have dominated" (p. 100). Reading Dana's *Two Years before the Mast*, one can imagine the attitude with which even a well-bred seaman might treat the Spanish Americans whom he saw on his voyage, and the impression of smug disdain that he must have left behind. Dana wrote, "There are no people to whom the newly invented Yankee word of 'loafer' is more applicable than to the Spanish American." While he was attracted by the fine manners and proud bearing of the Spanish Californians, he considered them "idle, thriftless people," given to extravagance, gambling, and corruption. Their political system was corrupt, subject to constant revolutions, with "no law but will and fear."[18]

It is certainly unlikely that the vast crowds of gold-seekers who came around the Horn or crossed Panama in the 1850s left very pleasing memories behind. Vicuña Mackenna recognized that they were hardly typical of North Americans and called them "those thieving bands which in 1849 and 1850 thronged Valparaiso in transit to San Francisco, who were not Americans but the trash of the world; our dockworkers did well by sweeping them off the piers with the handles of their oars" (p. 104). Sarmiento, however, with jovial cheeriness, took a different view. As he told it, Panama, before the building of the railway, was a ruined city which was revived and made prosperous by the coming of American ships and travelers across the isthmus. In fact, he claimed, Colombia had been so influenced by daily contact with the Americans that it had remodeled its political institutions (*Anthology*, p. 311).

### MISSIONARIES

To a negligible extent the Protestant missionaries in Spanish America helped to form images of the United States. There were few of them in the first half of the century, and they never became numerous. It appears that the first American Protestant services were held entirely for the benefit of the small English-speaking populations. In 1823, two American Presbyterians began meetings in Buenos Aires that continued until 1836. In that year a Reverend John Dempster was sent by the Methodists to found a church in

18. R. H. Dana, *Two Years before the Mast* (Garden City, N.Y., 1959), pp. 45, 75–78, and chap. 21.

the Argentine capital, and the Presbyterians joined his congregation, which, by Rosas' decree, was limited to the English-speaking colony. One can judge its restricted influence by the fact that this "Mother Church of Methodism in South America" had only twenty-six members in 1846 and that the first sermon in Spanish was not preached there until 1867. An American Protestant church was founded in Valparaiso by Rev. David Trumbull in 1846, but it also served the foreign colony for the most part and probably ministered to the sailors and passengers in transit on American ships. In 1856, the Presbyterians began their labors in Colombia, establishing a church in Bogota in 1861. They also proselytized in Mexico, beginning in 1872, and the Episcopalians started missionary work in Cuba in 1884. By then, there were American missionaries and mission stations in practically all of Spanish America, representing one or another denomination.

Beginning about 1860, mission schools were founded in many of the republics. By 1864, free Methodist schools for the poor, giving vocational instruction, were functioning in Buenos Aires, and in 1870 the same denomination established schools in Rosario, Montevideo, and Asunción. In 1876, the Presbyterians opened the Instituto Internacional (later called Inglés), and the Methodists opened Santiago College, both of which were to become splendid institutions patronized by leading Chilean families. An American school for girls was founded in Bogotá by the Presbyterians in 1869, and later one for boys was founded.[19]

Protestant missions naturally encountered opposition from the Catholic Church, especially in Colombia, Peru, and Ecuador. In a few cases, they were actively welcomed by the government authorities, either because of their educational activity or as a potential force in the liberal-conservative struggle over the official position of the Catholic Church. In Mexico, at least, the legend—which in this century became so common—that the missionaries were the vanguard of imperialism, was circulated at the time of the Mexican War. A Mexican historian, Francisco Cosme, wrote, "Protestant propaganda is an anti-patriotic enterprise and a real forerunner of the annexation of our country to the United States" (Onís, p. 141).

Possibly Sarmiento's reaction to the work of the American Bible Society in South America was representative of a general attitude toward missionary endeavor. Establishing its first agency in

19. I have relied on Robertson, pp. 298–317, for data on early missionaries and their schools.

Buenos Aires in 1864, its colporteurs became very active in distributing copies of the Bible, even in remote parts. Referring to the considerable expenditures of the organization, he said, "South America does not share in these gifts, however, nor would she accept them in that form. She needs to be instructed not in the written word, but in the practical spirit of Christianity." He pleaded with North American Christians to send teachers to Latin America and declared, "This is the crowning method of propagating the principles of the gospel" (*Anthology*, p. 331). Apparently the mission boards agreed with him, and increasingly toward the end of the nineteenth century emphasis was placed on the educational aspects of the missionary movement. Insofar as this was done, a more favorable opinion of the United States doubtlessly resulted.

### EMISSARIES OF ENTERPRISE

One manifestation of the restless North American spirit of activism during this period apparently had a good deal to do with the kind of opinion held by Spanish Americans of the United States. This was the presence in several South American countries of a group of Americans who stimulated the construction of railways and the establishment of steamship lines. Let us look briefly at the life and work of several of the outstanding and representative men in that group.

William Wheelwright was without question the best known. This New Englander captained a Yankee ship that was wrecked on the coast near Buenos Aires in 1823. Tarrying briefly in Argentina, he met Rivadavia and became interested in the new republic's transportation problems. Later, after a short tour of duty as American Consul in Guayaquil, he settled in Valparaiso and engaged in the coastal trade. While so occupied he conceived the idea of bringing steamships to the west coast of South America. Having interested British capital in the project, he became the moving spirit of the Pacific Steam Navigation Company, which began service to the western republics in 1840. Shortly thereafter, aroused by the possibilities of railways in Chile, he was responsible for the construction of a road in northern Chile; it was opened to traffic in 1851. Engineers, mechanics, and a locomotive were brought from the United States. At the same time, he secured a concession for a railway from Valparaiso to Santiago, which, with the major assistance of Henry Meiggs and another American engineer, Campbell, was completed in 1863. As early as 1850 Wheelwright dreamed of an international trans-Andean railway, a dream that he never realized; but he was successful in organizing British capital to construct an important segment of the international line from Rosario to Córdoba, opened in 1870. His last accomplishment was the building of a railroad between Buenos Aires and Ensenada, a plan that had occurred to him on his first visit to Buenos Aires.

For progressive South Americans, Wheelwright became a symbol of North American initiative and ingenuity, and he was held in high regard. In 1850 the Chilean government presented a gold medal to the enterprising *yanqui*, and later a statue was erected in his honor in Valparaiso.[20] In 1966 Chile honored him on one of its postage stamps. Alberdi considered him such an exemplary figure that he composed a very complimentary biography and described him as "a type of those personalities that South America requires in order that her rich soil may bloom."[21] Sarmiento praised him, along with Meiggs and Campbell (*Anthology*, p. 316), and Vicuña Mackenna called him "this enterprising doer of good to whom the Pacific [coast] owes so much" (p. 62).

Henry Meiggs was another North American who played an important role in railway construction in South America. His name is generally associated with the early history of railroads in Peru, where he was responsible for building the Arequipa-Mollendo line (1870), the extremely difficult road from Arequipa to Puno (1876), and the amazing railway from Callao to Oroya at the headwaters of the Amazon, one which was conceived in 1869 and completed in 1893. He was also active with Wheelwright in building the line joining Santiago with Valparaiso; referring to his part in this project, a Chilean writer said, "My country should be grateful to this son of the North who knew how to transplant to Chile the genius of his race in order to open for us a road of progress." The Peruvian government awarded him a medal, and his zeal and that of other American engineers was esteemed by Peruvian statesmen.[22]

Edward A. Hopkins belonged to the same breed of industrious American as Wheelwright. After acting as special United States agent in Paraguay in 1845, he tried in 1851 to promote a United States–Paraguay Navigation Company. Two years later, while American consul in Asunción, he bought a large tract of land for

20. There is a good account of Wheelwright and his achievements in Robertson, pp. 234–44.
21. Alberdi, quoted in Robertson, p. 242.
22. Quoted ibid.

his company, built a sawmill, and taught the Paraguayans how to cure tobacco. Although the dictator López put a stop to this activity, Hopkins continued for years to interest himself in the promotion of trade between South America and the United States. He helped the Argentines by preparing a special report on immigration and public lands and by promoting the establishment of steam navigation on the Paraná River. Hopkins also planned, organized, and saw to completion a railway from Buenos Aires to San Fernando. In 1864, he was named Argentine Consul in New York with the specific mission of negotiating the establishment of a steamship line to Buenos Aires, a task in which he was not successful.[23] Sarmiento, in his general eulogy of North American technical assistance to Spanish America, cited Hopkins particularly as a praiseworthy example (*Anthology*, pp. 316–18).

Although he was often mentioned by Spanish Americans, William Henry Aspinwall, the entrepreneur largely responsible for the construction of the Panama railway, was probably less highly regarded by them than Wheelwright and the others. Aspinwall came close to symbolizing the dangers of North American wealth and power. In 1832, Aspinwall became a partner of one William Howland in an import-export firm that built up a tremendous trade with Latin America, especially with Venezuela, Mexico, and Central America. Their fleet of clipper ships was well known in the principal Spanish American ports. In 1850, Aspinwall joined with other financiers in creating the Panama Railway Company, a million-dollar corporation. He, his brother Lloyd, and others obtained a concession for the railway from the Colombian government, and in 1855 the important line was in operation. The eastern terminus of the road was called Aspinwall. Later he was associated with others in forming the Pacific Mail Steamship Company, which was to play an important role in linking the west coast of South America with the rest of the world. Colombian liberals were pleased with the work of Aspinwall's company, and the Colombian Secretary of Foreign Relations said they undertook their task "with the intrepidity and valor which generally distinguish the North Americans." Camacho Roldán, exultant when the railroad was completed, wrote, "Our future depends upon the introduction of the capital and the arts of the rich and civilized peoples of the globe."[24] Other Spanish Americans, as we shall see, feared and objected to the *yanqui* presence in Panama.

23. Data on Hopkins are from the *Dictionary of American Biography*.
24. Both quoted in Robertson, p. 256.

## STUDENTS

It is improbable that there were a sufficient number of students from Spanish America studying in North American colleges and universities during this period to have significantly influenced opinion of the United States. In the early decades at least, Cuban students from good families continued to worry the Spanish authorities by their tendency to frequent Catholic schools in the North, and later in the century, as Protestants established schools in South America, a limited number of Latin Americans began to continue their education in denominational colleges. An occasional student of engineering found his way to the technological paradise; but the great majority of those educated abroad were drawn to Europe, and especially to France.

## SCIENTISTS AND EXPLORERS

Sporadically throughout this period, North American scientists and archeologists came to Spanish America on expeditions to relatively remote regions, and in a minor way they probably helped to draw a picture of the *yanqui* as a venturesome soul, energetically interested in expanding his knowledge and commerce. Four of these expeditions were organized by the United States government, which was careful to describe them as having peaceful objectives, made for the sake of extending "the empire of commerce and science," and not for conquest.

In 1838, Lieutenant Charles Wilkes was commissioned by the Secretary of the Navy to lead an expedition to Chile, Argentina, and Brazil in order to collect scientific data and explore trade routes. He was accompanied by a corps of scientists—a botanist, a philologist, a conchologist, etc. In 1851, Lardner Gibbon and William Herndon, officers of the navy, explored the possibilities of navigation on the Amazon, starting their travels in Peru. To judge from the travel book they later wrote, they were fully as interested in the culture of the local inhabitants as in their riverine explorations. Two years later, Lieutenant Thomas Page took a side-wheeler, the *Water Witch*, up the Paraná and its tributaries and returned with observations which were helpful in opening those rivers to steam navigation. In 1867, James Orton, sponsored by the Smithsonian Institution and Williams College, led an expedition through Panama, Ecuador, and the Amazon country.

The work of John L. Stephens, who with the English artist Catherwood discovered important Maya ruins in Central America and Mexico in 1839, and E. G. Squier, who in 1863 investigated cities of the ancient Incan empire, was particularly pleasing to many Spanish Americans for its revelation of the glory of their ancient history. Both gentlemen wrote careful accounts of their labor, and Stephens' book was translated and published in Mexico in 1848.

Two United States astronomers, Lieutenant James M. Gillis and Benjamin Gould, were early forerunners of scientific cooperation between Spanish and Anglo-America. Gillis was detailed by the United States Navy in 1849 to establish an observatory in Chile. With the close cooperation of the Chilean government, he arranged for a substantial exchange of plant seeds with Chilean scientists.[25] Some years later, Gillis was Alberdi's cicerone during the latter's visit in Washington, and the Argentine statesman said of him, "Never have I known a more modest scholar or a more hospitable man." Gould, a professor at Harvard, was induced by Sarmiento to come to Argentina to direct the observatory in Córdoba. His work, carried out in friendly collaboration with Argentine colleagues, was of great scientific value.

In his review of cultural relations between North America and Spanish America, in which he gave high praise to North American enterprise, Sarmiento specifically mentioned the names of Gibbon, Herndon, Page, Stephens, Squier, Gissis, and Gould (*Anthology*, pp. 322–24). One may assume that these and others added their modest contribution to the portrayal of the United States as a forward-looking and dynamic culture.

## The Influence of Books

We have already called attention to the fact that the cultural and intellectual orientation of Spanish Americans toward Europe during the greater part of the last century made it inevitable that they should have formed many of their notions of the United States from their reading of French and English authors. Tocqueville was a favorite source of information, but there is evidence that Captain Marryat, Mrs. Trollope, Herbert Spencer, Macaulay, Benjamin Constant, Jeremy Bentham, and others also contributed their mite to the North American image. Travel accounts by Spanish Americans had some vogue, and, although the editions were usually very small, they doubtless commanded attention. Sarmiento's writings

25. Wayne D. Rasmussen, "The United States Astronomical Expedition to Chile."

were particularly potent channels of information and opinion.

The translation and knowledge of books by North American authors increased substantially during the period, but a large segment of them, such as the volumes of Prescott and Irving, dealt with Hispanic history; aside from enhancing the intellectual prestige of the United States, they gave no picture of the northern republic. The popular writings of Benjamin Franklin certainly confirmed the image of the North American as industrious and thrifty. Cooper's novels, widely read, were popular because they were adventure stories, but they may have implanted ideas incidentally about the expanding frontier and its life as important elements in the North American saga. The constitutional *Commentaries* of James Kent and Joseph Story were translated in Buenos Aires (1865 and 1860, respectively), and Alberdi is said to have studied Judge Story's work with great care. These tomes carried on the earlier tradition of independence days when respect and esteem were attached to the basic North American political documents. Although Emerson and his essays were known to some of the leading Spanish Americans, his works were not available in Spanish translation, and his popularity in the southern republics was not achieved until the twentieth century.

Certainly the most easily identifiable and perhaps the most effective experience in Spanish America with books from the United States during the nineteenth century was related to the remarkable textbook publishing venture of Appleton and Company. Primarily as a commercial opportunity and without American government encouragement of subvention, this publishing house saw in the Spanish Americans' rising reverence for education a profitable market for translations and adaptations of North American textbooks. The company made a beginning in the 1840s with the publication of the translation of a new series of readers, prepared by Henry Mandeville and used in American schools. By 1858, its lists contained twenty-one elementary texts of various sorts. Thereafter the number of texts published in Spanish increased apace, and 134 titles were available to Spanish American educators and students by 1885. In that year the company had distribution branches in eighteen Hispanic American countries, and its well-organized distribution system and its Spanish-language catalogues contributed to its success. The origins of the textbooks varied. Some were classics of Spanish literature prepared for classroom use; a few primers of moral and religious instruction were translations from the French. Still others were original texts written by Spanish Americans; one of the best sellers was a geography prepared by a Venezuelan, Ramón Paez. Sarmiento not only published his book on North American education with Appleton (1866) and his *Vida de Abrán Lincoln*, but advised and assisted in making title selections. The majority of the titles, however, were either translations or adaptations of texts written by North Americans for use in schools in the United States; both Eugenio María de Hostos and José Martí, outstanding figures in Spanish American intellectual life, acted as editors and translators. Texts were listed in the widest range of subjects: spelling, grammar, literature, mathematics, the sciences, manners and morals, geography, teaching methodology, etc.

Aside from the profit element involved in this rather astonishing project, the publishers may have had broader objectives in mind, as indicated in the preface to one of the catalogues: "The Editors take pleasure in offering to those persons interested in education their new Catalogue of Textbooks for Teaching . . . with the object of promoting between the United States and Hispanic American countries those relations of friendship and commerce which are becoming each day more necessary and important."[26]

Without knowing the exact sales figures for these textbooks, one can assume, since it was not a purely philanthropic enterprise, that they achieved widespread circulation. If so, their significance in indirectly creating images of the United States in the minds of teachers and students can scarcely be overestimated. While a considerable number of the texts were practical books that must have confirmed the vision of the United States as a materially progressive nation, the fact that the whole series embraced the gamut of approaches to the cultivation of the mind and spirit must have planted an occasional suspicion that a complete and well-rounded culture was growing in the North. In any event, this publishing enterprise provided a basis for educational experience common to North and South. As Bernstein says, "Educators and students shared in a sort of hemisphere schoolroom."[27]

Unfortunately, Appleton's truly amazing undertaking began to falter in the 1890s. The difficulties of the Spanish American republics with dollar exchange were said to have been a factor in the decline and final extinction of the business, and it is more than

26. Bernstein, *Making an Inter-American Mind*, p. 60; see also James F. Shearer, "Pioneer Publishers of Textbooks for Hispanic America: The House of Appleton."
27. Page 61.

likely that the antagonism toward the United States which grew in intensity at the close of the century was also responsible.

Besides those discussed, other means of diffusion of knowledge and ideas about the United States played a role. An analysis of Spanish American newspapers and periodicals of the period would undoubtedly yield a good deal of material relating to the northern republic. In fact, some of the source material for this study was first published serially in newspapers. Diplomatic officers stationed in the United States sometimes wrote of their impressions; others passed them on by word of mouth.

In summary, the agencies by means of which Spanish Americans could form their concepts of North American life and civilization were more numerous and effective than might be thought at first. In spite of slow communications and transportation, the self-centered stance of the burgeoning republic of the North, the confusion of political adjustments in Spanish America, and the entire hemisphere's fixation on Europe, there was a frequent exchange between human beings, brought about by trade and navigation, political exile, and the printed page. These brought to Spanish America a respectable amount of knowledge about the United States, some of which was relatively accurate while portions were the common currency of stereotypes.

4

# Politics, Economics, and Imperialism

Before we inquire into the details of the Spanish American vision of American political institutions during this period, it will be useful to keep in mind the total picture of civilization in the United States which was so frequently present in the Spanish American mind. It is a picture shared by practically all observers, whether or not they were favorably inclined toward the United States, and it is painted with monotonous regularity. The northern republic was an epitome of dazzling progress, surpassing anything ever seen in Spanish America and making Europe seem slow and old-fashioned. Observers regarded with awe and amazement, some-times tinctured with fear, the utilization of seemingly endless natural resources and untiring energy to build railways, canals, steamships, factories, and cities with luxurious hotels. Fortified by strong political institutions and widespread popular education, this young, vigorous nation seemed destined to become the great-est power in the world, a miracle of material development. A few representative quotations will give some idea of the positive tones of this image of nineteenth-century North America.

"Everything in that country is colossal. . . . Industry there has made a surprising development; everything is done on a stupen-dous scale. . . . Men do not vegetate; they live as though possessed by an implacable demon—as if electric currents circulated in their veins. They accumulate such fabulous fortunes that it is impossible even to waste them away."[1]

"North American liberties are destined to exercise the more active influence on South America as European influences become suspect. . . . The former, moreover, are supported by the prestige

1. Ernesto Quesada, quoted in McGann, *Argentina*, p. 39.

56

of the ever more astounding wealth and power of the United States, by the spectacle of their increasing greatness, their imperturbable tranquility, and the peaceful invasion of every shore of South America by their industry and its representatives."[2]

"God has finally willed that there should be found united in one single die, in one single nation, virgin land to allow the people to multiply without fear of misery, iron to complement human energy, coal to move engines, woods to supply lumber . . . popular education to make each individual of the nation more productive, freedom of faith . . . in short, the republic, strong and growing like a new star upon the sky."[3]

"[American cities represent] the degree of perfection to which materialism can be used for the enjoyment of man. . . . Here everything is fresh, mechanical; everything is at hand; everything moves like a watch, obeying the will of the one who has the golden key which governs material pleasures."[4]

It is against the background of these visions of unbelievable prosperity and strength that we must analyze most of the images of the United States, whether they be of social life, culture, the national character, the imperialistic eagle, the economy, or the political institutions.

## THE MODEL REPUBLIC

Even though the Spanish American experiences in imitating the political institutions of their older northern brother were not turning out to be the golden dream of the founding fathers, a respectable group during the first half of the nineteenth century continued to regard these institutions as the ideal to follow. Manuel Dorrego, having studied the federal system of the United States during his exile there, warmly advocated it in 1826 as a model for Argentina.[5] Later, Juan Bautista Alberdi, in his famous plan for Argentine political reorganization, cited many of the fundamental North American documents and included many points in which the influence of the United States' constitutional theory and practice is evident.[6] Another Argentine enemy of the dictator Rosas, Esteban Echeverría, pointing to the errors of the revolution in

2. *A Sarmiento Anthology*, pp. 309–10.
3. Sarmiento, quoted in Onís, *United States*, p. 369.
4. Vicuña Mackenna, *Diario*, p. 86.
5. José Luis Romero, *Las ideas políticas en Argentina*, p. 117.
6. Robertson, *Hispanic American Relations with the United States*, pp. 89–92.

South America, idealized the North American political system: "Look at the United States: when the colonial bonds are cast aside, organized, splendid democracy appears; radiant with youth and intelligence, it comes forth from the head of the people, as Minerva from Jupiter's brow."[7]

Liberals like Lastarria and Bilbao of Chile and Sarmiento of Argentina continued this pattern of admiration for and faith in the political institutions of the United States, the pattern so common in the Independence period. Even as the optimism of revolutionary days began to sour in the face of internal strife and caudillo rule at home, their eyes remained fixed on the United States (and often on England) where democratic institutions seemed to have prospered and fulfilled a dream. Their continued reliance on North American models was usually accompanied by scorn for their Hispanic heritage on which they frequently laid the blame for failures in their homelands.[8]

Happily contradicting the prophecies of doom which had some currency in the early years of the century, the liberal admirers of North American institutions pointed to their enduring quality. Camacho Roldán described the American political structure as "the most solid and apparently the one with the best chances of enduring among all civilized nations" (p. 660). Refuting the gloomy predictions of Macaulay, Lastarria emphasized the fact that the Civil War did not destroy the republican form of government: "It trusted in the power of its institutions and in the judgment of the people. The institutions triumphed and, with the re-election of Lincoln, the people indicated that they wanted slavery abolished. They also proved that government founded in liberty and individual rights will not be harmed by demagogy or insurrection" (7:36). As in so many matters, these facts were undoubtedly a contrast in their minds to the often ephemeral nature of Spanish American governments.

## DIFFERENCES IN HISTORICAL BEGINNINGS

In an effort to explain the disparity between the apparently fortunate democratic development of the United States and the erratic

7. Quoted in Zea, *América como conciencia*, p. 136.
8. Lastarria, *Obras completas*, 7:152; *A Sarmiento Anthology*, p. 194; Francisco Bilbao, *La América en peligro*, p. 150. (Future references will be in the text.) Naturally, not all of the nation-builders advocated imitation of United States political forms. For example, the conservative Mexican historian Lucas Alamán was sternly opposed to such servility.

political life in their own countries, many of the commentators glanced briefly at history and decided that the colonial origins of English America were far more favorable to the growth of a stable republic than those of the Hispanic American community. For whatever consolation it could offer this idea became almost commonplace. Juan Montalvo, the Ecuadorian essayist, wrote, "The North Americans were rich, powerful, and civilized even before their independence from England. If they lacked a leader, one hundred Washingtons would have volunteered to fill the vacancy."[9] Alberdi, paraphrasing Tocqueville, praised the character of the founders of New England, noting that their goal was freedom from oppression, not gold (Onís, p. 153). Lastarria, in a sweeping generalization, described Spain's gifts to her colonies as corruption and enslavement while "Anglo-America came forth free and sovereign from its cradle" (8:170–71). Sarmiento put the contrast in his usual graphic manner: "Yanqui civilization was the work of the plow and the primer; the Cross and the Sword destroyed South American civilization. There they learned to work and to read; here we learned to loaf and to pray."[10]

## LIBERTY

In looking to the United States as a political ideal, the liberal thinkers differed somewhat from their revolutionary fathers in that they were not usually as interested in the specific details of the constitutional structure as they were in the practical existence of freedom, particularly freedom of speech and of religious belief. Bilbao said, "Freedom of thought, as an inborn right, as the right of rights, characterizes the origin and development of society in the United States. A restricted freedom of thought . . . was the mutilated freedom proclaimed by the revolutionaries of the South." Freedom of conscience, Bilbao thought, was associated with the flexible dogma and free examination encouraged by Protestantism.[11] Both Alberdi and Lastarria, contrasting the United States and South America, emphasized the practical kind of liberty enjoyed in the United States; industrial and commercial freedom, as well as the usual civil liberties, were considered to be the

9. Montalvo, "Wáshington y Bolívar," in Englekirk et al., *An Anthology of Spanish American Literature*, p. 304.
10. Quoted in Alberto Zum Felde, *Indice crítico de la literatura hispano-americana; los ensayistas*, p. 108.
11. Quoted in Zea, *The Latin American Mind*, p. 78.

natural base of society.[12] Adam Smith was obviously among their mentors.

Echoing some of the thinkers of the Independence period, several observers later in the century were wont to attribute the astounding prosperity of the United States directly to its panoply of freedoms. Bilbao believed that "such a complete and integrated development of the human faculties" in the northern democracy was the result of freedom of the spirit (p. 49). Alberdi agreed,[13] and Salvador Camacho Roldán, marveling at the prosperity and growth of Chicago (an amazing city to many of the visitors), decided that the secret lay not only in material factors but also in the exercise of political and religious liberty by mature and civilized people.[14]

In consonance with the type of liberalism so current in the mid-nineteenth century, most of the commentators admired a government most when it was least evident. In contrast to Europe and many of their own countries, the northern union kept governmental interference to a minimum. Traveling in the United States, Alberdi noted, "The amazing thing about public order in this country is that it runs by itself. One does not see or notice the government."[15] This observation was seconded by Camacho Roldán some years later (pp. 878–79).

### THE CANCER OF CORRUPTION

The golden vision of a model state did not last with all observers throughout the century. In the 1850s, and in succeeding decades, the defects of democracy in action on the American scene began to occupy their attention more and more. The evils of the spoils system, familiar to them on their home grounds, struck commentators as an ugly blot on a shining image. One witness writing in 1889 recorded that civil service reform legislation had been passed in 1882, but that several presidents had been laggard in making it effective (Camacho Roldán, p. 803). General administrative corruption was said to be rife. An Argentine traveler who visited the United States in 1881 said, "Republican ideas are far from being

12. Alberdi, quoted ibid., p. 81; Lastarria, 7:176.
13. Quoted in Zea, *The Latin American Mind*, p. 81.
14. Camacho Roldán, *Notas*, pp. 541–43; Raimundo Cabrera of Cuba, also impressed by Chicago's growth, attributed it to the genius of liberty, "which was manifest even in the pattern of home life" ("Chicago," p. 405).
15. Alberdi, *Memorias e impresiones de viaje*, p. 365.

put into practice here with the purity which is generally attributed to them. Administrative corruption is greater here than in any European country, or even any moderately well-organized South American country."[16]

The decline in dignity in political affairs and in quality of statesmen bothered some critics. José Martí, the great Cuban patriot, said, "A presidential campaign in the United States is a coarse and nauseating affair. . . . All sense of dignity is totally forgotten. . . . Mudslinging becomes rampant. Deliberate lies and exaggerations abound. . . . Every kind of infamy is judged to be legitimate. . . . An honest observer does not know how to analyze a battle in which all participants campaign in bad faith."[17] In 1856, Vicuña Mackenna decried the lack of truly great men in American politics. In contrast to the early presidents, all recent ones had been mediocre. Scorning Webster, Calhoun, and Douglas for one reason or another (but excepting Henry Clay), he declared that there was not a single man on the political scene who was eminent for his honesty and integrity. In the public eye, the great men were unscrupulous businessmen (p. 103).

Probably the most grievous charge against American political life, especially in the decades after the Civil War, was directed against what Martí decried as swindling in big business and gross corruption of politicians, which made a farce of democracy. Plutocracy, oligarchy, imperialism—these were the fearful diseases which were destroying the pristine purity of the American political structure, and were the more hateful to Spanish Americans because in them they saw danger for their own countries. Martí, whose journalistic campaigns against the evils in the North American political system would have done credit to the muckrakers, declared, "What is apparent is that the nature of the North American government is gradually changing in its fundamental reality. Under the traditional labels of Republican and Democratic . . . the republic is becoming plutocratic and imperialistic." On another occasion he referred to the American political structure as "the system in which the judiciary, the national legislature, the church, the press, corrupted by avarice, had in twenty-five years of alliance come to create within the freest democracy in the world the most unjust and shameful of oligarchies."[18]

16. Miguel Cané, *En viaje*, p. 301.
17. Martí, *Obras completas*, 31:12–13.
18. Ibid., 36:12, 37:56.

### DISILLUSION

While it was doubtless true that harsh criticism of the evils of democracy in the United States in the writings of such men as Vicuña Mackenna had overtones relating to the political situations in their homelands, and while Martí's condemnation was motivated in part by his obsession with the dangers of *yanqui* imperialism, it is sadly revealing to record that in the writings of some of the critics there is the sincere and anguished complaint of disillusioned men. They had pinned their highest hopes on an idealized white knight, their champion of democracy; then, as the century went on, they found that their idol had feet of clay, or at least was as human as the next sinful man.

Vicuña Mackenna is a good example of the disappointed admirer. At the end of his lengthy and well-written account of his extensive travels in the United States, he felt compelled to say, "I had come to that country filled with affectionate and ardent enthusiasm; I left it with disillusion in my heart. My affection for the people, my illusions of their social grandeur—all had fallen away from me little by little, buried along my road by the immense burden of materialism which is beating down this country, at the same time as it serves as its pedestal. I carried with me only my admiration for its power, but—I must confess it—admiration alone, without liking or enthusiasm" (p. 99). As a result, his book is a curious and sometimes baffling combination of praise and reproach. For example, after a particularly devastating denunciation of the mercantile spirit in American politics and life, he wrote on the next page, "the United States is a great country; it is the first nation of the globe, however much its race may justly be unlikeable to us. And indeed, who will fail to render tribute to you with his head erect and his breast filled with enthusiasm, as the only land in the world of greatness and liberty? Thou, cradle, refuge, and support for that supreme good, lost today in all nations; thou, fatherland of Washington, thou art also the manly, ardent protest raised against the leprosy of oppression and darkness which torments ailing humanity!" (p. 105).

In a less personal and rhetorical manner, Martí also spoke of the ambivalent attitude toward the United States, born of disappointment: "[Cubans] admire this nation, the greatest ever built by liberty, but they dislike the evil conditions that, like worms in the heart, have begun in this mighty republic their work of destruction. They have made of the heroes of this country their own heroes, and look to the success of the American commonwealth as the crowning glory of mankind; but they cannot honestly believe that excessive individualism, reverence for wealth, and the protracted exaltation of a terrible victory are preparing the United States to be the typical nation of liberty. . . . We love the country of Lincoln as much as we fear the country of Cutting."[19]

Writing at about the same time as Martí, Camacho Roldán—one of our most fervent admirers—said, "Accustomed, as we inexpert republicans of the South were, to regarding [American society] as the column of fire which long ago guided the Israelites across the desert, today it is impossible not to fear that there some upset has occurred in the progress of democratic ideas." He points to the bad influence of the post–Civil War millionaires in American politics and the shady deals and peculation which seemed to be so common (p. 806).

Even Sarmiento, whose flame of love and admiration for North American institutions was ordinarily so bright and constant, confessed on one occasion to some disillusionment after his first visit to the northern republic. Recollecting his early idealization of the United States, he said, "However, on studying it at close range, one finds that in many respects it does not correspond to the abstract idea which we had formed of it. Although humanity's ugliest ulcers have disappeared in North America, certain scar tissue still remains among European nations which here are turning to cancer, and at the same time new ailments have arisen for which no known remedy exists or is even being sought. Our Republic, therefore, liberty and strength, intelligence and beauty, the Republic of our dreams . . . that Republic, my dear friend, is still a desideratum. . . . Let us console ourselves nevertheless with the thought that these democrats have made the most progress of any nation on earth today along the road to the unknown political solution toward which Christian peoples are groping" (*Anthology*, p. 194). On the whole, Sarmiento's opinions about the United States carry the latter note of optimism rather than that of bitter disappointment.

## THE SECRET OF THE AFFLUENT SOCIETY

If some of the visitors from the south were disillusioned with the workings of the political system in the northern republic, their

19. Quoted in Manuel Pedro González, *José Martí: Epic Chronicler of the United States in the Eighties*, p. 67; see also p. 47.

astonishment at the economic progress there was hardly ever shattered. It was a habit of the serious-minded visitors of the time to fill out their travel records with abundant statistics, all of which went to prove the marvelous growth of population, railways, commerce, and industry. In spite of their occasional professions of loyalty to nonmaterialistic values, nearly all of the men whose writings provide our source material were greatly preoccupied with the problems of the material growth of their own republics, and their eyes were attentive to the enviable economic advance of the United States. Men like Sarmiento, Alberdi, and especially Camacho Roldán were eager to discover the formula for such material miracles so that their countries might do likewise.

As was the case during the Independence period, later nineteenth-century observers were not entirely in agreement about the answer to the chicken-and-egg conundrum in the American economy. Sometimes nature's largess—unlimited space, a fine coastline, navigable rivers, relatively flat land, varied natural resources—seemed to be the explanation of *yanqui* prosperity.[20] We have also seen that it was a commonplace to attribute that prosperity to the existence of political liberties, these leading infallibly to a material paradise. But more frequently American skill and energy appealed to them as the real answer. Camacho Roldán wrote, "Those people have acquired such a degree of energy in the struggle for life that their difficulties will be transitory. The wealth which they constantly produce, consume, and accumulate is of a magnitude such as is probably never found in any other country" (p. 575). And Sarmiento declared, "Nature brought the great territory of the Union into being, but without the profound economic science possessed by the Americans the work would have remained incomplete" (*Anthology*, p. 201).

As good disciples of British laissez-faire economists, many of them accepted the private initiative, free enterprise pattern of economic development as the best and indeed the natural system. According to Alberdi, the citizen of the United States, in contrast to the South American, manages his own work and business and is not a salaried servant of the state. He made out a case to prove that the material greatness of the United States was the result of "constructive egotism." The sum of all citizens working for themselves makes a great country. As a matter of fact, there are indica-

20. Vicuña Mackenna, after enumerating the natural blessings of the United States, exclaimed, "Why shouldn't this country be great!" (pp. 100–101).

tions that when the Spanish American observers talked about freedom and liberty in the United States they were thinking, at least in part, about freedom through untrammeled individual initiative to make money. The Colombian poet José Eusebio Caro managed to twist the old cliché about liberty being the cause of material prosperity into a new shape: When men are engaged in business, he argued, they have no time for the discord that naturally arises in a democracy. "Political liberty is not a beginning; it is a goal and a result; it is not this liberty that has brought about industry and trade; trade and industry have produced this liberty." Caro was not untypical of the Spanish American of the middle years of the last century. In the last letter of his life in 1853, he wrote of his faith in the kind of material progress he had observed in the United States—the railways, the ships, the telegraph networks—and he prophesied that the American would come to Colombia "with his enterprising spirit and will open doors and windows and give us light and life."[21]

## LANDHOLDING AND LABOR

In spite of their frequently imposing array of statistics, few of our witnesses took pains to analyze the detailed mechanics of the burgeoning economy of the United States. But there were at least two specific aspects of the economic structure which occasionally claimed their attention. One was the system of land tenure. Since during a part of the period North American wealth was largely agricultural, and since the economies of all the Spanish American countries were almost entirely based on products of the soil, it was natural that they should have particular interest in that aspect of our economy. And it was also natural that these observers, most of them liberals at home where the latifundia question was of great importance, should notice with triumph that American agriculture, particularly in the North and newly settled Middle West, favored small holdings of land worked by farmer-owners. Sarmiento commented with satisfaction on the system of taxing unused land and thus preventing the building up of idle latifundia (*Anthology*, p. 263). When he founded his model town of Chivilcoy in Argentina, he imitated the North American custom of parceling out the land in small units to settlers (Onís, p. 178). Camacho Roldán was delighted with the working of the Homestead Law

21. Alberdi quoted in Zea, *The Latin American Mind*, p. 81; Caro quoted in Manuel Torres, "The United States in 1850," pp. 7–8.

by which government land was distributed free in small parcels, thus overturning the age-long European type of land and social organization. This policy, he claimed, was of primary importance in American prosperity because it gave independence and personal dignity to the farmer, attracted immigration, stimulated the demand for manufactured products and the construction of railways, and gave real substance to the theories of liberty and equality. He admitted that large holdings can often be operated more economically than smaller plots, but argued that this difficulty could be solved by cooperative use of farm machinery (pp. 677–83).

From both a business and a humanitarian point of view, several commentators were interested in the treatment of industrial workers. Caro, when he found that living was expensive in the United States, attributed that fact to high wages, and noted that "this is the hardest country for the tramp and the prodigal and at the same time the most favorable country for the industrious man."[22] Sarmiento and Camacho Roldán in their wide travels found two industrial establishments of particular interest. Camacho Roldán was impressed by the works of the Pullman Company near Chicago, where the company furnished comfortable housing, schools, and recreation facilities for its employees, as well as offering them the opportunity to share in its profits (pp. 586–87). Sarmiento was fascinated with the textile mills in Lowell, Massachusetts, where he found that factories paying much higher wages than the English mills could nevertheless compete with them successfully. The explanation, he said, was simple enough: educated, well-paid workers equal more and better products. He marveled, as did other foreign visitors, at the young women workers—modest, decent, living in clean, comfortable quarters. Sarmiento called the Lowell experiment "a model of what capital, combined with the moral improvement of labor can accomplish in industry" (*Anthology*, pp. 241–42). We should remember that this was in 1847.

### THE GANGRENE OF WEALTH

Especially toward the end of the century, without denying the efficacy of the economic machine to produce wealth, observers began to see that such wealth was by no means equitably distributed. Even before the Civil War, Vicuña Mackenna was disgusted with wealthy high society summering at Saratoga Springs; the overdressed, snobbish women particularly offended him (pp. 79–

22. Quoted in Torres, p. 4.

80). Later, a Guatemalan traveler commented on the growth of luxury and ostentation in New York, the jewels and scandalously expensive dresses worn by the women; this frantic "keeping up with the Joneses," Milla mused, was an ironic contrast to the early, Spartan days of the republic. This obsession with wealth and display leads, he thought, to corruption, "the gangrene which is now invading the great Republic, just as it devoured ancient Rome" (pp. 155–57). The Colombian poet Rafael Pombo, in his sourly humorous poem "North American Girls on Broadway," described in detail the gaudy and pretentious parade of women on New York's fashionable artery, clothed in the finest Belgian lace, Persian shawls, silks from Damascus, pearls and emeralds from Spanish America.[23]

Commentators were shocked to contrast this vulgar display of wealth with life in the slums of New York and other large cities. José Milla, a Guatemalan literary man, painted a sordid, grim picture of the tenements in New York City: vagabond children wandered about the filthy, crowded streets; drunkenness was common; swarms of miserable, poverty-stricken people were jammed into dark basements; pathetic organ-grinders shivered and died in the cold. These people, he said, were far worse off than the poor in his native Guatemala (pp. 159–65). Camacho Roldán in 1889 described similar scenes of squalor in Cincinnati and New York, emphasizing the sunken eyes, the ragged dress, the vice in crowded, dark quarters. While these conditions he attributed in part to the low quality of southern European immigrants, he also recognized that they resulted from the increased concentration of wealth in a few hands, the progressive lowering of wages, and the growth of large-scale landholding (pp. 770–77).

So concerned was this Colombian Yankeephile about the imperfections in what he would have liked to regard as an ideal nation that he devoted a whole chapter to a detailed analysis of what was going wrong. He criticized the quick abolition of the high profit taxes imposed during the Civil War, the high tariff resulting in high prices and consumer distress, and the creation of trusts which raised and maintained high prices to the detriment of the common man. To my knowledge, he is the first Spanish American to launch a wholesale condemnation of the trusts, a theme which later was to become such a favorite among the critics

23. Rafael Pombo, *Poesías completas*, pp. 109–13. The lavish display of diamonds, even on garters, by American women also annoyed a Venezuelan visitor (Ricardo Becerra, "Crónicas yankees," 2:272, 320).

of the United States. Camacho Roldán, however, was not in the last analysis pessimistic about the outcome of the economic ills suffered by the great republic. He noted the creation in 1887, as a result of organized public opinion, of the Interstate Commerce Commission, which he believed would remedy some of the ailments. He also dwelt at some length on the growing power of the Grangers and the Knights of Labor, and believed that strong trade unions would in the end correct the abuses of the free enterprise system. A devotee of the idea of progress, he was confident that widespread systems of communications, public schools, the prevailing spirit of tolerance, and the habit of free discussion would cure the imbalance which seemed to be developing in the economic life of the United States (chap. 41).

### THE CLAW OF THE AMERICAN EAGLE

Most of the same men who were so astounded at the political stability and material progress of the United States were at one time or another profoundly fearful of the actual and potential dangers to the sovereignty of their homelands (or of Spanish America in general) presented by that growing giant. Although the graph of their fear reaction went up and down, depending to some extent on the giant's movements and the internal politics of their uneasy republics, one can say in general that apprehension increased notably during the period under discussion. Often the fear was motivated by specific actions on the part of the United States, but as frequently it was the result of the loud and boastful speech of North Americans in the wildly expansive mood characteristic of them during the century.

*The shearing of Mexico.*—The annexation of Texas and the Mexican War were the first major events to alarm our hemispheric neighbors. Naturally, the Mexicans, as the aggrieved party, were most vehement in their denunciation of what they considered naked aggression. Before the war, Mexican opinion was divided, the Federalists admiring the North American constitution as well as the education and progress of their northern neighbor, and Unitarians, such as Lucas Alamán, being often apprehensive of the expansionist tendencies of the United States. After the Texas affair, however, both liberals and conservatives united in attacking the union of the North, and even admirers, such as José María Bocanegra, contributed to the considerable literature of scorn for the United States. One Agustín Franco, in a book called *Ojeada sobre*

*Texas*, expressed the typical reaction: Stephen Austin, with his deceptive air of humility, had tricked the trusting Mexicans. The gringos, who had already shown their savagery in their decimation of the Indians and their treatment of their slaves, had brazenly taken Texas, "not unlike a viper that sinks her venomous fangs in the breast of the one who had given to it its life."[24]

In 1877, the Mexican poet Guillermo Prieto visited the United States and gave poetic form to his feeling:

> They can do everything;
> they can change the shreds
> of my unhappy country
> into splendid nations,
> —booty of deceit,
> victims of outrage!
> They can do anything!
> But they cannot tear
> from my native land
> her nobility, nor rob
> her shining beauty,
> her divine, heroic heart! (Onís, p. 120).

Some years later, the famous Mexican educator Justo Sierra warned his countrymen: "We must go from the military age to the industrial age. And we must go quickly, for the giant that grows beside us and creeps closer and closer to us . . . will come to absorb us and dissolve us, should we be weak. . . . Mexico destroys itself, while near us lives a marvellous collective animal, for whose enormous gut there is no food sufficient; he is ready to devour us."[25]

While South Americans were not uniformly full of admiration for their Mexican brethren, many of them were sincerely perturbed by the North American treatment of Mexico. Bilbao, whose general respect for the United States sometimes seemed unbounded, was keenly aware of the dangers for all of Spanish America implicit in the Mexican affair. He saw both Russia and the

24. Franco, quoted in Onís, p. 140; for a reasonably complete survey of Mexican reaction at this time, see Homer C. Cheney, "The Mexican–United States War as Seen by Mexican Intellectuals, 1846–1956," Ph.D. diss., Stanford University, 1959.

25. Quoted in Zea, *América como conciencia*, p. 137. Hatred of the *yanqui* invader is reflected in the popular Mexican ballads of the time; see Merle E. Simmons, "Attitudes toward the United States Revealed in Mexican *Corridos*," p. 34.

United States as eager to dominate the world. "Russia hides her claws to wait in ambush; but the United States stretches hers out further and further in this hunting expedition against the South. We have already seen fragments of America fall to the Saxon jaws of the boa constrictor which fascinates us and unwinds its tortuous rings. Yesterday it was Texas, and then the North of Mexico and the Pacific that greeted a new master" (p. 145). Another Chilean, Vicuña Mackenna, wrote that it was a calamity for Mexico to be situated so near the United States, "whose victim she had been, when she could have been her friend and pupil" (p. 28).

Sarmiento, whose total attitude toward the imperialistic tendencies of the United States was somewhat ambiguous, took—at least on two occasions—a view of the Mexican–North American imbroglio at variance with that of the majority. He observed that under Mexican rule, California was poor and backward and that with the coming of the Americans, bringing their legal system, the land was divided up and a prosperous state arose in ten years. Referring to American influence in occupied lands, he said, "It is noteworthy that wherever it has been tried, the chronic condition of revolution and uncertainty has ceased and freedom and prosperity have taken its place. Mexico burns in civil war, yet its three shorn-off branches [California, Texas, New Mexico] are flourishing beside it in peace" (*Anthology*, pp. 280, 313). Akin to this near justification for the predatory actions of the United States were certain observations of Camacho Roldán. Observing that the abolition of slavery in the Union had diminished the danger of North American aggression south of the border, he insisted that such remaining danger as there was came not only from the impetuosity of the Americans, but also from the weak government and lack of stability in Mexico and the backward political education of the Mexican people (pp. 725–45). Neither Sarmiento nor Camacho, however, completely condoned the territory-grabbing of the nation they so much admired.

*The filibusters.*—The next North American action to inflame Spanish American sentiment was the Central American adventure of Walker and his filibusters. Probably because of its barefaced insolence, Walker brought forth unanimous condemnation among our witnesses, and in some cases the most harsh and vituperative criticism. Far from being regarded as a wild, private venture, Walker's expeditions were considered by most Spanish Americans to be an affront to them by the American people and their government. José María Samper, a Colombian statesman, called *filibus-*

*terismo* "a discredit to the American Union, allowed by public opinion, encouraged by the press, and tolerated by the rulers and the Congress as a means of sure-fire expansion without any responsibility before foreign governments."[26]

Rafael Pombo's poem "Los Filibusteros" is a particularly unrestrained display of anger. Written in Costa Rica in 1856, the poet addresses Walker and his men:

> Come, filthy vomit of foreign debauchery
> with your benevolent mission of Americanizing,
>
> . . . . . . . .
>
> Come, heroes of industry, kind gift
> of the most prosperous North to its southern pupil.
> Come, robust saplings of the Anglo-Saxon tree,
> twisted, immense, athletic, gigantic, colossal,
> arbiter and infallible oracle of both worlds,
> the first and last pinnacle of absolute perfection.

He continues with an idyllic description of the beauty and wealth of Central America, "a garden lost by Adam and found by Columbus"; the filibusters profane this paradise, posing first as inoffensive guests, and then wielding their rifles and daggers to "substitute the Saxon code for that of Christ." The invaders drink prodigious amounts of whiskey to fire their enthusiasm and courage, but soon they will find out what the magic word "honor" means. The poet ends his doggerel by wishing them dead and their Union too.[27]

*How far beyond Panama?*—The apparent designs of the United States on the isthmus of Panama were a source of constant anxiety to Spanish Americans long before Roosevelt "took" Panama. Although the concession for the Panama Railway, built in the early 1850s by Aspinwall's company, was legally obtained from the Colombian government, the presence and transit of large numbers of Americans in Panama and the consequent imposition of American ways and habits, including drunkenness, irritated observers. Particularly galling was the *yanqui* attempt to fasten the name of Aspinwall to the eastern terminus of the railway, instead of

26. Samper, p. 364.
27. Pombo, pp. 763–66. For a discussion of other poems by Pombo referring to the United States, some critical and some favorable, see Hector H. Orjuela, "Rafael Pombo y la poesía anti-yanqui de Hispanoamérica." Other witnesses in this section who specifically mention Walker are Vicuña Mackenna, p. 107; Camacho Roldán, pp. 391–92; Bilbao, p. 158.

Colón.[28] Bilbao feared that the United States would completely occupy Panama and use it as a base for the eventual conquest of South America (p. 159).

In fact, it became somewhat common among Spanish Americans during this period, echoing the early, gloomy prophecies of Luis de Onís and indeed the expressed hopes of jingoistic publicists in the United States, to point to Panama as the future temporary terminus of North American expansionism.[29] They were not oblivious to the spirit of Manifest Destiny which was so loudly evident in the nineteenth-century United States. Many thought they saw the northern eagle's claw reaching out to grasp not only Mexico, Central America, and Panama, but Cuba and even South America.[30] As faithful readers of Tocqueville, they doubtless recalled his prediction about the inevitability of North American imperialist expansion: "It cannot be denied that the British race has acquired an amazing preponderance over other European races in the New World; and it is very superior to them in civilization, industry, and power. As long as it is surrounded only by desert or thinly populated countries . . . it will assuredly continue to spread. The lines marked out by treaties will not stop it."[31]

Concepts of racial superiority and inferiority, mentioned by Tocqueville and gaining increased currency in Europe in those years, often entered into the Spanish American's fear of conquest by the United States. Camacho Roldán, usually an affectionate admirer of the United States, asked whether the northern republic was destined to expand to the very ends of the continent "by means of conquest and annihilation of inferior races" (pp. 884–85). The Chilean Carrasco Albano, believing that North America had inherited from England its hatred of the Spanish race, predicted a race war between the United States and Latin America, and the Mexican Juan N. Pereda, advocating a defensive alliance of states of the Latin race, declared that it was threatened by absorption by the Anglo-Saxons of the North (Onís, p. 146). As we shall see, this concern with race became even more obsessive toward the end of the century and in the first decades of this century.

28. Vicuña Mackenna, pp. 106–7; Camacho Roldán, p. 319.
29. For example, see *A Sarmiento Anthology*, p. 199, and Vicuña Mackenna, p. 106.
30. José Martí particularly feared and fought against plans on the part of the United States to buy or otherwise acquire Cuba; see González, pp. 63–70.
31. *Democracy in America*, 1:449.

## MANIFEST DESTINY AND THE MONROE DOCTRINE

In contrast to most twentieth-century critics of North American imperialism, those of the last century generally laid the blame for the predatory activities on the American people themselves. When a Guatemalan visitor was leaving a New York school for physically disadvantaged children, the students bade him good-bye, hoping that his country would soon be part of the United States. This farewell was annoying proof to the visitor that the idea of absorbing the whole continent "is deeply embedded . . . even in the lowest classes." While the government has the same blueprint, it proceeds more cautiously and is willing to bide its time until "time and our own madness will see to it that what they call here the 'Manifest Destiny' of our race is fulfilled" (Milla, pp. 136–37). Camacho Roldán cited as one of the reasons for fearing further expansionist activities on the part of the United States the impatience of the American people, who grasped at all possibilities of gaining wealth, using fictitious excuses and disregarding the rights of weak nations. Journalists and the government were influenced by public opinion, and thus the popular demand for conquest was translated into policy and action.[32] The same writer identified the Louisiana Purchase as "the beginning of the dogma of 'Manifest Destiny' which dominates the obscure depths of the American mind and which seems to have within it so many dangers for the peoples of the Latin race on this continent" (p. 405).

While articulate Spanish Americans had diverse attitudes toward the Monroe Doctrine, a respectable number presaged twentieth-century opinion by regarding it as a cloak for sinister North American designs on the other America. Sarmiento, addressing the Rhode Island Historical Society in 1865, declared that the Monroe Doctrine could have been a good policy, but that it was being abused: "The Monroe Doctrine lost its sanctity and ceased to be a protective barrier of separation to become in itself a threat. . . . Who was to believe that there would come a day when the republic would cast shadows all around itself: slavery to the South, conquest to the West, a menace to the North [Canada], and a challenge to Europe" (Onís, p. 195).

Alberdi, who had a high opinion of some aspects of the United States but whose truest allegiance was to Europe after his native

32. This observation occurs in a lengthy and relatively moderate discussion of North American imperialism by Camacho Roldán, pp. 725–45.

Argentina, was severe in his criticism of the Monroe Doctrine. According to him, that pronouncement not only prevented such intervention on the part of Europe which could have been helpful to some of the Spanish American republics, but actually made them indirect colonies of the United States. "Even though the United States owes everything to Europe, it wants to isolate America from Europe, except insofar as Europe comes through the United States; it wants to become the only customs house for civilization coming from across the Atlantic." In Alberdi's opinion, Europe could offer Spanish America immigration, capital, machinery, and markets, and the United States could not. Convinced of the imperialistic ambitions of the United States, he proposed in 1844 a Hispanic American league, to be formed in agreement with certain European powers, and specifically excluding the United States.[33]

### ADMIRATION AND FEAR

Many of the critics who condemned American aggression against Mexico and feared the expansionist tendencies justified by the idea of Manifest Destiny were or had been otherwise more or less enthusiastic champions of the progressive civilization of the North. Once again we hear frequently enough a plaintive note of disenchantment and hurt puzzlement. Bilbao, who so often invoked the United States as a paragon worthy of imitation, sorrowfully confessed, "that nation, which could have been our star, our model, our strength, is day by day becoming more of a threat to the autonomy of South America" (p. 149). Vicuña Mackenna lamented that the northern Union could have been "the political regeneration of the world," but instead had violently thrust aside the weaker nations of America. "To assault defenseless neighbors, to usurp undefended territory, to involve apprentice nations in intrigues and bloodshed—that is the work of a cowardly, cunning vulture, not of the proud symbol which crowns her banners" (p. 106).

Sometimes the Spanish Americans managed to perform the somewhat difficult feat of wanting to emulate the United States and at the same time fearing and condemning the giant's future intentions toward them. Apparently their mental state was a kind

33. A good summary of Alberdi's thought on this point is W. W. Pierson's "Alberdi's Views on the Monroe Doctrine"; see also McGann, pp. 96–97.

of twilight zone where admiration shaded into awe and awe into dread. Alberdi, positive as he was about the wrongness of the Monroe Doctrine and the desirability of depending on Europe, was also a firm admirer of Wheelwright and other representatives of the technical and industrial talent of the North Americans, and at various times he proposed ways in which his fellow men could well imitate the United States. Carrasco Albano, even while pointing to the horrible phantom of race struggle with the United States, advised Spanish Americans to follow the Anglo-Saxons in their industrial development, their encouragement of immigration, and their railway construction (Onís, p. 146). Perhaps the most puzzling example of this schizophrenic mind was Francisco Bilbao; on one page he said, "that youthful colossus which believes in its empire, as Rome believed in hers . . . advances like a rising tide, its waters suspended ready to crash like a cataract on the South." Three pages farther, he changed his mood: "Let us feel boiling in our veins the seed of endless enterprise" (pp. 148, 151). We shall see that this same combination of fear of North American imperialism and esteem for the virtues of American society was present when the anti-imperialist fervor reached its peak early in the twentieth century.

Occasionally one comes across an attempt to dilute the blame attaching to the United States for her predatory attitude. We have noted Sarmiento's defense of the *yanqui*'s role in bringing prosperous civilization to former Mexican territories. Vicuña Mackenna, ordinarily an implacable critic of American materialism and aggression, recognized that imperialism as practiced by the United States was better than the European kind: "You have conquered without fastening colonial chains on the neck of the vanquished; instead you have given the embrace of your all-powerful Union. . . . You have overcome so many enemies without needing a craggy rock in the midst of the sea to disarm them; you unfurl your standard of fraternity to which a new star is added; thus the union of victors and vanquished is sealed forever." He also warned his countrymen not to think that all Americans are filibusters, and that many noble souls in the United States vigorously protested the Mexican War and Walker's activities (pp. 105, 108).

There is no question, however, that the dominant note in the Spanish American's attitude toward United States expansionism during the latter two-thirds of the nineteenth century was one of nervousness and outrage. A statement of Bilbao's is representative of their feelings: "Now we are beginning to hear the footsteps of the colossus who, fearing no one, stuns his neighbors more and more every year with his diplomacy, with that spawn of adventurers that he spreads abroad, with his growing influence and power . . ." (p. 149).

5

# Social Forces and Institutions

Although the political and economic systems of the United States, as well as its ominous imperialistic designs, were prime points of interest to Spanish American commentators, various aspects of the social scene also attracted their attention. Sometimes this interest was prompted by the odd and notable divergence between northern social habits and their own, as in the case of the role of women. More frequently, they searched the American social structure to discover clues explaining the bountiful progress of the United States which might be pertinent to their own circumstances.

## THE POWER OF THE IMMIGRANT

Among these clues they found particular food for meditation in the waves of European immigration inundating the eastern seaboard and spreading into the fertile Midwest. Observers from Argentina, Uruguay, and Chile were perhaps more attentive than others, since they were becoming hosts to increasing numbers of new European settlers. Sarmiento and Alberdi, among others, saw in immigration one of the magic keys for building a modern society in Argentina.

Sarmiento, outlining in *Facundo* the measures to be taken by a liberal regime when Rosas should fall, said, ". . . the new government will establish great associations to bring in population groups and distribute them in fertile territories. . . . And in twenty years there will come to pass what has happened in North America in the same length of time: cities, provinces, and states have risen as

77

if by miracle in the wild country where just yesterday herds of wild buffaloes were grazing." Alberdi in his well-known *Bases* likewise favored following the example of the United States in this regard. It is true that Alberdi was selective in his idea of the useful immigrant, believing that Spanish immigration would never make a republic, while Anglo-Saxon settlers, being identified with commerce, the Industrial Revolution, and the theory and practice of liberty, would be very suitable for his ideal.[1]

One of Sarmiento's expressed reasons for visiting the United States was to study the process and results of immigration. He apparently liked what he saw, or possibly retained his favorable preconceptions. In his travel notes he wrote, speaking of European newcomers in upper New York State, "The land soon puts its own stamp on them, and just as water, by rubbing the rough surface of various stones together, turns out pebbles as uniform as if they were all brothers, so, uniting and mingling with each other, these torrents bearing with them the fragments of old societies are forming a new people—the youngest and most daring republic in the world" (*Anthology*, p. 200).

The confidence of other commentators from various countries in the power of immigration to build a strong nation was bolstered by the American experience. Camacho Roldán, for example, prophesied in 1889, "There is no doubt that from the mixture of such varied elements there must come a powerful boiling reaction which, when it precipitates, will produce a liquor rich in vital juices and generous perfume" (p. 749). Although the Mexican Guillermo Prieto, writing in 1877, foresaw with some trepidation the day when the immigrants with their large families would blot out the Anglo-Saxon race, he believed that they added greatly to the nation's energy and that their influence would wipe out remnants of the aristocratic spirit to make a more perfect democracy.[2]

To a few of the witnesses, however, it was evident that immigration, along with its advantages, brought a cluster of grave problems to American society. Camacho Roldán, in his customary judicious and searching manner, listed some of these problems along with the benefits. Since the immigrants were ignorant of the language and customs of their new home and accustomed to an atmosphere of violent struggle with oppressive authority in the

1. Sarmiento, *Facundo o civilización y barbarie*, p. 272; Alberdi, *Bases y puntos de partida para la organización de la Confederación Argentina*, passim.

2. Prieto, quoted in Onís, *United States*, pp. 118–19; see also Milla, *Un viaje*, pp. 250–53, and Caro, quoted in Torres, "U.S. in 1850," p. 5.

old country, they were the cause, he observed, of much public disorder and were apt to be anti-social. Furthermore, their European habits being at odds with democratic processes, they lent themselves easily to political corruption, vote-buying, and machine politics. Much of the drunkenness in the United States, which scandalized this Colombian, was in his opinion a legacy of the immigrants. Nevertheless, on balance, Camacho Roldán believed that more good than harm would come from the inundation of foreigners. He observed that the second and third generations spoke English and were assimilated to the national mold, and that many of the evils of immigration, such as political corruption, were really the fault of the older Americans. He condemned the idea of restricting immigration, which was beginning to be general at that time (pp. 752–57, 777–86, and passim).

José María Samper, a countryman of Camacho's, carried his suspicions of immigration to the United States to rather fantastic extremes. Believing that the great immigrant mass represented the classes who were "the most miserable, the most oppressed, and most degraded by the vicious institutions of Europe," he concluded that they were instinctively imperialistic, nomadic, and rootless, ready for the invasion and annexation of other countries. His implication was that the immigrants were responsible for the Mexican War, the filibustering, and the voracious appetite of Manifest Destiny, having distorted the natural development of the original settlers.[3] As far as I know, Samper's views on immigration were unique among the commentators of his time.

Although it was overshadowed by the zeal of later generations for the secret of material progress, the concept so common among the early Spanish American defenders of the United States as an asylum for the oppressed was not entirely forgotten. Camacho Roldán listed it among the virtues of immigration (p. 785), and Sarmiento said that when God made the United States, "he knew very well that by the nineteenth century, the people being trampled, enslaved, and dying of hunger in other places would all come to join here and avenge humanity for so many years of suffering . . ." (Onís, p. 170).

## EDUCATION

Along with immigration, education was another social phenomenon which Spanish American observers of this period often relied

3. Samper, essay, pp. 362–63.

on to explain the growing greatness of their northern neighbor. Much of their own backwardness they tended to blame on the lack of widespread popular education, and consequently some of them looked carefully at the North American public school system as a pattern to follow in weaving their social fabric.

Sarmiento was, of course, the best known and the most tenacious and enthusiastic proponent of free public schools in the *yanqui* style. Largely self-educated, he was nurtured as a boy of sixteen, the keeper of a country store, on the homely wisdom of Franklin's *Autobiography*, and his zeal for popular education was no doubt derived in part from the practical precepts of that exemplary North American. Sarmiento confessed, "I imagined myself to be another Franklin; and why not? I was as poor and studious as he, and keeping my wits about me and following his footsteps, I some day could grow up to be like him, to be an honorary doctor as he was, and to make myself a place in the letters and politics of America."[4] In 1845, when he was an exile in Chile, he was commissioned by the Chilean government to go to Europe and to the United States to study educational systems and methods. He visited France, sharing the common view of the time that there was to be found the model of contemporary civilization; but after his sojourn there and his subsequent intellectual explorations in the United States, he revised his views and became convinced that the northern republic was the world's leader in education, as in many other aspects of social and political life. He became a worshipful disciple of Horace Mann, whom he called "the Apostle Horace" and "the St. Paul" of education. On his return to Chile, he wrote a lengthy book, *De la educación popular* (1849), setting forth his basic ideas on education, which he had formulated in the United States and which guided his life-long activity in trying to improve Argentine schools. Many of these concepts were later restated and reaffirmed in *Las escuelas—base de prosperidad i de la república en los Estados Unidos* (1866).

This is not the place to present a detailed analysis of Sarmiento's educational philosophy, but we should summarize some of the main points which he admired in the American system. As was the case in the United States, his conviction of the importance of education was linked with his adherence to the democratic form of government in which "every man, inasmuch as he is a man, is qualified to exercise judgment and will in political matters, and

4. Quoted in Englekirk, "Franklin en el mundo hispánico," p. 350.

in fact, he does so."[5] Assuming this premise, his emphasis on education followed logically: "From this inalienable principle, the obligation arises today for all governments to provide for the education of future generations, since they cannot compel every individual of the mature generation to receive the intellectual preparation presupposed by the exercise of the rights granted it. . . . The power, wealth, and strength of a nation depend on the industrial, moral, and intellectual capacity of the individuals who compose it, and public education must have no other purpose than to increase those powers of production, action, and direction, by constantly increasing the number of individuals possessing them" (*Anthology*, p. 292). Thus, the great virtue of the United States was that primary education was supported in good part by a general tax, and that the state assumed the responsibility, as a part of public administration, to direct and inspect the system of public instruction. He was particularly impressed by the educational concern evident in Massachusetts town meetings and expressed in the laws of that state.[6]

As a practical idealist, Sarmiento was aware of the importance to education of good buildings and good physical equipment, and he was struck by the care expended on schoolhouses in Boston. Such was their elegance, they seemed like temples. In his report to the Chilean government, he presented, as models for the construction of public schools, plans which he had collected in the United States. Years later, as Argentine Minister to the United States, he gathered together and sent back to his native land all kinds of educational equipment—maps, instruments, and books. During those years he arranged with the publishing houses of Appleton and Scribner to prepare books and maps in Spanish for use in Argentine schools (Onís, pp. 173–75).

The Argentine statesman found to his surprise that women were widely employed as teachers in North American elementary schools, contrary to the prevailing Spanish American practice. He further discovered that these young women were intensively trained in normal schools. These facets of the northern system he found worthy of imitation and, as president of Argentina, he was active in stimulating the establishment of normal schools. In order to set proper examples in these training centers, he was respon-

5. Watt Stewart and William French, "The Influence of Horace Mann on the Educational Ideas of Domingo Sarmiento," p. 18.
6. See Robertson, *Hispanic American Relations with the United States*, p. 286.

sible for contracting to bring to Argentina a number of women teachers from the United States, outstanding among whom was a Mary O'Graham (or Mary O. Graham); in Sarmiento's words, "The young ladies . . . have left bright trails behind them and sown a precious seed that will not be lost. For they have educated hundreds of girls and left their own spirit behind among those who have succeeded them as teachers."[7]

Sarmiento was also impressed with public libraries in the United States as a valuable instrument of public education, especially adult education, of which he was a firm proponent. "There is no country in the world," he said, "in which there is more reading or where books are more abundant."[8] He was instrumental in establishing public libraries in the Argentine provinces and in soliciting North American books (especially from Appleton) for them.

In summary, Sarmiento found in American education, and specifically in the system of primary instruction, one of the golden keys to the dazzling success of the United States. Repeatedly he insisted that education was the straight, royal highway to the kind of material success which he so highly valued.[9]

Another man who promoted North American ideals of education with great devotion in his native land was José Pedro Varela of Uruguay. Like Sarmiento, he visited the United States after touring Europe—in 1868. During his sojourn in North America he visited schools, observing methodology, buildings, and equipment, and accumulated a sizeable collection of educational publications. On his return to Uruguay, he lectured on his educational experiences and founded a society to promote popular education; it established a pilot school modeled on United States norms. In 1874, he published a book, *La educación del pueblo*, in which he set forth a compendium of educational theory and practice, largely based on North American achievements. Two years later, he was appointed director of schools of Montevideo and then national inspector of public instruction. In these positions he formulated and carried out a series of extensive reforms in Uruguayan educa-

7. *Anthology*, p. 300. See Tristán Enrique Guevara, *Las maestras norteamericanas que trajo Sarmiento*, and Alice Houston Luiggi, *65 Valiants* (trans. *Sesenta y cinco valientes: Sarmiento y las maestras norteamericanas*). It should be added, incidentally, that not all the American girls were successful in adjusting to Argentina (*A Sarmiento Anthology*, pp. 300–301).

8. Stewart and French, p. 24.

9. Robertson, p. 287. For accounts of Sarmiento and the United States in general, see Madeline Nichols, *Sarmiento: A Chronicle of Inter-American Friendship*; Amaranto Abeledo, "Sarmiento en los Estados Unidos"; and Edmundo Correa, *Sarmiento and the United States*.

tion, many of which reflected educational ideals and practice in the United States—free, compulsory instruction, the creation of local school boards, a wider and more practical curriculum, the use of the object method, the organization of normal schools and school libraries, and so forth.

The similarity of Varela's views to those of Sarmiento is apparent in the following quotation from his book: "The miracles which the United States has accomplished with respect to education are known: those are due to the united force of the authorities and the people, to the enormous sums which the state provides for that purpose, and to the enormous sums provided by the intelligent philanthropy of men of fortune! . . . A citizen of the United States believes that education is a necessity of the state, an exigency of society, and a convenience for all; and, realizing that many great sacrifices are necessary to assure the benefits of education to everyone, he disposes with pleasure of a part of his fortune in order to promote that great object!"[10]

Sarmiento and Varela were only two of a number of nineteenth-century Spanish Americans who found educational ideals in the United States worthy of study and adaptation. For example, J. Afredo Ferreira, an Argentine educator associated with some of the teachers imported from Massachusetts by Sarmiento, was greatly influenced by American educational doctrine. With the collaboration of two of those teachers, he set up model schools throughout Argentina.[11] Javier Prado, a Peruvian positivist philosopher and educational reformer, considered it a responsibility of the university to include in its teaching program elements which seemed to have contributed to the development and greatness of the United States. At the end of the century another Peruvian educator, Manuel Vicente Villarán, advocated educational reform along North American lines: "Peru should be . . . as the United States has been, a land of farmers, planters, miners, merchants, and workingmen," instead of a nest of intellectuals and bureaucrats. This was not an uncommon general attitude among the liberals. He suggested bringing American teachers into Peru, since North America offered a model for the educational organization of a free people, which the traditional European forms, with their aristocratic, monarchical, and clerical traditions, did not.[12]

10. Quoted in Robertson, p. 292; Robertson's account of Varela's life and achievements is valuable and well documented.
11. See Zea, *The Latin American Mind*, p. 210.
12. Prado quoted ibid., p. 191; Villarán quoted ibid., p. 192.

But by no means all Spanish American observers judged education in the northern colossus to be perfect. Coming from essentially patrician societies, some might grant that the widespread system of primary education was admirable enough, but they missed in the United States the educational attention which they thought should be paid to the elites. The Guatemalan diplomat Fernando Valero, writing in 1825, was amazed at how good and universal elementary education was. He believed, nevertheless, that the system in general was mediocre, producing a great many people with an average education but few really brilliant minds.[13] Vicuña Mackenna, visiting the United States some thirty years later, granted that most children got an elementary education and that consequently illiteracy was disappearing, but he criticized the lack of emphasis on a broad and liberal education (p. 95).

Later in the century, José Milla presented a fairly detailed and well-balanced picture of education in the United States. He was particularly interested in the fact that the system depended directly on the citizens, through their elected boards of education, and not on a centralizing Ministry of Education. With satisfaction he noted that education was supported in part by local taxes and in part by land-grant funds. Because of the structure of the system, he was impressed by the fact that the type of education varied considerably in different parts of the country and that frequent changes and reforms in methodology were being introduced. Like Sarmiento, he remarked on the fine school buildings, the presence of women teachers, the use of object lessons, the emphasis on physical education, and the fact that rich and poor mingled in the same school. Taking up a point frequently discussed by visitors of the time, he viewed coeducation with some alarm; it might be all right in the United States because of the customs and colder temperament of the people, but it would not be advisable in his country. On the whole, primary education was very fine, he thought; the schools were "real models of instruction."

Secondary and university education were not so praiseworthy in Milla's eyes. Although he was astounded and pleased by Vassar College with its remarkable endowment from a brewer's fortune, he found instruction in most universities far too encyclopedic; too many courses, many of them of a purely practical nature, clogged the curriculum: "It loses in depth what it gains in extension." Expressing a rather representative opinion, he said that secondary education and universities in Europe were much more thorough

13. Valero, *Bosquejo de los Estados Unidos de Norte América*, p. 39.

than and superior to the slipshod instruction in the United States (pp. 257–65).

The most forthright and all-inclusive critic of American education was José Martí, writing just at the end of the period under consideration. He found the whole theory and practice of education wrongly directed and set the tone for a good deal of later criticism which condemned education in the United States as utilitarian and overspecialized. According to Martí, "they stifle the individual in the child, instead of encouraging the movement and expression of originality that every creature bears within him. Thus they produce a sterile uniformity, a kind of liveried intelligence"; "The routine machine-man, very able in his special field, completely closed to all knowledge of or commerce and sympathy with what is human: that is the direct result of elemental and exclusively practical instruction. . . . In the public school they go no further than reading and writing and arithmetic."[14] This, of course, is a long way from the compulsive admiration of Sarmiento et al., and fits into a new pattern of images toward the United States, which developed so emphatically toward the end of the century, of a materialistic, soulless, imperialistic nation.

When one considers the type of education, principally French, to which most of our witnesses were accustomed, and how notably different its aim of educating gentlemen of the ruling class from the experimental, pragmatic, and more or less democratic approach of the Americans, it is hardly surprising to find basic criticism such as Martí's and Vicuña Mackenna's. Their views doubtless reflected an ambivalent attitude in their own countries. As professed advocates of republican institutions, they owed at least theoretical allegiance to popular elementary education. But their often aristocratic personal tastes did not find the rough-and-ready education of the United States very congenial, with its tendency toward mingling social classes. In spite of the efforts of such men as Sarmiento, educational systems in Spanish America to this day resemble European models a good deal more than North American ones.

## SOCIAL EQUALITY AND THE NEGRO

Rich and poor sat down side by side in American schools; this was only one of the manifestations of social equality in the United States which continued to startle Spanish Americans. A Mexican

14. Martí, *Obras completas*, 33:110, 32:68.

poet, Prieto, recorded his conviction that equality in the neighboring republic was not merely a theory but a practice; the lackey enjoyed the same privileges as his master; the masses were not regarded as rabble but as human beings, and the common man had achieved a sense of dignity previously unheard of (Onís, p. 119). Another poet, the Colombian Caro, speaking of the silk dresses worn by women in New York, said, "The craze of luxury has invaded all classes here, and the democratic spirit will not permit a maid to be less well-dressed than her mistress. That is why a servant here is a gentleman, and his service is as bad as it is expensive."[15]

In the record of his travels, Sarmiento often speaks of the lack of a social hierarchy. On American trains, for example, the European system of segregating passengers by social or economic class generally gave way to one-class coaches. Hotels were like palaces for the masses. He drew a graphic picture of equality among the people in dress, in manner, and even in intelligence. "The merchant, the doctor, the sheriff, and the farmer all look alike. . . . Gradations of civilization and wealth are not expressed, as amongst us, by special types of clothing. Americans wear no jacket or poncho, but a common type of clothes, and they have even a bluntness of manner that preserves the appearance of equality in education" (*Anthology*, pp. 206–8).

Vicuña thought that it was peculiar but typical of Americans that the sailors on a Mississippi River boat fraternized with the passengers, even though the latter were persons of distinction (p. 41). Valero was surprised that in public houses tea was served to country people with the same delicacy as to city dandies and that even common laborers and field hands read books.[16]

Against this background of free-and-easy social life, many observers considered it paradoxical that the Negroes, either as slaves or as free men, were pushed beyond the boundaries of any social class. Alberdi, when he visited his cherished Philadelphia and came forth from Independence Hall filled with the deepest emotion, was abruptly caught up as he saw a lavish carriage passing by, liveried Negro footmen exhibiting their menial state; he asked his companion how it was possible to reconcile that scene with the ideals of the republic.[17]

Pre–Civil War visitors unanimously believed that slavery was

15. Quoted in Torres, p. 4.
16. Valero, pp. 10–11.
17. Pablo Rojas Paz, *Alberdi*, pp. 173–74.

the great blot on the American escutcheon, and sometimes showed their familiarity with *Uncle Tom's Cabin*. Having abolished slavery in their own republics some decades before, they felt a virtuous horror at the peculiar institution and the cruelty attributed to it. Vicuña Mackenna, visiting a Louisiana plantation, recorded that slaves were treated like tools or animals and described the shame of a slave sale. He was nauseated to think that offending or runaway slaves were hunted down with dogs and burned alive (pp. 39–40, 102). Even Sarmiento, ordinarily tolerant of North America's faults, exclaimed, "Alas slavery, the deep, incurable sore that threatens gangrene to the robust body of the Union!" (*Anthology*, p. 265). Lincoln was generally praised as the Great Emancipator.

After the Civil War, it was apparent to Spanish American visitors that the Negro was not yet free in fact. The crimes committed in the name of lynch law scandalized observers, friendly and unfriendly alike. Social discrimination against the black man was as loudly decried by Spanish Americans then as now. Juan Montalvo, the Ecuadorian essayist of continental fame, wrote: "But a nation so extravagant and fantastic as the United States of America, where the customs run contrary to the laws; where the latter summon Negroes to the Senate, and the former refuse them entrance to restaurants and inns; where democracy reigns in institutions, and aristocracy in the form of pride and scorn excludes from the common society those whose color is not light enough; where neither talent nor wealth is of the slightest avail if the individual is stigmatized as quadroon or mulatto . . . this nation, I say, in the midst of its liberty, its liberalism, its progress, must inspire terror in the breasts of South Americans."[18]

Echoing speculation current in the United States at that time, some critics commented on the possibility of the establishment of a black nation in the South. Sarmiento believed that a racial war of extermination might be waged, or alternatively that there could be created a backward, black nation existing alongside a powerful and cultivated white republic (*Anthology*, p. 265). Camacho Roldán, in an exceptionally reasoned analysis of the Negro problem, also prophesied serious racial strife and discussed the idea of a separate Negro state being born; in his view, however, the only solution would be the fusion of the races (pp. 716–25). Milla, commenting on the injustice of racial discrimination, took refuge in a rather smug platitude: you cannot root out social prejudices in a day, and the passage of time is the only cure (p. 134).

18. Quoted in Crawford, *A Century of Latin American Thought*, p. 173.

WOMEN AND THE FAMILY

With regard to the position of women in North American society, the attitude of our hemispheric neighbors has varied remarkably little from the days of independence to World War II. They have shown continued interest in and surprise at woman's freedom and her importance on the social scene. In the period under discussion their fascination was generally tinged with respect and approval.

The physical charm of American women, of course, did not go unnoticed. Speaking especially of country girls, Sarmiento believed "their faces generally do honor to the human race," and, after visiting a physical education school for girls in Massachusetts, he gave high praise to the students' beauty and fitness (*Anthology*, p. 275). Miguel Cané, an Argentine observer, praised the elegance of the women of New York, and Pombo referred to the brilliance of their eyes and the scarlet of their cheeks, as well as the oriental luxury of dress of the "majestic army" on Broadway. Another Colombian poet, however, was less gallant; to him the New York women were long in the waist and flat-chested, and their feet were too big.[19]

Almost everybody remarked on the special respect and deference accorded women. They were put on pedestals by their men, and their freedom was given particular protection both by law and custom. "No one considers himself at liberty to speak to them, and anyone who should try to molest them would be liable to suffer the most serious consequences."[20] An Argentine litterateur was nonplussed and perhaps frightened when, on the train from New York to Buffalo, he looked from his upper berth and saw a lone lady traveler in the lower.[21] Sarmiento wrote, "The unmarried woman is as free as a butterfly until the moment of entering the domestic cocoon for the fulfillment of her social functions with matrimony. Before this period, she travels alone, she strolls through the streets of the cities, and publicly carries on chaste yet untrammeled love affairs under the indifferent eyes of her parents. She receives people who have not been introduced to her family, and at two in the morning, she returns home from a dance accompanied by the man with whom she has waltzed exclusively all night" (Onís, pp. 174–75).

19. Cané, *En viaje*, p. 291; Pombo, "Las norteamericanas en Broadway," in *Poesías completas*, pp. 108–13; José Eusebio Caro, *Epistolario*, pp. 97–98.
20. Milla, pp. 266–67; see also Cané, p. 289; Vicuña Mackenna, *Diario*, p. 59; and Jorge Vargas H., "Cartas importantes," 3:340.
21. Cané, p. 305.

Predictably, there was some difference of opinion about the higher education of women. Valero was astonished and favorably impressed; as a result of their education, women were thoughtful and had knowledge of benefit to society. He remarked especially on groups of young women going to Washington to learn about the political system.[22] Sarmiento was pleased to see poor girls borrowing money to go to normal school and repaying it when they found well-paid positions (*Anthology*, p. 240). Vicuña found the young Boston bluestockings to be "spiritual, educated but not pedantic, friendly but not pushing; they freely discussed all kinds of social themes." He was particularly gratified to discover that they opposed slavery and the Mexican War (p. 61). Milla, even though he admitted the virtues of feminine freedom, had reservations about coeducation and grumbled that young women studied too much liberal arts and not enough domestic science (pp. 267–68).

Two of our witnesses judged American women in harsh terms. Rafael Reynal, a Mexican politician, alleged that their complexion looked fresh only because of cosmetics, that they were too practical minded and considered love of little importance, and that they married only for wealth and position, regarding their husband as a kind of "second father."[23] Pombo accused his Broadway beauties of being capricious, cruel, domineering, and deceptive:

> All is passion and life 'neath their angel's brow,
> Like the fearful river in its fits of anger;
> Their heart? Look at it, list to its victims,
> Crying in that dark, silent, cold abyss![24]

As for the American family, the visitors of this period for the most part formed no very coherent picture, confining themselves to noting some differences between their own families and those of the North. They noticed, for example, that each family lived in its own house, not in the joint-family style; that relatively little importance was given to family life, each member going his own way and the home being simply a place in which one ate and slept; that the normal house had only one servant at the most; and that children were given a great deal of attention.[25]

22. Valero, pp. 45, 64.
23. Reynal, *Viaje por los Estados Unidos del Norte*, pp. 138–39.
24. Pombo, p. 113.
25. Vicuña Mackenna, p. 85; Prieto, quoted in Onís, pp. 118–19; Cané, p. 289.

The early independence of children was a shock to some observers. The fact that they became economically independent so young appeared as odd as the friendly, companionable treatment given by fathers to sons.[26] Sarmiento said, "The Yankee child horrifies the European by his assurance, his cautious prudence, his knowledge of life at ten years of age" (Onís, p. 174).

Divorce, which was to become such a point of censure in the twentieth century, was noted only by two of the writers who provide the sources for this section. One of them, Camacho Roldán, approached the question in a relatively objective, fact-finding mood, and surmised that the great increase in the divorce rate between 1867 and 1886 was due to industrialization, immigration, and the multiplication of transport facilities. Curiously, he concluded that the net effect of divorce would not be socially harmful: "I am inclined to believe that divorce will be a useful corrective for marriage, as much by making people more serious in the selection of their spouse as by regularizing relations in marital life. . . . As time goes on it will become a permanent institution" (pp. 860–77).

One gets the impression that most of the travelers never had an opportunity to know an American home intimately. Vicuña Mackenna was an exception; he was entertained in the Boston home of a North American traveling companion and retained that experience as his most favorable impression of American life. In the midst of an especially harsh denunciation of the evil wrought by mercantilism upon life in the United States, he paused to pay homage to the American home: "The moral sense, which is perhaps more pure and clear in the home of the man from the North than among us, is nevertheless kept firm only in the domestic corner, in the breast of the mother and her children. I have known noble souls and I have gone into the domestic sanctuary, the sacred home, and I have met only virtues to admire" (pp. 100, 104).

### RELIGION

Although religion was a basic factor in the nineteenth-century American home and in other social institutions, it aroused relatively little interest among our witnesses. We have seen that the spirit of religious toleration as an aspect of American political life continued to be highly regarded by liberal Spanish Americans,

26. Valero, p. 63; Prieto, quoted in Onís, p. 118.

and many considered Puritanism to be the mother of a number of estimable virtues which were evident in the social fabric. Sarmiento believed that the descendants of the Pilgrims inherited "their tradition of resignation and hard manual labor . . . the elaborator of the great moral and social ideas that make up the American nationality" (*Anthology*, pp. 227–28). Camacho Roldán, clearly differentiating the character and religion of settlers in the South from the Puritans in New England, described the latter as having "energetic characters, souls tempered in the fire of love for liberty, in which the feeling for family maintained austere customs" (p. 532).

Friendly observers sometimes discovered admirable qualities in American Protestantism. Sarmiento wrote, "It is of course astonishing to a lukewarm South American Catholic to see the high and extensive scale on which religion operates in the midst of that extreme North American liberty." Of the traveling preachers so common at that time, he said, "They are rough, energetic men who everywhere act as a stimulant to stir men's minds to a contemplation of the eternal verities. Theirs are as truly spiritual exercises as those of the Catholics—even more spiritual, for . . . the pastor or pastors at an open-air religious meeting . . . stir their dull minds and reveal the image of God in inconceivably grandiose proportions" (*Anthology*, pp. 226–27). Bilbao, as noted, praised Protestantism as a stimulant for freedom; he became, in fact, an outcast in his own country for his heretical beliefs. Milla, although uncomfortable in Protestant churches, where "worship appeals more to the reason than to the imagination and the senses," emphasized the morality and devotion to duty of the Protestant ministry (pp. 98–99).

Like Bilbao, Camacho Roldán linked North American political liberalism with Protestantism and found the combination good: "That freedom of interpretation and the independent, democratic organization of its religious institutions, instead of weakening or extinguishing religious fervor, has strengthened it." Religion, he continued, had great influence among educated people and talented men were attracted to the ministry. He observed that Protestantism was becoming less dogmatic and more open to the implications of scientific discoveries. He praised certain sects, such as the Congregationalists, for their liberalism, their opposition to slavery and the evils of drink, and their help to the Indians and Chinese (pp. 785–93).

As was true earlier in the century and also in more recent times, the strange behavior of Protestant sects was a fairly popular conversation piece. The strict social customs and the singing and dancing of the Shaker communities in New York State interested Valero. This same sect moved Camacho to remark on their splendid example in sacrificing personal desires for the common good. The Mormons, on the other hand, roused Milla to condemn their polygyny, their alleged cruelty, and intolerant fanaticism.[27] Sarmiento had high regard for Unitarians. In his first trip to the United States, he described theirs as a faith "that tends to unite in a common center all the subdivisions of sect and raise belief to the order of religious and moral philosophy." Years later, as Argentine minister, he again praised the Unitarians and admired "the deeply religious feeling that keeps the mind and heart of this nation active" (*Anthology*, p. 284). Camacho noted that Unitarians, while they were not "orthodox Christians," were firm upholders of moral virtues and wished religion to rise to the level of science (p. 792).

One of Sarmiento's more interesting pages is a description of a camp meeting, presumably Methodist or Baptist: "They send the women into the forest in one direction, and the men in another, to meditate alone and commune with themselves. . . . The effects of this moral leechcraft are strange and difficult to explain. The women become delirious and twist and writhe on the ground foaming at the mouth. The men weep and clench their fists. At length a religious hymn, chanted in chorus, slowly sweetens their holy visitations. Reason gains the upper hand, consciences are soothed, and faces show a deep melancholy, mingled with signs of moral benevolence, as though their feeling for justice had been strengthened by that mental catharsis."[28]

As is so often evident in this survey, those aspects of the American social structure which seem to have attracted the most attention among Spanish American commentators—at least those cited in this study—were matters which had particular relevance to significant problems at home. Hence education and immigration were favorite topics in their considerations of the United States, while such important questions as crime and the legal system,

27. Valero, p. 29; Camacho Roldán, p. 589; Milla, p. 47; Vicuña Mackenna, pp. 47–48, was outraged by the Mormons and saw their religion as the "sanctification of materialism."

28. *Anthology*, p. 227; José María Samper was not amused by the diversity of sects. In his eyes, it led to all the republic's ills—its materialism, its mindless cult of force and success, slavery, etc. (*Historia de una alma*).

social welfare, and the sociology of the westward movement went relatively unnoticed. On the whole, the image of the United States produced in the minds of these observers by what they understood of the social fabric was favorable and sometimes capable of providing models for action in their own countries.

6

# The Arts, Literature, and Philosophy

It is painfully apparent in the commentaries of this period that Spanish Americans did not look to the great republic of the North for inspiration in spiritual or artistic achievement. In varying degrees that republic, they believed, could point the way to useful political solutions and material progress, but it became almost axiomatic that such progress left little time or place for the work of the spirit, if indeed it did not actively inhibit it.

For the most part, the witnesses did not belabor this point, as have more recent Spanish American writers. They themselves were so interested in the marvels of a developing industrial civilization that generally their comments on high culture in the United States were limited. Caro, a poet, perhaps summarized their often unspoken impression when he said, "The Americans have everything: an immense and beautiful country, an admirable government, good laws, strict customs; they lack only what makes it all worthwhile; taste, sensibility, and appreciation of beauty. They are totally lacking in this last element. . . ."[1] With reference to a particular aspect of culture, Milla wrote, "The fine arts, that luxury of old societies whose civilization goes back for centuries, have not had time to develop in that young and perhaps too positivist people, which has given preferential attention to material advance" (pp. 255–56).

Occasionally, one finds citations of specific examples of the lack of artistic taste among Americans. Sarmiento, who was in no sense anti-American, was moved by the beauty of Niagara Falls (as were practically all Spanish American pilgrims), but recorded the sole

1. Quoted in Torres, "U.S. in 1850," p. 5.

reaction of a *yanqui* sightseer: "Those falls are worth millions" (*Anthology*, p. 236). Milla found New York's brownstone mansions monotonous and gloomy in their exterior and ostentatious within —all in bad taste (p. 256). Vicuña Mackenna attended theaters conscientiously in New York and elsewhere and found good taste sadly absent; the audiences seemed to prefer stupid histrionics and silly vaudeville to serious dramatic or musical art (pp. 6, 91). And, of course, the atrocious manners of *yanquis*, which we will consider as an aspect of the American character, were a constant reminder of bad taste and lack of culture.

The most fervent devotees of North American civilization sometimes felt obliged to reconcile in some way their great admiration for that civilization with its all-too-apparent neglect of traditional culture and the arts. At the best, their efforts in this direction were specious and not very convincing. Some took an obvious tack by declaring that artistic and cultural development would come in due time. Caro, noting the rapid establishment of centers of higher learning, believed that the state of cultural lethargy would change.[2] Camacho Roldán, admitting that the United States was feeble in great intellectual achievements, insisted that this was to be expected in such a young country (p. 673).

Sarmiento struggled valiantly against odds and with considerable sophistry to extenuate the charges of cultural backwardness in his beloved model republic: "Americans believe that they have no artistic feeling and affect to scorn works of art as the fruit of ancient societies corrupted by luxury. I believe, nevertheless, that I have been able to detect a profound and delicate feeling for the beautiful and great in this people marching rapidly in search of material comfort." He then proceeded to shift the field of the discussion from the fine arts to moral beauty, for which, he declared, the Americans had a keen and developed sense, as was evident in their efforts to eliminate ignorance, poverty, and moral and physical degradation. In Sarmiento's analysis, the Washington Monument (then being built) was a symbol of the *yanqui* artistic genius, of "the material desire to surpass the whole human race, all civilizations, and all centuries in daring." The contributions from citizens all over the Union to the building of the monument were "the clearest evidence, in my opinion, of the existence of a material artistic feeling." He gave a rather foggy definition of what he meant by "American art": "the manifestation of that constant aspiration on the part of the people for a national conception, embodied in

2. Ibid.

and revealed by every citizen through successive generations . . ."
(*Anthology*, p. 251).

Camacho Roldán also took a somewhat casuistic approach in
his defense of the spiritual quality of American life. Remarking
that it was usually believed that United States civilization was
only materialistic, he claimed that the truth was obscured by the
energetic bustling of Americans. Actually, he said, the development
of less materialistic faculties was abundantly evident in the sacrifices for idealism in the Civil War, in the widespread spirit of
philanthropy and mutual help, in the cosmopolitan interests of
the people as reflected in newspapers, and in the progress of applied science.[3]

### MUSEUMS AND ART APPRECIATION

Friends of the United States pointed to the establishment of museums and art galleries as proof of the increasing artistic interests
of North Americans. Sarmiento, although he granted that works
of art in these institutions were "barbarously mixed with curiosi-
ties brought back by mariners," insisted that the collections were
being enriched and embellished (*Anthology*, p. 251). Camacho was
pleasantly surprised to find good art museums supported by private donations in St. Louis and Cincinnati; he listed with satisfaction their European canvases (pp. 602–3). Vicuña Mackenna,
whose view of North American culture was pretty consistently
scornful, declared that American museums, with their collections
of oddities, were simply "temples of humbug" (p. 51).

During Martí's long residence in the United States, he visited
many art galleries in New York and wrote in South American
newspapers detailed and appreciative reviews of the exhibitions
he saw. Although he had little use for the wealthy patrons of art
in New York, he recognized their usefulness in fomenting the arts:
"Attracted by the smell of wealth, the world's art is flooding New
York. Rich people to boast of their luxury, municipalities to encourage culture, and saloons to attract the curious—all purchase
at fancy prices the most delicate and daring works produced by
European artists. If you do not know the pictures in New York,
you do not know modern art." He particularly appreciated the
Metropolitan Museum and wrote admiringly of its good lighting

3. Camacho Roldán, pp. 668–72; see also Milla, *Un viaje*, p. 255.

and splendid arrangement of collections. New York could well be proud of it, he wrote.[4]

Martí was also interested in and impressed by the progress made by American painters in freeing themselves from European models and creating an original style. Visiting an exhibition in 1880, he found it mostly imitative, although there were some American touches. Eight years later at a watercolor show he was amazed at the development. He recognized Winslow Homer (1836–1910) as an unmistakably American painter with "all the strength of primitive art." Other artists whom he considered outstanding were Eastman Johnson (1824–1906), Albert Bierstadt (1830–1902), Edward Moran (1829–1901), and Louis Tiffany (1848–1933). Although still in its cradle and lacking in polished technique, American painting was achieving a spontaneous, natural realism with a good instinct for color, Martí thought. The quality of American art was in contrast to the crudity and extravagance characteristic of some other aspects of American culture.[5]

Sarmiento presaged modern interest on the part of foreigners in the potentiality in the United States for mass democratic appreciation and support of the arts. He told of the traveling exhibition of a statue, "Venus in Chains," by an American sculptor, Popper; everywhere, in spite of the mutterings of Puritan prudery, it was received with interest and admiration and earned a good deal of money for the artist. "This popular ovation," Sarmiento thought, "bode more powerful stimuli and a more resounding glory to American art than kings have ever been able to stimulate when spending for the encouragement of the fine arts money not their own but wrung from the sweat of their people for their selfish pleasures." He prophesied that European artists would likewise take their works on American tours and thus educate *yanqui* artistic taste (*Anthology*, pp. 251–52).

## BEAUTY IN A MATERIAL CIVILIZATION

A number of critics, both benign and unfriendly, discovered beauty of an unpretentious kind in the growing cities of the Union. Camacho was enthusiastic about the esthetic charm of St. Louis

4. *Obras completas*, 43:180, 40:141. The paintings in New York's Hoffman House often attracted approving attention; see, for example, Vargas H., "Cartas," p. 339.
5. Martí, 40:141, 142–59.

—the tree-filled public squares, the wide streets, the fountains, and the flowering gardens with their statues (pp. 64, 66, 89). Vicuña, seeking beauty in a welter of noise and activity, found it in the tree-lined streets and parks of Philadelphia, in the Boston Common, and in cemeteries, especially Greenwood Cemetery in Brooklyn.[6] Sarmiento had a flexible idea of artistic pleasure and discovered it in contemplating many aspects of North America's material civilization. The villages of the Northeast, with their trim, well-proportioned brick houses adorned with green shutters and their little gardens enclosed within artistic white fences, pleased him as did the bright, red plows, the polished and ornamental harnesses of the horses, and the graceful, freshly varnished carriages. Even the commercial signs with their elegant gold lettering struck him as works of art (*Anthology*, pp. 202–5).

Both Sarmiento (*Anthology*, p. 214) and Vicuña Mackenna (pp. 41–42) thought the St. Charles Hotel in New Orleans was not only sumptuous, but also a manifestation of artistic splendor and good taste. Sarmiento considered it "a superb palace . . . which no civil or religious monument in the United States, except the Capitol at Washington, surpasses either in dimensions or good taste." The St. Nicholas Hotel in New York and Tremont House in Boston stimulated similarly favorable comment from Vicuña Mackenna (p. 84).

SPIRITUAL VALUES AND TECHNOLOGY IN THE BALANCE

The notion, later so widely propagated by José Enrique Rodó, that, while North America surpassed the South in technical genius, Spanish America was the guardian of human, artistic values appears to have germinated during this period. It was perhaps cultivated by reading the works of French observers of the American scene who frequently decried the materialistic civilization of the United States. In a letter to Francisco Bilbao, written in 1853, the liberal French churchman Lamennais said, "Providence has destined [Hispanic America] to be the counterweight to the Anglo-Saxon race, which represents and will always represent in the New World blind material forces."[7] Bilbao developed this theme: "We recognize the glories and even the superiority of the North, but

6. The cemetery in Brooklyn and the Laurel Hill Cemetery in Philadelphia were apparently on the Spanish American tourist route and prompted frequent comments on their beauty.

7. Quoted in Zum Felde, *Indice crítico*, p. 137.

we also have something to put in the balance of justice." Even though it was saddled with the Spanish heritage, he insisted that in Spanish America the Indians were made a part of the social body, slavery was abolished, and hearts had room for human love. "We have not lost the tradition of man's spiritual destiny." In Spanish America the love of art, beauty, and poetry was still alive. "There is what the Republicans of South America dare to place in the balance, alongside the pride, the wealth, and the power of North America" (pp. 151–53).

With a slightly different accent, Vicuña Mackenna expressed a similar viewpoint. In spite of widespread public education, he complained, intellectual life in the United States, although it was active enough, was superficial. "True education, the possession of knowledge which ennobles the intellect, the refined cultivation of the mind, is in my opinion very weak here when compared to ourselves who have an aristocratic and limited sphere of higher education, but one which is more profound and comprehensive." The Latin tradition of civilization based on reason and ethics, he said, was at least a venerable ideal in Spanish America, if not a reality in practice, while North American civilization rested on "cold calculation and depraved egoism" (pp. 95, 100).

The thought of Martí was impregnated with the conviction that his America stood essentially for beauty, spiritual truth, and idealism in contrast to the mounting scorn of those values in North American culture. It is noteworthy that Martí in many ways was a bridge between the literary and ideological patterns of the mid-century generations and the *modernista, yanqui*-scorning generation of the turn of the century.

### PHILOSOPHY AND SCIENCE

Our witnesses doubtless did not expect to find much in the way of profound philosophical speculation in North American culture. At any rate, except for their generalizations about materialism and an occasional reference to Emerson, philosophy hardly enters into their discussion of that culture. Alberdi, indeed, used the United States as an admirable example of how a new social and political order can develop without metaphysics: "No nation is less metaphysical than the United States, and no nation can suggest more material for speculation with its praiseworthy, practical advances, to philosophically-minded nations."[8]

8. Quoted in Zea, *América como conciencia*, p. 147.

Domingo del Monte, a Cuban writing in 1840, displayed exceptional knowledge of philosophical writing in the United States.
Combatting the common idea that "works on the higher branches
of philosophy" were unknown in North America, he pointed to
Jonathan Edwards' considerable reputation as a metaphysician
and cited a number of contemporary treatises on philosophy by
Americans now forgotten which "indicate that this type of studies
is not very neglected in the country." He added that the works of
European philosophers, such as Victor Cousin, were translated,
published, and read in the United States.[9]

Most of these writers did not rate North America very high as
a seedbed for scientific thought. Sarmiento, the persistent booster
of American achievements, saw astronomers, naturalists, archeologists, and geologists in the United States "undertaking to enrich and even remake science." But even he was probably more
impressed by the practical results of American applied science—
the lightning rod, the telegraph, and so on (*Anthology*, pp. 200–
201, 254). Camacho Roldán stated that, in contrast to Europe,
North America had not pursued the path of pure science but was
more concerned with the application of general scientific laws for
the satisfaction of human needs. He cited Franklin, Fulton, Edison, and Morse as the heroes of this kind of scientific endeavor
(pp. 673–74). Vicuña Mackenna flatly denied that North Americans
were outstanding in any kind of science, noting that their scientists were either foreigners or "specialists" (p. 63).

### LITERARY CREATIVITY

Literature, and especially historical writing, was without question
the best-known aspect of North America's life of the spirit among
Spanish Americans. While they might be ignorant of or scorn the
development of the plastic arts, philosophical speculation, music,
or pure scientific thought in the North, almost any literate person
was aware that the United States had produced a literature, and
many had read American authors in French or Spanish translation,
or sometimes in the original. It is true that a few scornful souls
denied the worth of that literature, especially in the later decades
of this period. Ernesto Quesada, an Argentine author, writing in
1883, stated that no one in Argentina knew anything of North
American literature or thought except a few students of constitu-

9. Domingo del Monte, *Escritos*, 2:252–53.

tional law,[10] but the evidence would contradict that allegation as far as Spanish America as a whole is concerned.

Bilbao regarded the literary production of the United States as "*sui generis*, a magnificent expression of the New World," and said, "Their literature is the purest and most original of modern literatures. It has the best historians, such as Motley, Prescott, and Irving; the best philosophers, such as Channing and Parker" (p. 49). Domingo del Monte wrote two detailed studies, "An Intellectual Sketch of the United States in 1840" and "Characteristics of Spanish Literature," in which he endeavored to prove to doubting Thomases that North American literature and books were a significant part of their culture. If we examine a number of individual North American authors in relation to South America, we can understand the extent of the reputation achieved by American literature.

While Benjamin Franklin was celebrated during independence days as a patriot and scientific genius, he came to be known later in the century primarily as the author of the *Autobiography* and *Poor Richard's Almanack*. Numerous editions of the *Autobiography* were published in South America about the middle of the century, and the *Almanack* was equally popular; a translation in verse was published in Lima in 1874, and a special edition for Argentine schools appeared in 1873. Sarmiento and many other Latin Americans of the time who were concerned with instilling the spirit of industry and order in the hearts of their fellow-citizens found in Franklin's life and writings nutritious fare. Sarmiento wrote in 1885, "Franklin has added three new precepts to the ancient Decalogue of Morality: Work, Order, Economy, in order to obtain and make secure liberty and equality on the earth, which is the aim of all morality and which becomes the way to live happily and make others happy."[11]

The writings of a whole group of American authors were prized by Spanish Americans partly because they dealt with Hispanic themes. Such was the case with Washington Irving. His *Life of Columbus* was translated and published in Spanish as early as 1833, and many editions—including several published in Spanish America—followed. The *Alhambra* was, of course, a favorite, and Domingo del Monte considered it worthy of comparison with Pérez de Hita's *Guerras civiles de Granada*. By the middle of the century Irving's works were well known in Spanish America and

10. Quoted in McGann, *Argentina*, p. 39.
11. Englekirk, "Franklin en el mundo hispánico," p. 352 and passim.

his name was invariably included in "the group dear to Spanish pride," as Pombo said.[12]

William H. Prescott also belonged to that chosen group. His *History of the Conquest of Mexico* was published in Mexico the year following its appearance in the United States, and successive editions appeared in Santiago de Chile, Madrid, and Jalapa (Mexico). His volumes on Peru and the Catholic kings also appeared quickly in translation, and were widely read. Vicuña Mackenna referred to Prescott as "that classical and likeable genius who had painted the epic of our conquest with such masterly art." He visited the historian in Boston and found him charming, thoughtful, and impressive. Ordinarily not given to praising the North American genius, Vicuña said of Prescott, "As a historian he is without doubt the most highly regarded that America has produced" (pp. 61–62). Domingo del Monte praised him as an industrious author and marveled at his good faith and diligence in examining old archives and "the ability with which he has been able to understand and interpret them."[13] Other historical writers who were respected were George Bancroft and Jared Sparks.

George Ticknor was likewise admired and praised. Sarmiento called him the greatest scholar in the field of Spanish American literature, and Andrés Bello also eulogized him (Onís, p. 161). Del Monte, without knowing the *History of Spanish Literature*, commended the exquisite and scholarly nature of his articles.[14]

Among the novelists, James Fenimore Cooper was probably the best known. His novels are reported to have been popular in Peru as early as 1834, and in 1852 an American naval officer traveling in South America stated that Cooper was better known there than in the United States. *The Last of the Mohicans* continued throughout the century to be a widely read favorite, especially among children. *Uncle Tom's Cabin*, of course, enjoyed wide popularity and was translated in Mexico only two years after its initial publication. In the same year it was printed as a pamphlet by *El Comercio* of Lima, doubtless more for its social interest than its literary value. Although Louisa May Alcott was introduced to Spanish American readers by Martí late in the century, her tales do not appear to have been translated until the twentieth century. The

12. Monte, vol. 2, "Caracteres de la literatura española"; Pombo, "Las dos Américas," *Poesías completas*, pp. 982–85; Sarmiento and Vicuña Mackenna specifically mention Irving as outstanding.
13. Monte, 2:162.
14. Ibid., p. 165.

stories of Mark Twain began to appear in periodicals as early as 1877,[15] but his fantastic popularity in Spanish America was apparent only after the turn of the century.

In poetry, Longfellow had no northern peer for Spanish Americans of this period. He was the first North American poet to be translated into Spanish, and the roster of literary men, especially Colombians, who tried their hand at this poetic task includes a great many names prominent in the literary history of Spanish America. Rafael Pombo, a talented Colombian poet, was the first of this distinguished group to put Longfellow's verse into Spanish, making his translation of "The Psalm of Life" in 1864 while he was living in New York. Other poems which were commonly liked and translated were "Evangeline," "Excelsior," and "Daybreak." Numerous critical studies of Longfellow were also made by Spanish Americans; one of them called him "the patriarch of American letters." Recalling his interest in French and Spanish literature, Monte referred to Longfellow as a "poet who was as inspired as he was scholarly."[16]

William Cullen Bryant was less well known than Longfellow, although some of his poems were translated by such eminent poets as José María Heredia and Pombo. His visit to Spanish America late in his life helped to spread his fame; Vicuña called him "the poet of enthusiasm and art."[17]

Poe, who was to exercise such a significant influence in Spanish American literary life in the present century, was not generally known as a poet until 1887, when a volume of translations by the Venezuelan poet Juan Antonio Pérez Bonalde appeared, with an enthusiastic introduction by Santiago Pérez Triana. His tales, however, which were published in multiple editions in Spain, beginning in 1858, were quite popular. It is said that some of his tales were printed in the Lima press as early as 1847.[18] Just at the end of the period under discussion, Poe began to assume the position of North America's most celebrated man of letters.

Oddly enough, Emerson, whose idealism has had such appeal

15. Estuardo Núñez, *Autores ingleses y norteamericanos en el Perú*, pp. 159–60, 170, 188.

16. Englekirk presents a detailed study of Longfellow in Spanish America in "Notes on Longfellow in Spanish America, and "El epistolario Pombo-Longfellow."

17. Vicuña Mackenna, *Diario*, p. 63; see Manuel Pedro González, "Two Great Pioneers of Inter-American Cultural Relations."

18. Estuardo Núñez, *Autores*, p. 175; see Englekirk, *Poe in Hispanic Literature*.

to thoughtful Spanish Americans in this century, was relatively
unknown to Spanish American observers during the Concord sage's
lifetime. Sarmiento apparently had heard about him during his
first trip to the United States in 1847, but did not meet him until
1865, when he presented him with a copy of *Facundo* and dined
with him. The Argentine statesman described Emerson then as "a
public monument, wreathed with the aura of public admiration."
On Emerson's death in 1882, Sarmiento published a moving tribute to the essayist, referring to him as "a Greek head on square
Yankee shoulders, who for forty years, after suffering opposition
to his doctrines for twenty, has given direction to North American
spiritual life and has seen the birth of a school of Emersonian
ideas."[19] The sage's death also brought forth another exceptionally
eloquent eulogy by Martí; it was filled with such worshipful
phrases as "He lived face to face with nature as if all the earth
was his home, the sun his own sun, and he the patriarch"; "His
mind was priestly, his tenderness angelic, his anger sacred"; "His
mind was not for hire, nor his pen, nor his conscience. Like a star,
he irradiated light. In him the human being attained the highest
degree of dignity." It is strange that these panegyrics, and another
by Enrique José Varona, had not been preceded by some appreciation of Emerson during his lifetime. His essays were not translated into Spanish until the twentieth century.[20]

19. Englekirk, "Notes on Emerson in Latin America."
20. Martí, pp. 1053–54; Varona, *Obras*, 2:287–314. These and other data on
translations introduced in this section were taken from Englekirk, *Bibliografía de obras norteamericanas en traducción española.*

7

# The American as a Person

As in earlier years of the century, commentators of this period were so engrossed in the institutions and collective life of the United States that generally they made only a few shorthand notes on the American character. The traits they associated with that character were nearly always directly linked with their opinions of the political, economic, and social institutions and progress of the northern republic.

## A LOVER OF MONEY

In view of their concept of the United States as a prosperous giant, it was not unnatural that Spanish Americans should jump to the conclusion that the individual citizen of that republic was obsessed with a craving for money and material possessions. This trait was by all odds the most common among those attributed to the North American character by the critics during this period. There was little variation in their expression of this conviction and a few representative quotations, arranged chronologically, will reveal the almost universal tenor:

"The dominant passion in that land is commercial wealth. The labor and effort put into gaining it are excessive" (1825). "[The North American] can be identified by a strong and exaggerated love for riches" (1834). "[The Americans] are men whose only God was gold" (1848). "Money is their idol, but it is an infamous, stupid idol which the intellect of this people worships in the most absurd way" (1856). "For this wealthy, enormous, mixed-up people life is nothing more than the conquest of fortunes: this is the

105

disease of its greatness. . . . It is upsetting, making ugly, and deforming everything" (1889).[1]

Some of the observers found this appetite for money all the more incomprehensible since the North American in general, it seemed, had no pressing needs and was not by tradition ostentatious or a lover of luxury (Vicuña Mackenna, p. 101). Camacho Roldán placed a passion for business alongside cleanliness as the two most distinguishing characteristics of the American, but was somewhat puzzled because he did not seem in the least miserly or niggardly in spending his money; his wife especially always had all the money she wanted to spend (pp. 882–83).

The passion for wealth, in the opinion of a few of the commentators, led to other associated vices. Even Sarmiento thought that the Americans' materialism had led them to be unscrupulous in money matters (Onís, p. 176). Prieto cited as proof of their lack of scruples in financial affairs the prevalence of questionable bankruptcy and insurance cases, and believed that love of money was the root of all evil in both religion and politics in the United States (Onís, p. 120). We have seen that Martí feared that the purity of American democracy was being polluted by the buying of votes and the disproportionate influence of the robber barons in the political processes.

Many were disgusted because North Americans seemed to judge a man's worth by his financial status and not by his moral qualities. "How much is he worth?" was the decisive question. Martí disliked the servile admiration for those who had obtained money, no matter how, and the scorn for those who had failed or were not interested in the race for riches.[2] Perhaps the most harmful effect of the money complex in Spanish American eyes was that it seemed to overwhelm all spiritual values. Camacho Roldán, who appeared to have real affection for North Americans, ventured to counsel them on this point: "Man does not live by bread alone. There are eternal, transcendent goals the contemplation of which raises up one's character and gives temper to the soul's strength." Americans should pay more attention to delicate sentiments and to the mysterious worlds of the unknown, and less to their common daily occupations. They should nurture more Emersons, Longfellows, and Prescotts. "It is high time that the American mind should pause to think about the end to which his present race is

---

1. Valero, *Bosquejo*, p. 60; Reynal, *Viaje*, p. 150; Pérez Rosales, quoted in Onís, *United States*, p. 124; Vicuña Mackenna, *Diario*, p. 101.

2. See also Reynal, p. 159.

taking him." "The American people," he continued, "must seek their credentials to win the respect of history, not only in the accumulation of millions [of dollars], but also in the accumulation of acts of selflessness, abnegation, and justice toward humanity" (pp. 883–84).

A few Spanish Americans like Camacho thought that they recognized two conflicting tendencies in the American character: idealism and materialism. He observed that unlimited greed worked alongside philanthropic sentiments and love for humanity. Sometimes in the same individual North American one could see, he thought, the mania for making money coupled with a spirit of self-sacrifice and a desire to become one with the rest of humanity (pp. 588–89). Even Martí, who was a much more bitter critic of the United States, recognized this duality in the nature of Americans: "Which spirit," he asked, "will prevail in North American civilization? The Puritanical one, which represents the most judicious and transcendental affirmation of human rights, or the Carthaginian one of conquest and sordid profits?"[3]

## THE ACTIVIST

Another characteristic of the *yanqui* about which Spanish Americans seemed to agree, as they surveyed the miracle of progress in the United States, was his unlimited energy and his robust vitality. Vicuña Mackenna could hardly believe "the devouring activity which there is in this country, the fire which burns this land, in which it seems that men were going about breathless from an excess of life, seeking the highest peak in their incessant race. . . ."[4] In this characteristic Sarmiento discerned the heritage of the New England colonial settlers: "the iron energy to struggle against and overcome difficulties" (*Anthology*, p. 228).

Examples of how that dynamism was rapidly conquering nature and its obstacles were noted at every turn, especially in the West. Camacho saw the dredging and flood control of the Mississippi as an unprecedented burst of human effort and genius (p. 457), and Sarmiento, marveling at the growth of Chicago, exclaimed, "In the West things are attempted that seem superhuman, inconceivable, and absurd" (*Anthology*, p. 278). Vicente Pérez Rosales, a Chilean

3. Quoted in González, *Martí*, p. 49; "Carthaginian" or "Phoenician" were favorite terms to describe the *yanqui* trader.
4. Vicuña Mackenna, p. 200; see also Alberto Blest Gana, *De Nueva York al Niágara*, p. 271, and many other witnesses.

writer who followed the gold-seekers to California, was amazed that as soon as the *yanquis* arrived there they began with feverish activity to build roads, schools and churches (Onís, p. 124). Milla, having visited Chicago just after the great fire, saw in the quick recovery from that disaster proof that Americans will not let themselves be defeated in adversity. The completion of the transcontinental railway was for him further evidence of the tenacity and energy of North Americans (pp. 49, 56–57).

The will to overcome obstacles by heroic effort was, incidentally, considered by some a trait worthy of imitation by the Spanish Americans. Milla said, "Let us pay our tribute of admiration and respect to the people that has been able to carry out such prodigies, and let us take inspiration from their wholesome example" (p. 57).

## The Cold and Boastful *Yanqui*

Much less admirable in Spanish American eyes was the chilly haughtiness of the North American, which they believed was particularly apparent in his dealings with citizens of other American republics. In contrast to the quick and visible expression of feelings and ideas so customary to Spanish Americans, the undemonstrative mien, even among friends and members of a family, and the seeming aloofness of the American repelled many of the observers. The stiff man of the North often appeared to be unsociable and lacking in the jovial cordiality which they attributed to their own character and culture. As they saw it, even the seriousness of Americans revealed no deep passion or feeling.[5] In a humorous vein, Sarmiento recounted an experience in a Pennsylvania hotel. Having suffered some contretemps in his money arrangements, he flew into a good Latin rage, gesticulating and swearing in Spanish; the Americans, prim and "little accustomed to manifestations of Southern passion," were frightened out of their wits (*Anthology*, p. 257).

More distressing, however, than the general glacial manner of Americans was their attitude of disdainful contempt toward Latin Americans. It was Vicuña's opinion that the Anglo-Saxon's scorn for people of Latin origin was a modern form of the disdain with which the Vandals regarded the Romans. He cited the example of an American soldier who, during the Mexican War, had urinated

5. *A Sarmiento Anthology*, p. 231; Valero, pp. 62–63; Vicuña Mackenna, p. 80.

in the Mexican halls of Congress to symbolize the North American attitude (p. 106). *Yanqui* ignorance of Latin America was considered symptomatic of this contempt. The North American took little interest in the nations to the south or their problems and often asked silly questions about what language was spoken there, what kind of government they had, or how the people dressed, "as if they were talking about an African tribe."[6]

To Vicuña Mackenna, as to many foreign visitors in the nineteenth century, the American habit of boasting was particularly irritating. He found that there was practically no limit to their national pride. Everything in the United States—buildings, ships, men, children, and even lies—were the biggest and best in the world (pp. 99, 103).

The self-glorification of the North Americans was often a point scored against them in the Spanish Americans' fears of imperialism. Bilbao wrote, "by looking at themselves and finding themselves so great, they have fallen into the temptation of Titan, convinced that they were the arbiters of the earth and even the possessors of Olympus."[7]

## THE BOOR

Closely associated in the Spanish American mind with the American's arrogance were his roughness and his bad manners. José María Samper found this characteristic even in diplomatic representatives of the United States: "The United States has almost always sent us ministers who seem to be more qualified as plantation bosses than for the austere and delicate functioning of diplomacy: rough of character and manners, imperious, exacting, and snobbish about the prosperity of their country, their favorite thesis has been that our people of color can serve only as slaves. . . . They are ostentatious toward what they consider a servile race."[8]

Several standard examples of North American bad manners, perhaps fortified by the outrage of such European travelers as Mrs. Trollope, were often brought up. One was the eating of apples in the halls of Congress by the Congressmen.[9] Chewing peanuts, apples, and tobacco in the theaters was also frowned upon. To-

6. Vicente Quesada, *Los Estados Unidos y la América del Sur*, p. 63; Milla, *Un viaje*, p. 93.
7. Quoted in Zea, *The Latin American Mind*, p. 98.
8. Quoted in Mary Chapman, "Yankeephobia," p. 10.
9. Congressional apple-chewing was mentioned by Reynal, p. 87, and Vicuña Mackenna, p. 102.

bacco chewing and spitting in public places were considered filthy habits of the *yanquis*. In fact, Pombo wrote a whole poem attacking the customs. After a preamble praising the enterprising spirit, the self-reliance, the industry, and the public morality of Americans, he pleaded with them—before they brought the blessings of industry and peace to his country—to desist from "the horrible mania of coughing and spitting." "If your weapon of annexation is the spitting cannon, no fortification can resist such a bombardment." He added that chewing tobacco and keeping time with their feet should also be barred.[10]

Sarmiento humorously described still another oddity of American manners when he drew the vivid picture of seven dandies in conversation, two with their feet on the table, and the others with their feet draped over the chairs at various angles. He also noted the habit of eating meals in a great hurry, with all the food in one plate. But in the judgment of this great admirer of the United States such manners were to be excused, and the North Americans were really civilized people: "The Europeans make fun of the rough manners of the Americans, more put on than real," he wrote, "and the Yankees, because of a spirit of contradiction, become obstinate about the matter, and pretend that it is the prerogative of liberty to behave as they choose. . . . The only cultured people that exists in the world, the last product of modern civilization, is the North American" (*Anthology*, p. 218).

Occasionally and especially early in the century the rusticity of American manners was associated with the vision of republican simplicity and unpretentiousness that was a conscious rejection of the ceremony and etiquette of aristocracy and monarchy.[11] Regarded in this way, such manners fitted into a liberal ideal and were found praiseworthy. Alberdi noted with approval that the style of the Americans was so simple that even elegant men wore straw hats, and that the American government had unsuccessfully tried to persuade foreign diplomats to wear simple clothes. The plain clothing and manners of American presidents in the White House astonished and pleased Vicuña, and he remarked on the unheard-of circumstance of the president going to shop for groceries.[12]

10. Pombo, "Pajas en ojo ajeno," *Poesías completas*, pp. 820–25.
11. Reynal, p. 150.
12. Alberdi, *Memorias*, pp. 366, 368; Vicuña Mackenna, p. 72; see also Onís. p. 175.

### THE GENEROUS PHILANTHROPIST

However much of a rough-hewn money-grabber the North American was made to appear, few had any doubts about his benevolent liberality in helping his less fortunate fellows. Camacho Roldán was very favorably impressed by the unparalleled generosity of Americans in assisting the victims of the Chicago fire in 1871, when the contributions from all states totaled some $60 million. During his visit to St. Louis, he noted with gratified amazement the philanthropic donations to schools, hospitals, libraries, museums and public parks (pp. 578–79, 519). Vicuña, after castigating North American materialism, nevertheless praised in warm terms the charitable institutions founded by Americans and cited statistics to indicate their magnitude; he was particularly struck by the substantial aid given to the victims of the Irish famine in 1847 (p. 104). Martí composed an emotional obituary for Peter Cooper, the industrialist and philanthropist who had done so much for the education of the poor in New York. "I loved him as a father," he wrote.[13]

In a personal way Sarmiento discovered American generosity. When he found himself temporarily without funds in the Pennsylvania Alleghenies, a stranger, "a guardian angel," spoke to him in French and Spanish, lent him books to read, and advanced him twenty-five dollars. Later, on the train, a lady from near New Orleans offered him her home as a refuge in case he should need it (*Anthology*, pp. 257–60). Camacho Roldán was also delighted with the helpfulness of his American hosts: "In this country there is much courtesy toward foreigners and most people consider it a duty to lend them all kinds of assistance" (p. 579). Even Vicuña Mackenna, who was no great admirer of the American character, was delighted with the hospitality of his Boston hosts and said that he was made to feel entirely "at home" (p. 99).

### THE OPTIMIST

Akin to the Spanish Americans' bewilderment at the unbounded energy of the North American was their astonishment at the spirit of self-reliance and confidence which seemed to characterize the people. Vicente Pérez Rosales, after his rough experiences in California, declared that the essence of the American spirit was its

13. *Obras*, 15:57–67.

daring, constancy, and faith in the immediate future.[14] Vicuña Mackenna said, "They believe that there is nothing which they cannot undertake and nothing that is out of their reach; and with this confidence they embark on every enterprise and with it they always get the fruit that they had promised themselves" (p. 99). Sarmiento, being something of a self-made optimist himself, was especially aroused by the American's self-confidence. In his opinion, the progress of the United States was not due to its size alone, but to certain qualities of the spirit, principally self-reliance, which was a real fetish among Americans. "The American male," he wrote, "is a man with a home, or with the certainty of owning one, beyond the reach of hunger and despair, able to hope for any future that his imagination is capable of conjuring up . . . a man who is his own master" (*Anthology*, p. 222). Vicuña summarized the *yanqui* character thus: "That is the way the *yanquis* are: they have conquered nature and they have overcome themselves, the first by planning, the second as a duty, and all as a matter of custom" (p. 58).

### MISCELLANEOUS TRAITS

A few other characteristics of North Americans were occasionally mentioned by observers, but none of them with the frequency of those outlined above. Intemperance in the use of strong drink, particularly whiskey, was sometimes remarked upon with disapproval.[15] Several observers mentioned the North American's addiction to speed, apparent in his eating, his marriage (propose on Monday, get married on Tuesday), his catching a train, and the races of Mississippi river steamers. As one of them remarked, "He is always in a hurry and never stops to look at the shop-windows or the girls, as the Frenchman does."[16] A trait that has attracted the close attention of Spanish Americans in the present century— the American's penchant for organization—was sometimes noted in the nineteenth century, especially with reference to the large number of fraternal organizations like the Odd Fellows.[17] This trait competed with the famed individualism of the *yanqui*. Curiously enough, the cleanliness of the North American people and

14. Pérez Rosales, *Recuerdos del pasado*, p. 124.
15. For example, Reynal, p. 47, and Pombo, "Los filibusteros," *Poesías*, pp. 763–66.
16. Camacho Roldán, pp. 881–83; *A Sarmiento Anthology*, p. 217.
17. For example, Prieto, quoted in Onís, p. 119.

their towns, which was such an object of curiosity and admiration among those of the independence generation, was only mentioned specifically by one of our witnesses; Camacho Roldán singled it out as one of two outstanding impressions received during his trip. He liked the clean clothes, the freshly shaven faces, and the combed hair of North American men; the shining trappings of carriages and horses; and the swept streets and freshly painted houses which he had seen (p. 880).

All in all, although their images of the *yanqui* were not as varied or as discerning as those developed by later commentators, the Spanish Americans of this period had a reasonably detailed likeness of the North American person in their minds. There were elements of the stereotype in this picture, it is true, and perhaps too often they saw the flesh-and-blood North American through the lens of their concepts about American institutions or their fear of political domination by the northern colossus. They were very often impressed most by those traits which seemed to contrast directly with their own self-image—the coldness, the dynamism, the materialism, the quaint if not out-and-out bad manners.

# Part Three
## 1891-1960

# 8

# The Intellectual Background and Ways
# of Communicating

Obviously, Spanish American attitudes toward the United States in this century have been shaped in part by frequent difficulties and times of tension in hemispheric international relations and by the economic and sometimes military presence of North America in the southern republics. But the facts of intergovernmental quarrels, interventions, and American economic expansion are not enough to uncover fully the background of the complex images of the United States in Spanish America. The external events of the international scene have been construed and colored in subtle but important ways by several psychological factors and intellectual developments at work within the opinion-making groups of the Spanish American republics.

## ANGLO-SAXONS VS. LATINS

During the last half of the nineteenth century, many Spanish American thinkers, their ears attentive to intellectual fashions in Europe and especially France, were attracted to the scientific determinism of European naturalism. This attraction became evident in their allegiance to various interpretations of positivism.[1]

1. *Positivismo*, as used by many Spanish American critics, is often not pure Comte but an eclectic and elastic term embracing social Darwinism and other aspects of Spencerian sociology, the raciology of Gustave Le Bon, and other scientists' doctrines. A short, informative account is in W. J. Kilgore, "The Development of Positivism in Latin America." Leopoldo Zea's important works on positivism (*Dos etapas del pensamiento en Hispanoamérica* and *El positivismo en México*) have been criticized for the above-mentioned semantic confusion: William Raat, "Leopoldo Zea and Mexican Positivism," *Hispanic American Historical Review* 48:1–18 (1968). Actually,

Both Comte and Spencer were regarded as authorities on the nature of human society. The addiction to the apparently scientific formulae of positivism and its related European social theories took various forms in Spanish America. One of the most interesting for my purposes was the widespread preoccupation with the ideas of Comte de Gobineau, Gustave Le Bon, and others about the deterministic influence of race, and to a lesser extent of geography and climate, on the nature and progress of societies. Naturally, the Spanish Americans were especially concerned with the much publicized proposition that the Nordic or Anglo-Saxon race was superior, not only to the colored races, but also to the Celtic, Slavic, and Latin peoples. Their reaction to this supposedly scientific thesis was varied and provided a dominant theme for intellectuals, notably during the first three decades of the twentieth century.

A few agreed fully with the racist hypothesis and concluded that Spanish America, with its complex mosaic of peoples, was doomed to inferiority. Not only was the Hispanic element outside the magic circle of Nordic virtue, but the vast indigenous population in so much of the area was thought to be on an even lower rung of the racial ladder. To this dogmatism regarding the ethnic base there were often added pessimistic pronouncements about geographic handicaps. Thus the whole trend amounted to a most discouraging deterministic picture.

Alcides Arguedas in his *Un pueblo enfermo* (1909) drew dismal conclusions about the future of his native Bolivia and other republics with their masses of Indians whom geography and racial heritage, he insisted, had made morally and physically inferior. The Argentine Carlos Bunge presented in *Nuestra América* (1903) a "scientific" survey of the ethnic ingredients of the Spanish American mélange and concluded that it was characterized by three primary traits: arrogance, laziness, and sadness. A better breed, to be introduced through European immigration, Bunge believed, was the only hope for his America. The Mexican *científico* Francisco Bulnes was more of a believer in the determinative power of environment than a racist, but his outlook was as pessimistic as Bunge's. His book, *El porvenir de las naciones hispanoamericanas ante las conquistas recientes de Europa y los Estados Unidos* (1899), developed the idea that the character of a race depends

many so-called positivists, such as José Ingenieros, Justo Sierra, and José Enrique Varona, had a notable and contradictory admixture of metaphysical idealism in their thought (see Zum Felde, *Indice crítico*, pp. 187–205).

on the kind of foodstuffs it eats: wheat-eaters are progressive, and corn-fed peoples are lacking in mental and physical energy. He then proceeded to analyze the defects of Spaniards, Indians, and mestizos and to castigate the sorry society they have produced in America.[2]

It is significant for the theme here that these gloomy critics tacitly or explicitly conceded the superiority of North American civilization on the assumption that it was Anglo-Saxon. In a sense, their writings were an extreme expression of the premises on which Sarmiento and many other liberals based their thinking: Let Spanish America come as near as it can through imitation and immigration to the hemisphere's stronghold of Anglo-Saxon virtues. As we have seen, these premises did not exclude fear of United States imperialism.

Not all of the *pensadores* who were influenced to a greater or lesser extent by European theories of superior and inferior races and of the determining effects of geography reached the glum conclusions of Arguedas and his pessimistic confreres. For example, Francisco García Calderón, a cosmopolitan Peruvian essayist, accepted the proposition that the Negro and Indian elements in the Latin American population were indeed inherently inferior. He decried their vitiating effect on Latin American progress but prophesied that European culture and immigration would in the long run overbalance the retarding weight of the colored races. The question of Anglo-Saxon and Latin racial differences usually became in his thinking two conflicting traditions or "spirits," and his net attitude toward racialism seems confused or ambivalent.[3]

José Vasconcelos, well known throughout Latin America for his original and sometimes erratic thinking, was very conscious of the variation of traits and abilities among races and many of his ideas were molded within the framework of race. But he refused to go along with deterministic conclusions about innate superiority or inferiority. In the several phases of his intellectual career he actively promoted the cause of the Indian in Mexico and glorified the Hispanic "race" as blessed by particular spiritual virtues. In contrast to most racists, he believed that miscegenation, far from being harmful, gave variety and richness to a culture. In fact,

2. For lucid discussions of the ideas of Arguedas, Bunge, and Bulnes, see Crawford, *A Century of Latin American Thought*, pp. 103–8, 252–60; Martin S. Stabb, *In Quest of Identity*, chap. 2; and Zum Felde, chaps. 2–5.

3. *Les democraties latines de l'Amérique*; *La creación de un continente*; and "El panamericanismo, su pasado y su porvenir."

one of his dreams was the eventual emergence in tropical America of a fifth and "cosmic" race, the result of racial blending, surpassing all others. In some respects, Vasconcelos represented an increasingly optimistic trend in twentieth-century Spanish American thought, a denial of the fatalism manifest in such writers as Bulnes.[4]

Even during the 1880s and 1890s, when racist theories were particularly in vogue, there were brilliant dissidents. Manuel González Prada (Peru, 1848–1918) was an ardent believer in the Indian's potentiality, and José Martí (Cuba, 1853–95) rejected out of hand all arguments of racial determinism.[5]

### THE REJECTION OF POSITIVISM AND THE SEARCH FOR NATIVE ROOTS

Although the tendency to think in terms of race has by no means disappeared among Spanish American intellectuals, the pessimistic determinism of race, geography, and climate has become outmoded in recent decades. The lessened prestige of such theories was part of a general reaction against the kind of nineteenth-century Spanish American positivism that esteemed material and utilitarian values and relied on the deterministic conclusions of a questionable science and that so often had held the material progress of the United States as its model and goal.

A brilliant essay by the Uruguayan José Enrique Rodó, *Ariel* (1900), was the bible of the new idealism that summoned Spanish American youth to forsake its servile attempt to ape the imperfect civilization of the North and urged it to build a future based on spiritual values, appreciation of beauty, and the aristocracy of enlightened thinkers. Rodó's followers, the *Arielistas*, preached his gospel in their several versions, all expressing hope and faith in the possibilities of a Latin American culture growing from its own roots and peculiar talents. A Colombian disciple, Carlos-Arturo Torres, sounded the dominant note when he said, "A close and constant examination of the great European civilizations leads the Hispano-American observer to be sincerely persuaded that, aside from exceptional cases of excellence . . . the average intellectual and moral level of the civilized population of our young states is not by any means inferior to that of the old European societies;

4. *La raza cósmica* and *Indología*.
5. See Martin S. Stabb, "Martí and the Racists."

this is an extremely fruitful conviction for high endeavor and a potent one for rekindling the fires of enthusiasm and faith in ourselves—fires which have been burning low during long days of testing and depression."[6]

The reaction against the deterministic interpretation of positivism and the affirmation of a more idealistic view of life was stimulated by the reading of Bergson, William James, Unamuno, and others. Intuition, an appreciation of mystic insights, and the exaltation of individual emotions entered into this philosophical revolution, which was represented by Antonio Caso and José Vasconcelos in Mexico, Manuel Díaz Rodríguez in Venezuela, Torres in Colombia, Alejandro Deústua and García Calderón in Peru, Enrique Molina in Chile, and José Ingenieros in Argentina, among others.[7]

*Ariel* was an exceptionally important book, not only for its intrinsic grace and message, but also because it was a timely answer to a widespread need. To a generation dejected by pessimism and a creeping sense of inferiority, and exasperated by the admonitions of men like Sarmiento to become more progressive like the North Americans, *Ariel* offered a confident affirmation of a set of values peculiarly Latin American. "It was the longed-for reply of this weak, backward America," said another Uruguayan critic, "to the titanic potentiality of the North; its self-justification, its compensation, its retaliation." The same writer called *Ariel* "the most representative expression of the general state of mind . . . in all the countries of the continent. Rodó's book was just as much the result of a latent spiritual state in Latin America at that time as it was a determining factor in the definition of that state of mind."[8]

An Ecuadorian educator's recollections of his youth in the 1920s illustrate vividly the psychology of a generation nurtured by Rodó and his followers: "And thus, rather proudly, we made our vow of faith to our race and we held aloft, amidst our sufferings, our poverty, anarchy, and chaos, the banner of our illusions. We evoked the symbols of our glory and the goals of our past. . . . It

6. Carlos-Arturo Torres, *Idola fori*, p. 144; Agustín Alvarez, an Argentine contemporary of Rodó, was also an early opponent of the idea of the eternal damnation of Spanish America because of racial inferiority (Crawford, p. 102). Perhaps the most complete refutation of racism in Spanish America is Fernando Ortiz' *El engaño de las razas*.

7. See Luis Alberto Sánchez, *Balance y liquidación del 900*, chap. 6; Stabb, *In Quest of Identity*, chap. 3; and Zea, *The Latin American Mind*, passim.

8. Zum Felde, pp. 290, 292.

all uplifted our souls and flung the windows of the future wide open."[9]

Subsequent *pensadores* have disagreed with some of Rodó's ideas and emphases, criticizing his indifference to economic factors and his aristocratic, ivory-tower aloofness.[10] Nevertheless, his hopeful quest for the basis for a true Spanish American identity has been a major trend in twentieth-century thought. In a wide diversity of forms, this search for intellectual, social, and economic independence based on qualities natively Spanish American has preoccupied the majority of thoughtful people during the major part of this century. It is often called nationalism, although one hesitates to use the word because of its cluster of imprecise connotations. In literature, theoreticians and creative writers wrestled with the problem of *americanismo*—the incorporation into novels and poetry of the distinctive stuff which may mark off Spanish America from the rest of the world.[11] In the plastic arts and music, artists have been at pains to introduce themes typical of life in their respective native lands, often exploring the Indian background or contemporary Negro cultures. In social and political life men like the *aprista* leaders and those of the Mexican revolution have sought ways of making the Indians and other depressed groups a part of the distinctively national pattern. In economics there has been much talk and a little action in the direction of throwing off the dependence on foreign capital and exploitation of resources.

As far as attitudes toward the United States are concerned, what have been the net results of, first, the ideas of racial determinism in Spanish America, and, second, the idealistic reaction to positivism? One important outcome of both trends of thought has been to magnify the conviction that the abyss between the two Americas is indeed deep and perhaps unbridgeable. In accordance with their theories, those who believed that the quality of a society is determined by racial factors saw the United States as formed by the Anglo-Saxon race, which in almost every sense was a contrast to the Latin and indigenous races. While the new seekers after national identity have rejected such a simplistic concept, they too

9. Alfredo Pérez Guerrero, *United States of America: Objective or Beginning?*, pp. 12–13.

10. See, for instance, Sánchez, *Balance y liquidación*, pp. 15–36, and Stabb, pp. 40–43.

11. See John T. Reid, "Recent Theories of Americanismo."

have customarily conjured up their own vision of Caliban *vs.* Ariel. It is true (although often overlooked) that Rodó hoped for an eventual meeting and fusing of the best traits of the northern republic and those of the Latin tradition. But most of his contemporaries and followers proudly stressed the vital differences between the two parts of the hemisphere.[12]

The various manifestations of twentieth-century nationalism have certainly had their effect on attitudes toward the United States. In particular, extreme economic nationalism has often been the rallying point for sensational exhibitions of anti-*yanqui* feeling. But Americans tend to quickly identify all forms of Latin American nationalism with anti–United States sentiment. That is not necessarily the case, and as will be evident in later pages of this study, the views of representative intellectuals have covered a wide range of responses and are often quite complex.

## PAN HISPANISM AND PAN LATINISM

One of the noteworthy elements which entered Spanish American currents of thought, especially during the first decades of this century, was the concept of Pan Hispanism. As thinkers began to consider an Anglo-Saxon North America as an antagonistic, material civilization from which their own ideal culture must be clearly separated, some turned to Spain as the sacred fountainhead from which values and traditions flowed, different from and purer than those of the North. The antipathy toward Spain which characterized the nineteenth-century liberals was now transformed by many into filial pride for an illustrious mother. The disaster of 1898, by which the Anglo-Saxon racial foe added several more notches to the stock of his imperialistic gun, aroused sympathy for the ancestral race and praise of its shining virtues.

As early as the 1850s, Spain had started an official Pan Hispanic propaganda campaign that continued in one form or another well into this century. Books, subsidized organizations in America, cultural junkets, lecture tours, scholarships, congresses—the usual panoply of an official cultural offensive—were used to promote

12. For examples of consciousness of extreme differences in the witnesses of this section, see Josá María Vargas Vila, *Ante los bárbaros*, p. 184; Benjamín Subercaseaux, *Retorno de U.S.A.*; Antonio Gómez Robledo, *Idea y experiencia de América*, pp. 107–8; and Daniel Cosío Villegas, "México y Estados Unidos," *Cuadernos Americanos*, p. 9.

the theme of cultural and racial solidarity between Spain and her former colonies.[13] But in reality such effect as these government-sponsored activities may have had was largely due to the fact that the Spanish American intellectual, caught in the tricky net of racial theories, felt an inner necessity to identify and glorify his racial origins. That there is no such thing as a Hispanic race and that their America was in fact an amalgam of numerous ethnic stocks appeared to be matters of little consequence for men like Roque Saenz Peña (Argentina), Rubén Darío (Nicaragua), or Carlos Pereyra (Mexico).

The literature produced by these spirits in search of a race was abundant and grandiloquent from 1898 to about 1930, and was current particularly in the first decade of the century. Starting in the 1930s, when Pan Hispanism became the *Hispanidad* movement directed by the Spanish Falange, the concept of blood ties with Spain became predominantly and merely a political issue; conservative and Catholic elements tended to support the *Hispanidad* conception, while liberals and radicals abandoned it.[14]

Inherent, of course, in the ideology of Pan Hispanism—both as an official Spanish campaign and as an eagerly clutched staff of security for bewildered Spanish American intellectuals—was an undercurrent of scorn and animosity toward the United States, its foreign policy, and its culture. In its nature, it could hardly have been otherwise, since it was an offensive operation against the fabricated superiority of the Anglo-Saxon race.

Occasionally and with the gentle stimulus of official French cultural activities, the idea of some kind of Pan Latin solidarity was expressed.[15] Speaking of this movement, Gómez Robledo, a Mexican historian said, "Born . . . in literary circles under the direct and strong influence of French culture, it was used by our elite groups as a defense of our spirituality against a 'North-Americanization' which . . . was bursting upon us in its most repulsive aspects." But this very logical tactic in the essentially unreal war of the races gained little favor in comparison with the soul-satisfying beauty of the unity of the Hispanic race. The Argentine novelist Manuel Gálvez expressed the consensus well. Speaking of the "new

13. For detailed accounts of the Pan Hispanic movement see Rippy, *Latin America in World Politics*, chap. 12, and his "Pan Hispanic Propaganda in Hispanic America."

14. Bailey W. Diffie, "Ideology of *Hispanidad*."

15. For example, Vargas Vila, p. 87.

race" being born in his native land, he said, "Despite the mixtures, it will be a Latin race. . . . The men who come to populate this country are Latins in an overwhelming majority. Our spirit and our culture are Latin. But within our Latinism we belong, and will eternally belong, to the Spanish caste."[16]

### CONTINENTAL SOLIDARITY

Inherent in this eager pursuit of a Spanish American personality has been the conviction, at least at the theoretical level, that such a personality must be that of the whole of the Spanish-speaking republics, and sometimes of the complete Latin American family. It is true that Mexican and Argentine writers in particular have worried a good deal about the national characters of their respective countries,[17] but in general the tendency has been to revert to a spiritual version of Bolívar's political dream of a federated Spanish America.

In the earlier years of this century, one of the professed purposes of Latin or Spanish American solidarity was to combat the *yanqui* peril. The Chilean poetess Gabriela Mistral expressed the idea very neatly: "Today we are Mexico, Venezuela, Chile, the Aztecan Spaniard, the Quechuan Spaniard, the Araucanian Spaniard, but tomorrow our common suffering will weld us into one. Let us devote all our activity, like an arrow, toward that inevitable future: one only Spanish America united by two stupendous factors —the language God gave us and the misery which the United States gives us." Both Blanco-Fombona and Vargas Vila seriously advocated some kind of a Latin American league to beat off the northern invader. Rodó, although not so fearful of *yanqui* political imperialism, was also a firm supporter of Latin American unity.[18]

With the inspiration of José Vasconcelos and under the leadership of the Argentines José Ingenieros and Alfredo Palacios, an organization called the Unión Latino-Americana was actually established in Buenos Aires in 1922. For some years this society

16. Gómez Robledo, p. 73; Manuel Gálvez, quoted in Davis, *Social Thought*, p. 424; his *El solar de la raza* (1911) is an eloquent example of an attempt to identify Argentina with the Spanish "race."

17. See especially the writings of Ricardo Rojas and Eduardo Mallea (Argentina) and Samuel Ramos and Octavio Paz (Mexico); chap. 6 of Stabb's *In Quest of Identity* is a good summary of the Argentine situation.

18. Gabriela Mistral, quoted in Donald M. Dozer, *Are We Good Neighbors?*, p. 318; Rodó, quotations in Sánchez, *Balance y liquidación*, pp. 86, 90.

carried on a campaign of propaganda in favor of juridical, economic, and even political confederation among Latin American
nations and against North American imperialism.[19]

In more recent years, "the Western Hemisphere idea" has continued to find frequent expression; it has sometimes lost its anti–
United States character and has become a conventionalized concept of spiritual or cultural kinship. One occasionally comes across
the notion that the United States could be part of the hemispheric
brotherhood. The Ecuadorian poet Carrera Andrade has written
in rather vague terms, "The American of our day—both in the
North and in the South—has a new and original vision. His feeling
of human fraternity logically leads him to his yearning for universal solidarity."[20]

## AMERICA'S DIVINE MISSION

Intimately linked with the idealistic reappraisal of the Spanish
American character and its potentialities that began with Rodó,
and associated also with the concept of continental solidarity, has
been the commonly voiced conviction that America (usually Latin
America) has a destiny to fulfill in world history. This is a modern
version of an old European concept which also had its adherents
in the United States.[21]

In the older commentators, the messianic mission of America
was usually restricted to that part which enjoyed the blessings of
the Latin "racial" heritage. Vasconcelos said, "Those peoples
which are called Latin, because they have been the most faithful
to America's divine mission, are those destined to carry it out. . . .
In order to create that changeable, malleable, ethereal, deep and
essential fabric [the Cosmic Race], the Ibero-American race must
become steeped in its mission and embrace it as if it were a mystic
vision." Vargas Vilas' assertions were equally unqualified: "The
race is everything—our powerful, tropical race—made up of all
the human varieties which have entered into its formation. There
is the source of our amazing and hidden organic potentiality for
the future."[22]

19. Clarence H. Haring, *South America Looks at the United States*, pp.
142 ff.; *Por la unión latino-americana* (Buenos Aires, 1922) by José Ingenieros
is a representative manifesto of this movement.
20. Jorge Carrera Andrade, *Rostros y climas*, pp. 119–20.
21. See Hans Kohn, *American Nationalism*, pp. 21 ff.
22. Vasconcelos in Englekirk et al., *An Anthology of Spanish American
Literature*, pp. 665–66; Vargas Vila, p. 122. For other examples of the divine

Both world wars served to reinforce the mystique of the New World's mission of carrying and brightening the torch of civilization while the Old World languishes and decays. A Chilean philosopher, not long after World War I, said, "The apparently incurable maladies of Europe have made us think of America as a land of promise where a new humanity may flourish and which may reach an ideal of perfection impossible for the Old World precisely because she carries within her the dissolution engendered by hatred and age-long feuds."[23]

To the student of inter-American attitudes it is significant that, particularly during and occasionally since World War II, the Spanish American dream of a golden destiny for America has sometimes included the United States. An Ecuadorian publicist wrote in 1939, "The two Americas are fulfilling a single destiny: a political organization and a social way of life built within the norms of respect for human liberty. . . . The culture of these peoples of America—peoples and cultures which are now being formed—will have as its peculiar and highest quality a perfected political organization in which order, discipline and social duty will coexist with respect for human liberty."[24] A Cuban journalist, writing in 1954, developed at some length the idea that the New World, under the leadership of the United States, has been called upon to carry out a civilizing mission in the world; Europe lives in the past, is full of prejudices, and cannot be counted on for future direction.[25]

Jorge Mañach, a Cuban essayist, presented in 1959 a well-reasoned belief for the "vocation for newness" of North and South America: "The essential feature of the American spirit, in the South as well as the North, is an attitude, at once critical and creative, of hope for a better world." Mañach proceeded to analyze the common traits and interests of Americans of the South and North, to point to the different qualities of each group worthy of imitation by the other, and concluded, "Only by helping and learning from each other can we Americans of the North and South overcome our particular defects and demonstrate that ours is indeed the promised land dedicated to the full fruition of man."[26]

---

mission theme, see Rufino Blanco-Fombona, *La lámpara de Aladino*, pp. 476–77, and Enrique González Martínez, quoted in Samuel Guy Inman, *Latin America*, p. 382.

23. Enrique Molina, *Por los valores espirituales*, p. 133.
24. Gerardo Gallegos, "El destino de América," pp. 36–37.
25. Nicolás Bravo, *El destino humano y las Américas*, chaps. 19, 25, and 40.
26. Mañach, essay in Franz M. Joseph, *As Others See Us*, pp. 340–45; César

## THE RISE OF MIDDLE GROUPS

The search for identifying qualities and a true mission among Spanish Americans that we have been describing began in a group of thinkers belonging for the most part to the old aristocracy, men like Rodó and García Calderón. But this intellectual ferment, often called nationalism, has in the last two or three decades in many Spanish American countries spread among members of the developing "middle groups," as American scholars like to call them. The growing importance of the middle class is especially apparent in countries like Mexico, Argentina, Uruguay, and Chile, although its composition and net effect on national life cannot be neatly defined.[27]

In general the middle groups appear to be made up of government bureaucrats, other white-collar workers, small-scale industrialists, merchants, army officers, journalists, university professors and students, and other scattered elements. Most observers agree that a sense of national pride, sometimes exaggerated, and a receptivity to change in economic and social patterns, incongruously allied with a kind of provincial traditionalism, are characteristic of these groups.

What effect the emergence of the middle groups has had or is having on the Spanish American image of the United States is a question without a simple answer. On one hand, although they lack the coherence of the United States middle class, they are apt to count in their ranks eager imitators of certain North American middle-class ways of life. On the other hand, some of their spokesmen—university leaders, journalists, intellectuals—in their nationalistic fervor resent the influence and power of the United States and develop anti-*yanqui* feelings. Their deep desire to live in an economically and culturally independent Spanish America leads them on occasion to lash out against the economic and even the cultural forces of the North which seem to hold them in bondage or to frustrate their new class ambitions.

---

Graña, "Cultural Nationalism," gives a comprehensive although somewhat confusing account of the Spanish American version of Manifest Destiny.

27. For discussions of the middle groups see Thomas W. Palmer, *Search for a Latin American Policy*, pp. 121–22; Kalman H. Silvert, *The Conflict Society*, chap. 14; John L. Johnson, "The Political Role of the Latin American Middle Sectors"; and especially Unión Panamericana, *Materiales para el estudio de la clase media en la América latina.*

## INTERNATIONAL COMMUNISM

The relationship of the international Communist offensive as manifested in Spanish America to the subject of this study is fairly simple and obvious. Pursuing their usual tactics, the Communist parties of all varieties in the other American republics have attempted to make capital of those aspects of indigenous ideology which are useful for their immediate and long-range purposes. Thus, they have seized upon the chauvinistic and extreme aspects of growing nationalism, fear of United States political, economic, and cultural imperialism, and resentment against the alleged exploitation by American business interests.

It is important to note that the Communists invented none of these weapons of the propaganda war. As we have seen, the manifestations of the Spanish American effort to find an identity and a future, with their frequently concomitant animosity toward the United States, developed in the Spanish American mind many years before Communist groups appeared in the early 1920s, and long before the advent of the cold war. The only new theme in the Spanish American Communist's book is a glorification of the Soviet Union (or Communist China or Cuba), and that has not usually proved to be one of his most effective tactics.

Having found their slogans and propaganda themes to a large extent ready-made for them, the Communists and their fellow travelers have, except during the five years following the Nazi attack on the Soviet Union, consistently hammered away on the anti-*yanqui* front. In the zigzagging course of the party line this particular message has been fairly constant, and the articulate support of an influential group of intellectuals and literary men, such as Pablo Neruda (Chile) and Nicolás Guillén and Juan Marinello (Cuba), has lent some prestige and strength to the anti-American propaganda. To what extent their efforts have been successful in forming an unfavorable image of the United States in the Spanish American mind is problematical.

In the United States even fairly well informed people have often been inclined to label and fear any manifestation of anti-*yanqui* sentiment in Latin America as evidence of Communist activity and power there. Without denying that the Communists have been busy and often successful, especially among labor and university groups, in fanning flames of resentment against the United States, it is inaccurate to attribute all such sentiment to "Communist agitators." For one reason or another that resentment has been sincerely felt by many non-Communist sectors in Spanish American society and by many persons who are actively anti-Communist. To confuse condemnation of North American economic imperialism by indigenous Spanish American reform groups with subversive Communist activity is not only naïve but harmful to the achievement of a viable inter-American modus vivendi.[28]

### THE IMPACT OF THREE WARS

While it is apparent to anyone who reads the Spanish American press over a period of time that events in the tortuous course of international relations have their effect—often evanescent—on Spanish American opinion of the United States, we will mention here only three high points of the history of the United States' involvement in world affairs, during the period 1898–1960. They are singled out because the reaction to them of articulate Spanish Americans joined with the prevailing psychological climate to produce significant attitudes toward the United States.

The first of these points was the Spanish American War. Inasmuch as that war was waged with the ostensible aim of freeing Cuba from Spanish rule—a goal greatly cherished by both Cuban and other Spanish American patriots—one might have expected approval of, if not enthusiasm for, the North American role in the struggle. Actually, although there were some Spanish Americans who expressed such approval, a great many more took the part of Spain. In their mood of pessimistic despair concerning the future of Spanish America, they saw the war as another episode in the offensive to impose Anglo-Saxon superiority on the Latin "race" and other "lesser breeds," and as an affront to the spiritual tradition of the Hispanic peoples. Victor Pérez Petit, a Uruguayan colleague of Rodó's, expressed very honestly their devious line of thought: "We waited and longed for the liberty of Cuba. . . . But what we could in no way accept was the intervention of North America. It was true that it was favorable to the independence of Cuba; but we were not grateful for the favor. What did that for-

28. Reasonably factual studies of the activities of the international Communist movement in Latin America may be found in Robert J. Alexander, *Communism in Latin America*, and U.S. Senate Committee on Foreign Relations, *Soviet Bloc Latin American Activities and Their Implications for U.S. Foreign Policy*.

eign nation have to do with the conflict among peoples of another race? Why did it have to interfere in something that for us was a family affair? In that struggle we were for Spain. An independent Cuba—certainly; but not as a result of North America's favor or interest. This manner of reasoning, as you can see, was a little complicated; but that's the way it was. Among us feelings have the upper hand."[29]

The retention of Puerto Rico and the Philippines at the war's termination and the passing of the Platt Amendment simply served to confirm the Spanish American's suspicion that *yanqui* cultural and political imperialism was on its way to destroying the independence of the Hispanic family. First McKinley and then Theodore Roosevelt with his "big stick" policy became the symbols of the villainy of the Colossus of the North.

Such was the prevalent attitude of Spanish American intellectuals toward United States foreign policy until World War I, and it was aggravated during the years between the wars by our intervention in the affairs of republics bathed by Caribbean waters. The entry of the United States into World War I and particularly the idealistic pronouncements of President Wilson, however, brought about among some intellectuals a new and favorable attitude toward the United States as a world power. It is true that only eight Latin American republics—seven of them the so-called banana republics—allied themselves with the United States in the war, and that particularly in Argentina writers in such a prestigious intellectual journal as *Nosotros* continued to excoriate the United States.[30] In Mexico, Wilson's aid to Carranza was certainly not appreciated by such intellectuals as Antonio Díaz Soto y Gama. But an influential group of Rodó's disciples, including Víctor Andrés Belaúnde and Francisco García Calderón (Peru) and Joaquín V. González (Argentina), found in Wilson a new idealistic hero. Youthful ears accustomed to hearing the United States identified with Caliban and imperialism now listened to hymns of praise for this ex-professor who was leading his country in the crusade for self-determination and justice. The admiration for Wilson, added to the fact that France, the spiritual home of so many intellectuals in those days, was one of the allies, and that the United States was seemingly destined to take Europe's place as the center of world

29. Quoted in *Panorama* (1963), no. 5, pp. 187–88; for other statements of animosity toward the United States as a result of the Spanish American War, see Blanco-Fombona, *La lámpara*, pp. 402, 225–30.
30. See Percy Martin, *Latin America and the War*, p. 25.

power, brought about for some and for the time being an attitude of esteem and respect for the United States.

But this little honeymoon did not last into the 1920s. Marines continued to land on Spanish American shores, even in Wilson's administration, and the activities of American business in Latin America grew enormously. The Fordney-McCumber tariff legislation (1922), which hurt Latin American trade, and the near-apotheosis of Sandino as the hero persecuted by *yanqui* "overlords" in Nicaragua helped to revive and intensify the old grudge against *yanqui* imperialism.

World War II created once again among many Latin Americans a more cordial mood toward the United States. This time the path for such a mood had been cleared by the Good Neighbor Policy. Historians may debate the actual origin of that policy and the abandonment of intervention in Latin American internal affairs, but in Spanish American eyes the Good Neighbor Policy and Franklin D. Roosevelt are practically synonymous. Although some leaders of opinion—especially among the *apristas*—had their initial suspicions of the sincerity and durability of this *yanqui* change of heart, there is no question that the Good Neighbor Policy and its translation into concrete foreign policy realities had a tremendous and favorable effect on Latin American opinion of the United States. As Duncan Aikman said, "there was an emotional atmosphere not unlike that of a reconciliation between quarreling lovers." FDR became a folk-hero, in a way that Wilson could never have been.[31]

This era of good feelings lasted fairly well throughout World War II. There were pockets of sympathizers with the Nazi-Fascist regimes, but in general the hearts of liberals, reformers, and leftists were turned toward the United States and its allies in the struggle against Fascist totalitarianism. Even the gringo-baiting of the Communists was muted; and the *apristas'* hard opposition to economic imperialism was subordinated to respect for the nation leading the fight for democratic freedom. This changed climate of opinion was abundantly reflected in the books written during the war by Spanish Americans about the United States and its civilization.[32]

31. Aikman, *The All-American Front*, p. 316. On the welcome accorded the Good Neighbor Policy, see José Vasconcelos, *¿Qué es la revolución?*, pp. 36–44; Luis Alberto Sánchez, "A New Interpretation of the History of America"; and Bryce Wood, *The Making of the Good Neighbor Policy*, chaps. 12 and 14.

32. Representative of such books are Luis Alberto Sánchez, *Un sudameri-*

In the postwar years the close cordiality of the days of the Good Neighbor Policy and the war was considerably dissipated. As far as the official policy of the United States toward Latin America is concerned, there has been outspoken criticism of our apparent support of dictatorial regimes and of our emphasis on economic aid to countries outside the hemisphere to the neglect of massive assistance to Latin America. There have been other bones of contention such as Guatemala in 1954 and Castro's Cuba. To what extent the Good Neighbor image and the cordiality developed during World War II are still live factors is a question open to debate.

CHANNELS OF INFORMATION

During the twentieth century and especially in recent years, the ways in which Spanish Americans receive their impressions of the United States and its citizens have multiplied so rapidly that in the following pages we can only give a summary review of them, restricting the presentation to facts and when possible some estimate of the type of impression generated through the particular channel.

*United States business interests in the other American republics.* —The phenomenal growth of American investments and business activities in Latin America during this century has provided one of the more important sources of images of the United States for both the average Spanish American and the intellectual. In 1897 our direct investments in Latin America amounted to only $308 million; by 1919, partly as a result of the effects of World War I, they increased to nearly $2 billion, and by 1929 they reached a total of more than $3 billion. Between 1950 and 1960 the average annual rate of investment was about $325 million, and the total direct investment rose steadily until in 1960 it reached some $9 billion.[33]

For our purposes, the important facts to note are that this large-scale invasion by United States private capital brought with it a substantial human invasion of American businessmen, managers,

*cano en Norteamérica*; Manuel Seoane, *El gran vecino*; Emilio Uzcátegui, *Los Estados Unidos como los he sentido yo*; and Luis Quintanilla, *A Latin American Speaks*.

33. Whitaker, *The Western Hemisphere Idea*, p. 113; *New York Times*, June 7, 1946; Joseph Grunwald, "Change Does Not Mean the End of Profits," p. 35; a useful general survey of American investments is U.S. Senate Committee on Foreign Relations, *United States Business and Labor in Latin America*.

and technicians, and the realization on the part of Spanish Americans that the control of the economies of some of their republics was predominantly in the hands of North Americans. Particularly since World War II, the United States has been an almost exclusive source of foreign capital. From an economic point of view, this situation may have had some advantages for the Spanish American republics: capital lacking for the development of natural resources became available and economic growth was accelerated. But attitudes are not determined only by purely economic considerations. The net effect of North American business enterprise in Spanish America has been to help create a threatening image and an antagonistic attitude toward the United States among large groups of Spanish Americans.

The most common complaint has been that the United States business community does not enter into friendly social relations with the people of the host country, keeping itself disdainfully aloof and making little effort to learn Spanish.[34] Another has been the allegation that North American employees are accorded treatment different from that given to native employees. The latter are socially segregated and are not paid on the same scale as American workers engaged in the same labor. Furthermore, it sometimes has been said, talented young people of the country are often excluded from good positions in the enterprise by the presence of United States citizens.[35]

Particularly in the first decades of the century, North American business interests, allegedly with the aid of American diplomatic missions, were accused of meddling in the internal politics of the republics and even of fomenting revolutions when it seemed to their advantage.[36] In fact, a good deal of the resentment against North American business enterprises has arisen from a generalized feeling that the political and economic destinies of some of the republics were not really in their own hands, that foreign interests were in effect robbing them of their patrimony, national sovereignty, and pride.

Finally, American concerns in Latin America have been charged

34. Among many examples of this complaint see Bravo, p. 145; Mañach, p. 339; Quintanilla, p. 48; and Wood, pp. 299–300 (quoting a Foreign Service despatch from Bogotá).
35. Enrique Bernardo Núñez, *Viaje por el país de las máquinas*, and S. Walter Washington, "A Study of the Causes of Hostility toward the United States in Latin America," p. 23.
36. Manuel Ugarte, in Englekirk et al., pp. 658–59, and D. H. Radler, *El Gringo: The Yankee Image in Latin America*, chap. 4.

with making exorbitant profits from their operations, taking most of those profits out of the country, and bleeding the republics of their natural resources without due benefit to the people. Since the major part of United States direct investments were in the extractive and plantation industries—sugar in Cuba, oil in Mexico and Venezuela, fruit in Central America, and copper in Chile—these charges have seemed the more self-evident to the Spanish American critics.

One can hardly overemphasize the intensity of the resentment aroused by these accusations—justified or fictitious—not only among intellectuals and students, but among the common people. The Mexican *corridos* (popular ballads) of the 1920s, for example, were filled with bitter invective against American oil companies, using as their principal themes the unjust exploitation of natural resources, intervention in Mexican politics, and the mistreatment of Mexican employees. According to one song, the Mexican oil workers were so angry that "they want to eat nothing but gringos, raw and also roasted."[37]

In recent years, most American companies, like United Fruit, have taken measures to brighten their sullied image in Spanish America. Improvement of workers' housing, construction of schools and hospitals, sharing of managerial responsibilities with nationals of the country, more careful training for American employees, some reinvestment of profits in the national economy, and public relations programs were some of the steps taken.[38] To what extent these efforts succeeded is a matter of conjecture. While responsible critics were perhaps not as virulent as the old-timers of the first part of the century, Communist propaganda and intense nationalistic concern kept the old stereotypes in circulation, and honest patriots still had doubts about the wisdom of surrendering to further exploitation of national wealth by *yanqui* capitalists. May and Plaza, in their survey of the United Fruit Company's operations, concluded, "Latin American esteem for the United Fruit Company and its works is far from universal. The farther one moves away from those who have first-hand dealings with United Fruit, the lower is its repute. . . . Its worst reputation is in the Latin American republics with which it has no active relationship. . . . To the average man in the average Latin street,

37. M. E. Simmons, "Attitudes," pp. 35–36.
38. The activities of the United Fruit Co. and the Creole Petroleum Co. are illustrative; see Stacey May and Galo Plaza, *The United Fruit Company in Latin America*, and *Time*, May 22, 1964, p. 96.

the name of the United Fruit Company conjures up an image not unlike that of the Abominable Snow Man."[39]

José Figueres, twice president of Costa Rica and generally friendly toward the United States, said not long ago, "The history of foreign companies in our midst, in spite of recent and praise-worthy improvements, is not a story of efforts for the well-being of our people. . . . We should be skeptical of investors who come to Latin America exclusively to tap sources of low wages."[40]

TOURISTS

Even though the number of American tourists going to Spanish America has never, except in the case of Mexico, been nearly as large as the contingent in Europe, they have nevertheless left their marks on the picture of the North American character. To judge from the available testimony, their contribution has not ordinarily been a very favorable one. Tourist traffic has greatly increased in recent decades. American tourists going to Mexico and South America in 1961 spent about ten times as much as those going in 1929.[41]

Particularly in Mexico, the American tourist may be fawned upon as a source of easy money, but the popular opinion of him is far from complimentary. According to one authority, the usual Mexican concept of the tourist from the North is that of a rich, discourteous person, devoid of sensitivity and culture, and very aloof to the common people of the host country.[42] Cosío Villegas, a prominent Mexican economist and educator, said of the American abroad, "He appears then as a noisy, stupid, meddling, inconsiderate, and childish being. And more than by his display of childishness, he impresses people by his incapacity to adapt himself to his surroundings, and consequently to understand them."[43] Eighty-eight of one hundred Mexican journalists, in reply to a questionnaire, stated that the impression left by American tourists was mainly unfavorable. Forty-three of this same group claimed that they received their impressions of the United States from tourists.[44]

39. Pp. 239–42.
40. Quoted in Davis, pp. 473–74.
41. *Statistical Abstract of the United States*, 1963, p. 214.
42. Norman D. Humphrey, "The Mexican Image of Americans," p. 117.
43. In Joseph, p. 297.
44. John C. Merrill, *Gringo: The American as Seen by Mexican Journalists*, pp. 21–22.

Comment from other parts of Spanish America on tourists was scanty. A Colombian observer portrayed the American traveler in conventional terms: he is naïve, a spendthrift, dresses in outlandish clothes, and gets belligerently drunk. According to this commentator and others, the wild behavior of the American tourist is simply the result of breaking loose from the dull, mechanized monotony at home.[45] A well-informed North American noted that most American tourists in Latin America fail to appreciate the countries they visit because they do not know Spanish and because they are too busy grousing about poor accommodations and other travel annoyances.[46]

There have been a few defenders of the maligned tourists. Surprisingly, a goodly number of Mexican students in the United States believed that the majority of American tourists were well behaved and sincerely eager to learn more about Mexico.[47] A Cuban journalist expressed a very unorthodox view. In his opinion, the tourists' charmed fascination with strange customs delighted the Spanish American; he concluded, "What this influx of tourists means for better mutual understanding is inestimable."[48] On the whole, however, it seems likely that the impressions made by tourists, certainly in Mexico and probably in the other republics, have served to mold a strange and not very respectable image of the United States.

## STUDENTS AND TEACHERS

In comparison with the nineteenth century, when the sons of the Spanish American elite almost invariably went to Europe for their higher education and when only a sprinkling of would-be engineers attended North American universities, this century has seen a gradual flood of young men and women come to our private secondary schools and universities. During the years 1919–55, inclusive, a total of nearly 43,000 Latin American students studied or trained in institutions of higher education in the United States.[49]

There can be little doubt of the effectiveness of this channel of communication in creating images of the United States, both in

45. Jesús Arango, *Estados Unidos: mito y realidad*, pp. 84–88; Subercaseaux, p. 155.
46. Stephen Duggan, *The Two Americas: An Interpretation*, p. 249.
47. R. L. Beals and N. D. Humphrey, *No Frontiers to Learning*, pp. 94, 107.
48. Bravo, pp. 197–98.
49. Kenneth Holland, "Statistics and Comments on Exchange with the United States."

the students' minds and among wide circles of listeners and readers at home. Indirectly, some of the severest anti-imperialist critics of the Colossus of the North provided testimony to this effect. Manuel Ugarte warned his fellow Spanish Americans: "It is an ordinary occurrence . . . for very young students who have gone from us to follow a course in the universities of the Union, to have their heads turned by their new surroundings, or the material conveniences which they offer, and to return to their native land contemptuous and arrogant, proclaiming in English the necessity for submission."[50]

Many United States friends of Latin America have had almost blind faith in the power of student exchange to bring about good relations and mutual understanding between the Americas. Stephen Duggan, for example, wrote, "The more students and teachers from the Latin American countries study and teach in our institutions of education . . . the more will they remove the misconception existing among many in Latin America that our civilization is but a brutal materialism devoid of the finer elements of life. . . . Everywhere are to be found returned graduate students teaching in the institutions of Latin America, enthusiastic over their studies in American institutions and strong adherents of better understanding with the people of the United States."[51]

That returned students are effectual agents in communicating their impressions to influential groups of their compatriots is borne out by several surveys of ex-grantees. Of a substantial group of Mexican returned grantees, 72 per cent reported they had presented their experiences and impressions in the press, on the radio, and in formal talks. Eighty per cent had discussed their experiences with groups and 91 per cent believed that their listeners were interested and accepted what they heard as true.[52]

While there is little doubt that student exchange is a powerful medium of communication or that many Spanish American students in our schools may have helped to present a better picture of the United States than that of the popular stereotypes, several qualifying factors must be taken into account. A minority

50. Ugarte, *Destiny of a Continent*, p. 14.
51. Duggan, pp. 260–63; Clarence Haring, "The Two Americas," p. 378; and Carleton Beals et al., *What the South Americans Think of Us*, p. 87, are examples of the confident optimism in the value of exchanges so current among Americans concerned with Latin American affairs.
52. International Research Associates, "A Study of Reactions to the State Department Exchange Program among Returned Mexican Grantees," pp. 12–17.

of students for several reasons return from their educational experience with a bitter taste in their mouths. They can be very effective in denigrating certain aspects of American civilization. Others on return find themselves at odds with their native environment and without jobs commensurate with their self-esteem. They can be a negative force as far as transmitting a good image of the United States is concerned. Finally, there are those who because of their unbounded and uncritical enthusiasm for the United States are discredited by their countrymen and lose influence as reliable communicators.

With regard to the creation of favorable images of the United States, the conclusions of a pair of anthropologists who studied Mexican students' reactions before and after residence in the United States are pertinent: "Insofar as their attitudes altered and their knowledge increased, the changes were selective in nature. With growth of knowledge and understanding, many shifted from being hostile critics to being friendly critics. But they remained critics in some degree."[53] In general, this same statement could be applied to many of the Spanish American visitors to the United States whose opinions are cited in this study.

## INTELLECTUAL COOPERATION

Although the term has come to have some fuzzy connotations, "intellectual cooperation" is still a useful category to embrace a number of activities that during this century brought thousands of citizens of both Americas together in common tasks involving common interests. In contrast to the mass media, they have not been the means of affecting the image of the United States among large and heterogeneous groups of Spanish Americans, but certainly they have helped to mold the image in the minds of highly selected and influential people.

Usually reference to conferences sponsored by the Pan American Union or the Organization of American States calls up a picture of formal meetings of foreign ministers dealing more or less successfully with international political problems. In reality, the scores of conferences held under official inter-American auspices during the period of this survey dealt with a range of fields—science, history, medicine and sanitation, law, education, aviation, architecture, agriculture, labor, and others. Their participants were not only politicians and statesmen, but also experts, leaders in the

53. Beals and Humphrey, p. 97.

particular field, discussing problems which were familiar to them all. Under these circumstances, Spanish Americans came to know directly the calibre of their North American colleagues and to estimate North American achievement with some accuracy. Those familiar with such meetings may object that much time seems to be frittered away in quibbling over organizational procedures, and that they are low on tangible results. However that may be, they have been an undeniable force in determining attitudes toward the United States. A Chilean statesman and diplomat who should know what he is talking about said, "These gatherings have brought together leading men and women in all activities of the twenty-one republics; they remain in contact, they become friends, they link their work and their plans. They may do more in the long run to unify the twenty-one nations through broad foundations of mutual interest than did the leaders at the top of the pyramid in a century."[54]

The same remarks apply to the scores of inter-American congresses and meetings sponsored by a large number of non-governmental societies and federations. The variety of their interests may be seen in a random selection of their names: Inter-American Society of Psychology; Inter-American Press Association; Institute of Ibero-American Literature; Inter-American Hotel Association, and so on. Almost all of these periodically have held assemblies or congresses, which in some cases may not have been much more than junkets or vacations for the participants. In any case, they represented excellent occasions for becoming personally acquainted with nationals of the other American republics. Furthermore, many of these organizations have published bulletins or other periodicals which probably were valuable channels of information. These non-governmental organizations and conferences multiplied particularly since World War II.

The work of certain American foundations in the Spanish American republics provided an even better opportunity for Spanish American specialists to work and become acquainted with their colleagues from the North. The Rockefeller Foundation, for example, beginning in 1915 and continuing for the next thirty years, carried on an important campaign to eradicate yellow fever in Ecuador, Peru, Colombia, and Venezuela, employing a large staff of scientists from both Americas. Both the scientists and the average citizen of those countries were thus in an advantageous position to have direct contact with outstanding representatives of

54. Carlos Dávila, *We of the Americas*, p. 172.

North American intellectual life. In 1943 the same foundation entered into an agreement with the Mexican government to establish a joint agricultural program in that country. By 1950 eleven American scientists were working successfully with some sixty Mexican experts to develop better strains of corn, wheat, and other plants. The institute established for this purpose trained not only Mexicans for agricultural research, but also citizens of other republics; in addition, scholarships to the United States were made available. Particularly during and since World War II, the foundation's highly selective fellowship programs included substantial numbers of Spanish Americans.[55]

The Carnegie Endowment for International Peace was also an early agent in the field of intellectual cooperation with Latin America. Its activities beginning in 1914 included the sponsorship of trips to South America by such American savants as James Scott Brown and George McBride; the presentation of United States books to Latin American libraries; grants to educational missions from the Spanish American countries to visit the United States; the publication of a journal of inter-American opinion (*Inter-America*); assistance in founding the American Institute of International Law; and many other projects that have helped to make the United States better known to Spanish Americans. Other foundations which indirectly aided the cause of inter-American understanding were the Guggenheim Foundation (an annual average of fifteen very generous fellowships for Spanish Americans) and the W. K. Kellogg Foundation.

Several agencies of the United States government have engaged in the same type of activities as were carried on with such success by the foundations. There is some reason to believe, however, that the latter may have been more acceptable to thoughtful Spanish Americans than governmental efforts, and consequently may have been channels through which a clearer and more favorable image of the United States was presented. Manuel Gamio, the Mexican anthropologist, praised the "altruistic and disinterested" nonofficial scientific work sponsored by the Rockefeller Foundation, the American Geographic Society, and the Carnegie Institution of Washington, contrasting it with the official efforts of our diplomatic missions.[56]

55. See Raymond B. Fosdick, *The Story of the Rockefeller Foundation*, chap. 5 and pp. 184, 91.
56. Manuel Gamio and José Vasconcelos, *Aspects of Mexican Civilization*, pp. 182–84.

To catalogue all the scientific projects, unilateral and cooperative, in which citizens of the United States have come in close
contact with Spanish Americans would demand a whole volume.
Projects in the fields of archeology and anthropology have been
especially numerous. It is more than probable that thousands of
Spanish Americans have derived some of their concepts of North
Americans and their culture from association with these scholars.
The details of these concepts would include many diverse elements, but doubtless the general attitude has been one of respect
for North American civilization and its scholarly achievements.

### THE MISSIONARY'S TRAIL

Protestant missionary endeavor, largely under the auspices of
United States churches and organizations, continued to expand in
Spanish America during the twentieth century. It was characterized by these noteworthy developments: the trend of missionary
work was increasingly toward educational and medical service,
although the purely evangelical function was not neglected; sects
such as the Pentecostalists, Assemblies of God, Jehovah's Witnesses and other so-called faith missions came to predominate in
many countries over the more historic Protestant churches; nationals of the several Spanish American republics were trained
to carry on the ministry in such a way that the foreign missionary
was no longer the dominant symbol of Protestantism; the impact
of all missionary activity was increasingly felt more among the
lower middle class than among the elite; efforts were also directed
toward isolated Indian groups.

There is no way of knowing with any certainty what the net
effect of American Protestant activity was on Spanish American
attitudes toward the United States. In the early decades of the
century, Protestant missionaries appeared to a group of the foes
of imperialism to be simply forerunners and instruments of *yanqui*
domination. This was particularly characteristic of the thought of
José Vasconcelos. One North American commentator said in 1943,
perhaps with considerable exaggeration, "It [missionary activity]
is the most formidable single cause for anti-American propaganda
and for sowing suspicion and dislike for everything North American."[57]

57. Vasconcelos, *Hispanoamérica frente a los nacionalismos agresivos de
Europa y Norteamérica*, passim; John White, *Our Good Neighbor Hurdle*, p.
51; see also Alexander, *Communism*, pp. 234–35.

Quite aside from the linking of Protestant missionary endeavor with imperialism, the fact that the vast majority of Spanish Americans were at least nominally Roman Catholic led inevitably to resentment and antagonism against the "heretical" intruder. There were some conservative Catholic intellectuals, such as Víctor Andrés Belaúnde, who reacted strongly in this way. Oscar Lewis, in his anthropological studies of Mexican families, tells in detail of the social ostracism of one family which had turned to Protestantism and of the accusations of immorality and racial haughtiness directed against missionaries.[58]

A few tolerant souls spoke out in favor of evangelical missions. Gabriela Mistral's opposition to *yanqui* imperialism did not extend to Protestant activities in Spanish America. "Our church," she said, "should remember its essential unity of interest with Protestantism and consider that it loses infinitely less when the free-thinker is evangelized than when the youth of Catholic blood embraces atheism with the fervor of a Roman gladiator." Benjamín Subercaseaux advocated Protestant missionary activity in Latin America as useful in reaching people otherwise untouched by Christianity. There is some indication that those of the Catholic hierarchy who were trying to revitalize the Church's position saw in Protestant activity a needed stimulant to reform.[59]

Understandably, Spanish American attitudes toward the educational and medical efforts of the missionaries were far more favorable than toward their purely proselyting activities. The medical work and the agricultural schools of the Seventh-Day Adventists were relatively well regarded, as was the social service work of the Friends Field Service. Such schools as the American Institute of La Paz, Santiago College in Chile, the Colegio Internacional in Asunción, Crandon Institute in Montevideo, and others commanded respect from Spanish Americans of all classes and frequently were recognized as models of progressive educational practice.[60]

Amanda Labarca, the Chilean educator, recalled that her attitude toward the United States on the eve of her first visit was mixed: "I had completed my courses in the University of Chile

58. Belaúnde, *La realidad nacional*, p. 4 (this Peruvian diplomat was generally favorably disposed toward the United States); Lewis, *Five Families*, pp. 41–45.

59. Gabriela Mistral, quoted in Inman, p. 181; Subercaseaux, pp. 269–70; see *The Christian Ministry in Latin America and the Caribbean*, ed. Wilfred Scopes, p. 26.

60. Robertson, *Hispanic American Relations with the United States*, pp. 298–315, and Haring, "The Two Americas," p. 72.

and—like all the youth of that period—was impressed by the books of the Uruguayan Rodó, especially by his *Ariel*. . . . But I had also studied for a short time in Santiago College, an establishment of high calibre maintained in Chile by members of a Methodist mission . . . and there I had known generous, idealistic, and liberal teachers. My spirit vacillated, then, between my admiration for Rodó and my regard for North American professors and friends."[61]

While the YMCA and the YWCA originally entered Latin America in 1891 as allies of the missionary movement, their early emphasis on the training of nationals as leaders and the consequent nationalization of the associations in the respective countries largely exempted them from the stigma often stamped on Protestant missions. Their nondenominational character, their social services, and their complete acclimatization to the local scene won them general praise rather than censure.[62] In fact, the tendency of most missionary endeavor in recent years to rely on native personnel and organization more than on foreign emissaries, as well as the increasing emphasis on medical and educational work, blunted much of the earlier criticism of Protestant missions.

### UNITED STATES GOVERNMENT PROGRAMS

During the period 1939–60, the number and kind of officially directed American activities in the Spanish American republics were so great that we can hardly do more than enumerate them here and make some uncertain surmises about their effectiveness as channels of communication. These activities fall into four general categories: economic and scientific cooperation and assistance, educational and cultural exchange, information programs, and support of cultural centers. Aside from some archeological and other scientific expeditions to Latin America sponsored by the Smithsonian Institution, the United States government did not until 1938 concern itself with the activities mentioned.

From the establishment in 1938 of the Interdepartmental Committee for Scientific and Cultural Cooperation to 1960, agencies of the United States government carried out with the Spanish American republics hundreds of cooperative programs that were intended to advance the health, economies, and education of those republics. At first these programs were under the direction of

61. Labarca, essay in Joseph, pp. 309–10.
62. Robertson, pp. 318–20.

agencies specifically created to extend technical assistance to Latin America (the Institute of Inter-American Affairs and the Inter-American Education Foundation). Later they became a part of worldwide efforts to assist developing countries and were continued under agencies bearing various symbols—"Point 4," ICA, AID, and so on. In Latin America the assistance programs customarily were concerned with public health, agriculture, primary and secondary education, and engineering projects.[63]

Evaluation of these programs in relation to the North American image in the Spanish American mind is difficult if not impossible. The very fact of giving assistance, one assumes, would reinforce the idea of generosity as a national characteristic. Day-to-day working relations with dedicated North American specialists doubtless led to an appreciation of some of the Americans' more laudable virtues, and, of course, the training of technicians in the United States presented a sizeable group with a more complete picture of our civilization. On the other hand, some American specialists whose knowledge of Spanish was limited, whose adaptability to alien cultures was weak, and whose feeling of superiority was exaggerated, merely confirmed, according to some reports, unfavorable stereotypes about North Americans. Furthermore, the disparity between the size of the foreign aid program in Latin America and that of programs in other parts of the world since the end of World War II aroused considerable and articulated antagonism.

Although Spanish American students have been enrolling in American colleges and universities for nearly a century and a half, the United States government did not officially sponsor student and professor exchange until the Division of Cultural Relations was established in the Department of State in 1939. Since then, with varying budgets and changing organizational structures, the department continued to implement a substantial program of educational exchange, stressing, in addition to purely academic exchange, the travel of "leaders" from both Americas. The visits of leaders—prominent men and women in the professional and cultural fields—doubtless had considerable influence in determining the sort of picture of the United States that was seen by Spanish Americans in recent decades.

As an extension of the general exchange program of the department, traveling exhibits of American art and tours by musical,

63. See Charles A. H. Thomson, *Overseas Information Service of the United States Government*, pp. 117–57, 161–64, and Donald Rowland, *History of the Office of the Coordinator of Inter-American Affairs*, passim.

dramatic, and dance groups were sponsored, not always with complete success. Designed to increase respect for North American cultural achievement, these efforts may have had some positive effect.[64]

As in the case of cultural exchange, official government information programs, using the several mass media, did not come into being until World War II. During the war, a fairly extensive campaign of informational activities was improvised by the Coordinator of Inter-American Affairs, with the assistance of the Department of State. It included the use of press features, publications, radio programs, and motion pictures (mostly documentaries). While the natural emphasis at that time was on war issues, backgrounds of American life and culture were not neglected. After the war, official information activities were continued, first by the Department of State and after 1953 by the United States Information Agency. The stress on topical questions of foreign policy still remained a dominant note, particularly as the cold war developed. Nevertheless, a mainstay of the information operations in Spanish America was the dissemination of ideas and concepts about the basic nature of American civilization and culture, and in this sense they played a role in molding the image of the United States.[65] How significant this role was in the total complex of communication and information channels and in view of the handicap of the official label is a question to which both the USIA and Congress devoutly yearn for a definitive answer.

In 1941, the United States government started to lend support to cultural institutes (or binational centers, as they were later called) in various Latin American countries. These institutes were autonomous organizations, incorporated under the laws of the respective countries and governed by a binational board of directors. Their activities varied to suit local needs, but generally included English language classes, the operation of a library of North American books, lecture and seminar programs, and social events. Government support consisted of the assignment of one or more American "grantees" or USIA officers to assist in management and teaching, a supply of books and other materials, and in some cases the donation of building funds. Although it varied from center to center, financial support usually constituted a substantial part of the total income of the organizations. Before the gov-

64. Thomson, pp. 164–71.
65. Ibid., passim.

ernment interested itself in these institutes, eight had been established in Latin America under the private initiative of American citizens and nationals of the particular country, the Instituto Cultural Argentino-Norteamericano in Buenos Aires being the oldest.

In addition to the binational centers, six American libraries (often called "information center libraries") and some reading rooms were established entirely under government auspices. The oldest and best known of these institutions is the Benjamin Franklin Library in Mexico City. Some type of official support was also given to a considerable number of schools in Spanish America established by American citizens.[66]

In some respects the work of all these institutions may have contributed as much as any other single official endeavor to the opening of channels for the understanding of the United States and its civilization. The libraries alone were a continuous and dependable medium for laying the factual basis for such understanding. Let us take as an example the question of American literature. The library collections in the binational centers naturally had varying holdings, but they averaged perhaps 1,500 books per center and their monthly circulation may have averaged between 200 and 300. Many of the centers also sponsored lectures or classes on American literature. These facts may furnish one explanation for the phenomenal increase in the interest in and knowledge of American literature.

### PRESS AND PUBLICATIONS

An important source of Spanish American impressions of the United States has been, of course, the newspaper. By 1960, most foreign news, including that of the United States, was furnished by two American news services, the Associated Press and the United Press.

The dominance of American agencies did not always exist. Until 1902, the French Havas had exclusive news distribution rights in Spanish America. In that year Associated Press began to operate in Central America and the Caribbean area, and in 1916 and 1919,

---

66. Ibid., pp. 167–68; for details about various pertinent government programs I am indebted to a mimeographed study prepared by R. E. Murray, in the files of the Department of State: "Review and Evaluation of Inter-American Cultural Programs and Activities Undertaken by the United States prior to 1956," April 1956.

respectively, AP and UP initiated their services to South America. At the beginning of this century Havas reigned almost supreme; such news about the United States as it dealt out emphasized riots, murders, and disasters, and favorable stories were the exception. It was doubtless through this medium that so many literate Spanish Americans acquired a prejudiced concept of *yanqui* civilization as being very violent.

Following their entry on the journalistic scene, North American news agencies were sharply criticized both by North American observers and by intellectuals in Spanish America. The former not infrequently blamed the news agencies for peddling too much material about gangland killings, sensational divorces, lynchings, the Ku Klux Klan, etc., in the United States and not enough about scientific and cultural developments.[67] On the other hand, some of the more rabid South American foes of *yanqui* imperialism portrayed the news agencies as a dangerous tool in the hands of Wall Street and the State Department, helping in devious ways to subjugate the Spanish American republics.[68]

Whatever may have been the truth in the past, the charge that the news services distort the image of the United States by overemphasis on sensational and scandalous stories does not seem to be supported by the facts concerning more recent output. A content analysis made in 1959 of twenty leading Latin American newspapers showed that about 12.5 per cent of the total news space was devoted to the United States. Of this coverage, 40 per cent was devoted to questions of government and politics, principally foreign relations, 12 per cent was given over to economic affairs, 12 per cent to sports, and 11 per cent to entertainment. The remaining 25 per cent covered a wide range of subjects—social problems, human interest, science, accidents and disasters, and so on. A very small amount of space was given to stories of crime or sensational frivolities. This pattern of coverage corresponded roughly, although not exactly, to the emphasis given in the raw material provided by the news services. On the other hand, items about cultural life and science in the United States were insignificant in number. If distortion took place, it apparently was in the overwhelming attention given to foreign relations and economic ques-

67. Wood, pp. 299, 417, citing despatches from United States missions in Latin America; Haring, *South America Looks at the United States*, p. 136; Carleton Beals, *The Coming Struggle for Latin America*, p. 181.

68. Vargas Vila, p. 152; Rufino Blanco-Fombona, "Noticias yanquis," in Englekirk et al., pp. 652–55.

tions at the expense of such matters as educational, scientific, religious, and cultural developments.[69]

Another source of information (or misinformation) about the United States was the numerous feature articles written by Spanish Americans who visited or resided in the United States. A good part of the material used as the principal source for this study was first published in the Spanish American press. Naturally, such material varied in quality and in attitudes displayed toward the United States. An American scholar writing in the 1920s points to such articles at that time as being a significant medium for the diffusion of a dismal picture of North Americans and their culture, in which emphasis was placed on divorce, on the evils of prohibition, on the Ku Klux Klan, and on the crude, uncultured American.[70] On the other hand, during World War II, a number of visitors from Latin America sent back for newspaper publication relatively flattering accounts of the *yanqui* and his country.[71]

Some impression of North American life and culture must have been conveyed to the Spanish American reader through the considerable number of periodicals in English and especially in Spanish which were edited in the United States and had substantial distribution in Spanish America. Particularly popular have been Spanish editions of *Reader's Digest, Life en Español,* and *Popular Mechanics.* In the absence of special studies in this field, the kind of impression of the United States made by these periodicals is difficult to determine. One may guess that *Reader's Digest* left a vague idea of North Americans who were optimistic, eager for clean living, and idealistic—probably a generally favorable view. Some Spanish American intellectuals, however, dismissed the *Digest* as trivial and superficial. *Mecánica popular* may have strengthened the stereotype that Americans are fond of mechanical gadgets; apparently there were a good many Spanish Americans with like tastes.

Translation and publication in Spanish America of books by North American authors has increased enormously during this century. In recent years the great majority of these books have been scientific volumes, mostly in the field of applied science. In descending order of the number of titles published, other cate-

69. This information and other useful material about the news services in Latin America are to be found in Wayne Wolfe, "Attitudes toward the United States as Revealed in the Latin American Press," chap. 2.

70. Haring, *South America Looks at the United States*, pp. 134–36.

71. For example, Germán Arciniegas, *En el país del rascacielos y las zanahorias*, Manuel Seoane, and Uzcátegui.

gories are literature (including great quantities of detective and adventure fiction), the social sciences, history, and biography.[72] Some comment on the possible images created by the publication of American literature is included in a later chapter. As for the other fields, it can be safely surmised that in general the flood of North American titles in translation was in itself a reflection of respect for American achievement, especially in medicine, engineering, and other applied sciences.

### COWBOYS, GANGSTERS, AND MICKEY MOUSE

There is little question that the motion picture of North American origin was in the first half of the century an increasingly potent factor in Spanish American life. Using Argentina and Mexico as yardsticks, the following figures tell the story of the popularity of American films: in 1920, the United States exported to these two countries a little over 14 million linear feet of exposed movie film; in 1940, the footage had more than doubled; by 1963, the figure had reached approximately 40 million linear feet.[73] American movies were generally more welcome than those of any other country, although Mexican films offered competition and intellectuals and sophisticates tended to prefer the European product; they were shown not only in cities but in all but the most inaccessible rural communities.

Most commentators, both North and Spanish American, appear to agree that American films were an exceptionally active medium for the formation of stereotypes of the United States, and that the stereotypes were mostly unfavorable. Such categorical statements about the effect of motion pictures made in the United States are, however, open to question. It is undoubtedly true that well-educated, sophisticated Spanish Americans found many North American films infantile and not true to life; but for that very reason it is not likely that they formed their ideas of the United States from those films. On the other hand, anyone who has sat through the showing of an American cowboy or adventure film in a provincial Spanish American town has been impressed with the often noisy enjoyment of the films by the audience. It may be

72. Data from Library of Congress, Hispanic Foundation, *Spanish and Portuguese Translations of United States Books.*

73. Department of Commerce, *Foreign Commerce and Navigation of the United States,* 1920, 1940; *United States Exports of Domestic and Foreign Merchandise,* 1963.

doubted that the audience is particularly conscious of any representation of American life in the films; they are part of a world of make-believe, recognized as such by all but the most slow-witted, a world akin to that of folk-tales or of the Mexican films. If, however, some in the audience are carried away by the pseudo-realism of the picture, they seem to regard that reality as exciting and even enviable. Some conservative older people may have complained about immodesty and immorality and perhaps associated those alleged attributes of certain films with characteristics of North American life. Also, the general impression of skyscrapers and relatively luxurious living as characteristic of the United States may have been a cumulative result of seeing many American films. It should be added that during the sixties in urban communities in most countries, television, which often uses adapted American or American-style programs, began replacing the movies as entertainment.[74]

## A Preliminary Note on the Sources for This Chapter

Because of their abundance, the choice of commentators for the period 1891–1960 has been more difficult than for the earlier years. Greatly increased opportunities for travel and the growth of the publishing industry in Spanish America are factors that significantly multiplied the number of accounts and studies of North

### Geographic Distribution of Sources

| Countries | Principal | Other | Total |
|---|---|---|---|
| Argentina | 7 | 7 | 14 |
| Bolivia | 1 | | 1 |
| Central America | 1 | 3 | 4 |
| Chile | 7 | 2 | 9 |
| Colombia | 6 | 1 | 7 |
| Cuba | 2 | 4 | 6 |
| Dominican Republic | 1 | | 1 |
| Ecuador | 3 | 4 | 7 |
| Mexico | 6 | 6 | 12 |
| Peru | 4 | 2 | 6 |
| Uruguay | 3 | 3 | 6 |
| Venezuela | 2 | 1 | 3 |
| Total | 43 | 33 | 76 |

74. See Oscar Lewis, *Five Families*, pp. 82–83.

American civilization among Spanish Americans. Some of these accounts were fairly detailed and covered many aspects of life in the United States; they constitute the principal sources of this section. Many other writers made passing remarks about the United States, usually relating to specific subjects; a few of them have been cited in this section and are considered as "contributing" witnesses. The views of forty-three principal and thirty-three incidental commentators have been recorded.

In spite of conscientious efforts to provide a reasonable geographic coverage in the choice of sources, the various republics are somewhat unevenly represented. This fact is evident in the table.

The impressions of prominent Spanish Americans have been supplemented in this part of the study by the results of a few opinion surveys conducted among special groups, by a press-content analysis, and occasionally by reference to the writings of attentive North American observers of Latin American affairs.

# 9

# The Modern Image: Political, Economic, and Social Questions

The dominant attitude of many if not most Spanish American intellectuals toward the United States as a nation for a good part of this century has been that of an alarmed and resentful opponent of what was universally called imperialism. In the first years political imperialism was the primary target. The fear that the Colossus of the North was plotting to absorb the weaker Spanish-speaking republics into its expanding empire became a conviction among a number of very articulate critics of the United States, filtering down in the form of slogans from them to sizeable segments of the population. Later, economic and cultural domination became the dreaded spectres.

We have recorded that anxiety about North American expansionism dates back to the Independence period and that it grew in intensity during the nineteenth century. The Spanish American War ignited a conflagration, fueled by the acquisition by the United States of Spanish-speaking territory and growing psychological tensions within Spanish America. While the fear of political absorption has diminished, some form of opposition to northern imperialism has been a fairly constant note to this day in opinion about the United States.

There is no need to recount here the details of the events that aroused widespread and vehement opposition to America's foreign policy with regard to Latin America since it has been told often by competent authorities.[1] If we recall the occupation of Puerto

1. Samuel Flagg Bemis, *The Latin American Policy of the United States*, presents the essential facts, although his tendency to justify the actions of the United States is obvious.

Rico and the Philippines, the Platt Amendment to Cuba's constitution, the American role in the birth of the Republic of Panama, interference in the events of the Mexican Revolution, and the frequent interventions, armed and otherwise, in the affairs of several Caribbean republics, we have the basic framework on which was built the movement of opposition to political imperialism.

We will also refrain from attempting to present a comprehensive listing of the dozens of books and articles that appeared in the early years of the century attacking the actions and policy of the United States. An exhaustive accumulation of examples would not be especially illuminating except as an illustration of the scope of the campaign, since, for the most part, they were cut from a single pattern.[2]

The broadsides aimed at *yanqui* imperialism by José Vargas Vila and Rufino Blanco-Fombona are probably the most devastating of the collection, and a brief survey of their invective will give a useful idea of the extremes of the campaign. Vargas Vila, a Colombian novelist, compressed most of his anti-*yanqui* venom into an impassioned prose-poem called *Ante los bárbaros*. Its pages are studded with epithets of opprobrium: North Americans were "the barbarians of the North," "the drunken mobs," "a voracious, unfriendly, disdainful race," "a band of adventurers." Their policy toward Latin America was "the doctrine of plundering, robbery, and conquest." American conduct in the Philippines was "a wave of fire and blood," and the Panama affair was nothing but "insolent, tricky piracy." In summary, wrote Vargas Vila, "A great nation becomes a burly bandit, cutting the throats of weak nations. Washington's ghost becomes a pirate. And the banner of liberty becomes an immense shroud cast over the heads of those peoples." While British imperialism, he declared, was at least a civilizing force, the North American brand was simply brutalizing and destructive, "the sport of savages . . . the madness of prosperity."[3]

Rufino Blanco-Fombona, a Venezuelan litterateur of substantial and continental reputation, was equally outspoken in numerous publications. When he heard that President McKinley had been assassinated, he felt that justice had been done. The dead leader, he wrote, had fostered North American imperialistic ambitions,

2. Yankeephobia of the anti-imperialist kind is thoroughly examined in Rippy, "Literary Yankeephobia in Hispanic America," and in his "Pan Hispanic Propaganda in Hispanic America." See also Mary Chapman, "Yankeephobia."

3. Vargas Vila, *Bárbaros*, pp. 149, 159, and passim.

and "his hangman's fingers" had marked out Hispanic America for northern greed. "May his wounded flesh taste lead" was his requiem, "may the man who unleashed tragedy in the Philippines, in Cuba, and on the sea know what tragedy means."[4]

Manuel Ugarte, an Argentine essayist and perhaps the most persistent and dedicated of the literary foes of imperialism, devoted a good part of his life to proclaiming the dangers which threatened on the northern horizon. More temperate in his expression than Vargas Vila or Blanco-Fombona, he was probably the most influential of the anti-imperialist guild in spreading indignation against the expansionist course of the United States. He propagated the idea, which became almost a cliché, that there was a North American master plan for dominating its southern neighbors, a skillfully coordinated conspiracy involving Wall Street and the Department of State, plotted with diabolical shrewdness.[5]

Other writers, such as Carlos Pereyra and José Vasconcelos of Mexico, were especially brilliant among anti-imperialistic luminaries; in fact almost everybody who pretended to literary prominence from 1900 to 1925 felt the urge or the obligation to condemn and warn against the expansionist designs of the Colossus of the North.[6] Even poets from time to time forsook their fine-spun theories and Parisian bohemias to lend their talents to the verbal offensive against *yanqui* imperialism.

The poem "A Roosevelt," by Rubén Darío, the best known representative of the new *modernista* movement in poetry, was a particularly memorable poetic reflection of concern in the face of the northern menace. University students are said to have learned it by heart. Published in 1904, this poem expressed in vivid terms the common fear not only of political engulfment by the United States, but also and more pointedly of the annihilation of the cultural personality and even the language of Spanish America.

4. Blanco-Fombona, *La lámpara de Aladino*, p. 402; see also his *La evolución política y social de Hispanoamérica*, and his essay on Sarmiento in *Grandes escritores de América* (Madrid, 1917).

5. Ugarte, "La nueva Roma," in Englekirk et al., *Anthology of Spanish American Literature*, pp. 656–57. Four books by Ugarte are important landmarks in the anti-imperialist campaign: *El porvenir de la América latina* (1910); *Mi campaña hispanoamericana* (1922); *El destino de un continente* (1923); and *La patria grande* (1924).

6. For a fairly complete bibliography of anti-imperialist writings, see Rippy's introduction to Ugarte's *Destiny of a Continent*, pp. 293–96. Particularly significant works were Pereyra, *El mito de Monroe* (1914), Arturo Capdevila, *América: nuestras naciones ante los Estados Unidos* (1926), Alfredo Palacios, *Nuestra América y el imperialismo yanqui* (1915), and Vasconcelos, *Bolivarismo y Monroismo* (1935).

Addressing Theodore Roosevelt as the personification of American imperialism, Darío said, "You are the United States—you are the future invader—of that ingenuous America which has Indian blood —which still prays to Christ and still speaks Spanish." Describing Roosevelt as haughty, able, energetic and self-confident, the poet glorified his own America, which "lives on light, fire, perfume, love" and prophesied that the "free cubs of the Spanish lion" will never be conquered.[7] Although Darío also occasionally criticized the United States in his journalistic articles,[8] he was neither a consistent nor a convinced anti-imperialist. In fact, shortly after the publication of "A Roosevelt," he composed "Salutación al Aguila," which was a somewhat banal hymn to Pan American friendship and cooperation. Darío had gone to Rio de Janeiro as Nicaraguan delegate to the Third Pan American Conference, and there, possibly under the influence of Elihu Root's personal charm and the cheery brotherhood of champagne, he wrote this rather friendly tribute to the United States, a poem that angered Blanco-Fombona, a less fickle opponent of the imperial eagle.[9] Darío's last important poem, "Pax," was a plea for the union of all American republics—"The Star-Spangled banner with the [Argentine] blue and white."[10]

José Santos Chocano, a Peruvian poet often described as a literary Yankeephobe, also held a somewhat ambiguous attitude toward North American power. In his "La epopeya del Pacífico" he wrote lines that became well known in Spanish America: "The United States, like a bronze pillory, tortures the foot of America against a nail. . . . Let us distrust the man with the blue eyes— when he tries to snatch us from the warmth of our hearth—and beguiles us with a gift of buffalo skins—nailed down with disks of sounding metal." But then the poet granted that hard work is the only way to enjoy a lost Eden, implying that Spanish America should imitate the industrious virtues of the blond-haired Saxons. While the Panama Canal will be built by Negro labor, not by white northerners, it will surely be a boon to Spanish America,

7. Darío, in Englekirk et al., pp. 426–27. Fear of cultural imperialism has been a frequent theme in other commentators; see, for example, Ernesto Mario Barreda, poet and novelist, *Nosotros*, 2a epoca, 1:52–57.

8. E.g., *La caravana pasa*, pp. 240–49, and "Edgar Allan Poe," in *Los raros*, in *Obras completas*.

9. See Fred P. Ellison, "Rubén Darío and Brazil"; Luis Alberto Sánchez said that Darío's opposition to imperialism was purely "decorative" and that he lacked "social sensitivity" (*Balance y liquidación del 900*, p. 49).

10. Darío, *Poesía: libros poéticos completos*, pp. 479–84.

Chocano concluded.[11] There is evidence that Chocano's ideal was the harmonization of the exuberant Latin imagination with the persevering energy of the North.[12]

The defeat of Spain in 1898, considered by many as a blow aimed at the Latin or Hispanic "race," and the landing of marines in Central America and the Caribbean republics stirred up a swarm of protests in verse which were more significant as polemic than as poetry.[13] Poems written later by the Cuban Nicolás Guillén and the Chilean Pablo Neruda, in which the United States came under heavy fire, were in an entirely different category. Because of the universally recognized poetic genius of the authors (Neruda is regarded by some as Latin America's greatest bard), their denunciations of American imperialism, following the Communist line pretty closely, have in all probability carried a good deal of weight. Neruda's series of intricate poetic criticisms of Anaconda Copper, Standard Oil, and United Fruit is impressive verse, even though its basic theme is well within the established pattern; the poems have likely had influence, particularly among Chilean and other Spanish American young people.[14]

One of the most remarkable literary manifestations of the fear and detestation of *yanqui* imperialism was a series of novels attacking North American economic and political penetration. The first of these, *El problema*, by the Guatemalan Máximo Soto-Hall, was published in 1899, and they have continued to appear steadily ever since. Our record, which is doubtless incomplete, lists twenty-seven such novels, principally anti-*yanqui* in theme. (The list with pertinent details appears in Appendix 3.)

With a few exceptions, such as César Vallejo's *Tungsteno* and one or two novels of Miguel Angel Asturias, this fictional offensive is of slight literary quality. The plots are melodramatic and the characters are usually caricatures. Like our western novels and like folk-tales, they are compounded of a group of familiar motifs or elements that occur with remarkable regularity. A few of the earlier novels, such as those of Soto-Hall and the Costa Rican Carlos Gagini, deal with the dreaded possibility of political and

11. Chocano, in Englekirk et al., pp. 468–69.
12. See Chocano's poem "El canto del porvenir" and Estuardo Núñez, "El poeta Chocano en Nueva York."
13. See selections by Calixto Oyuela (Argentina), Luis Andrés Zúñiga (Honduras), and Santiago Argüello (Nicaragua) in Alberto Cabrales, *Política de Estados Unidos y poesía de Hispanoamérica*.
14. Neruda, *Obras completas* (Buenos Aires, 1956), pp. 423–27; Guillén, *West Indies, Ltd.* (Havana, 1934).

cultural absorption by the United States. Most, however, are concerned with the penetration of North American companies into
Spanish America for oil, mining, or fruit. It is not unexpected
that a large number of works are the product of Central American
pens and that the villain is the United Fruit Company. Some of
the recurring elements in most of these stories are the cold, heart-
less *yanqui* businessman or manager, often disdainfully conscious
of race, the hateful, servile native overseer or foreman, the seduc-
tion of a native maiden by these lustful bullies, the collusion with
national politicos to steal the nation's economic birthright, the
"cultural" invasion by the *yanquis* with their whiskey, aspirin,
victrolas, strange language, and immorality, and, above all, the
cruel and pitiless exploitation of the national worker.

The authors of some of these novels were Communists (e.g.,
Carlos Luis Fallas) and they naturally used the party's stereotypes
as their building blocks. Nearly all of them, party members or not,
followed a generally uniform pattern; a number of these novels,
in addition to their main anti-imperialist theme, included plentiful
material illustrative of local folklore and customs, particularly
those of Miguel Angel Asturias. The tendency may be one facet
of the intense nationalism which inspired these novels.[15]

Historians and other North Americans concerned with inter-
American relations are often so astonished, shocked, or conscience-
stricken when they realize the extent and effectiveness of the anti-
imperialist sentiment embodied in the writers we have discussed
that they fail to heed several very noteworthy although secondary
aspects of this literature. It will be worthwhile to review briefly
these aspects.

Almost without exception, in the tirades against *yanqui* imperialism, the attack was directed not particularly at the people of
the United States, but rather against the government of the Colossus of the North in unholy alliance with the greedy interests of
Wall Street. In their broadsides some of the more rabid crusaders,

15. See Eneida Avila, "Las compañías bananeras en la novelística centroamericana." This comprehensive study attempts to collate conditions as described in the novels with present-day realities as revealed in a large number
of field interviews with personnel of the United Fruit Company. The results
indicate little correspondence between the fictional presentations and the
actual situations. For a brief survey of anti-*yanqui* fiction, see Luis Alberto
Sánchez, *Proceso y contenido de la novela hispanoamericana* (Madrid, 1953),
pp. 531–34; Harold Urist, "Portrait of the Yanqui"; and Anson C. Piper, "El
yanqui en las novelas de Rómulo Gallegos." (Gallegos, a distinguished novelist and statesman, portrayed admirable *yanquis* as well as villains.) See
Appendix 3 for a list of such novels.

such as Vargas Vila, pilloried our whole civilization and its people, but a good many of the critics specifically absolved the ordinary North American citizen of responsibility.

Carlos Pereyra, a Mexican historian and one of the most implacable foes of imperialism, explained that the American people have been deceived by politicians with regard to the true and dastardly intent of the Monroe Doctrine.[16] In one of the most explicit anti-imperialist novels of Central America, Máximo Soto-Hall's *La sombra de la Casa Blanca*, the White House and Wall Street are as usual bracketed as vicious flaws in North American life. But, the novelist continued, "as for the people, I am never weary of repeating that they are fine. The clean seed brought by the 'Mayflower' has been borne by the four winds throughout this vast continent and has flowered and borne fruit. When the scalpel cuts out the flaws, this will really be a marvelous nation."[17]

The Argentine poet Leopoldo Lugones wrote in 1938, "In the United States there is a breed of ignorant, brutal politicians and they are the proponents of the famous 'big stick.' But there is another more numerous and better kind of individual for whom inter-American harmony is no vain clap-trap." Benjamín Subercaseaux, a Chilean writer, believed that the people of the United States are the best intentioned in the world, but that their rulers do wrong to Latin America.[18] A contemporary Argentine castigator of imperialism denounced American bankers, politicians, and monopolies in the old-fashioned way, but declared that imperialistic ventures find no favor or support among the common people of the United States and arouse active opposition from a distinguished academic group.[19]

Related to this belief that the villains of imperialism are the politicians and bankers, and not the man-in-the-street, is the curious fact that many of the most ardent opponents of *yanqui* highhandedness in the Caribbean draw a clear line of demarcation between the alleged imperialism of the United States and the civilization and national characteristics of that country. A few, like

16. Pereyra, p. 22.
17. Quoted in Avila, "Las compañías," no. 57, p. 118.
18. Lugones, "La América Latina," p. 67; Subercaseaux, *Retorno de U.S.A.*, p. 180. Future references to Subercaseaux are in the text.
19. Ramón Oliveres, *El imperialismo yanqui en América*, p. 50. Other commentators of the caliber of Alfonso Reyes and Luis Alberto Sánchez exempt the American people from imperialistic guilt. See Beals and Humphrey, *No Frontiers*, p. 94, for the belief of Mexican students in the innocence of the common man.

Blanco-Fombona, simply damned our whole culture with all its ways and works. But more frequently one finds unqualified censure of imperialism alongside frank admiration for certain aspects of the *yanqui* character and its culture. Darío, while making Theodore Roosevelt the symbol of the dangers of North American expansionism, also expressed a scarcely veiled esteem for his energy, culture, pride, and capability—all presumably representative qualities of his country.[20] Ugarte, the arch-enemy of the United States' Latin American policy, did not equivocate in expressing his high regard for the virtues and cultural advance of the United States. Francisco García Calderón (Peru), after making the customary charge against North American perfidy in dealing with Latin America, proceeded to describe North American society with equanimity, giving full credit to its praiseworthy aspects.[21]

A particularly clear example of the tendency to separate the government from the American people is provided by Colombian attitudes following the Panamanian revolt and Theodore Roosevelt's arbitrary action with regard to the canal. Colombian opinion at the time and subsequently showed continued respect for United States contributions to republican progress and generally placed the blame for Colombia's grievances on Theodore Roosevelt and his cohorts. Their treachery, many maintained, did not represent the desires of the American people.[22]

Some of the *apristas*, passionately defiant of economic imperialism, found much excellence in the North American way of life. For example, in Luis Alberto Sánchez' voluminous survey of the United States as he knew it, there is a chapter which could pass as a typical pamphlet attacking Manifest Destiny and Dollar Diplomacy. But the bulk of this Peruvian *aprista*'s book contains a fairly objective and mostly favorable account of life and culture in the United States.[23] A most striking illustration is the lengthy book about the United States by Colombian educator Jesus Arango. It is divided into two parts. The first 115 pages are a sober examination of American civilization, with clear emphasis on its laudable

20. Darío, "A Roosevelt," in Englekirk et al., pp. 426–27. Darío later admired Roosevelt even more fully when he learned that the president honored poets (ibid., p. 427). See José Balseiro, "Rubén Darío and the United States," p. 76.

21. Ugarte, *The Destiny of a Continent*, pp. 169, 285; García Calderón, *Latin America: Its Rise and Progress*, pp. 298–306.

22. Joseph L. Arbena, "The Image of an American Imperialist: Colombian Views of Theodore Roosevelt."

23. Sánchez, *Un sudamericano en Norteamérica*, chap. 2 and passim.

features. The remainder is a forthright condemnation of the imperialistic monster.

A third important aspect of the clamor about North American
imperialism is the fact that attacks on the iniquity of the United
States have almost invariably been accompanied by severe casti-
gation of their fellow citizens and especially of their rulers by the
Spanish American writers themselves. In the writings of men like
Ugarte, the blame for intervention in the political life of Latin
American countries by the United States is assigned as much to
the governing classes in the south as to the northern meddler.
According to Ugarte's thesis, to disparage and hate the United
States leads nowhere; the Spanish Americans' energy must be
directed to united and patriotic efforts to make their own coun-
tries strong. In the midst of his diatribes against the "modern
Carthaginians" (North Americans), Vargas Vila in like manner
took time out to excoriate Spanish American politicians as blind,
lazy, and submissive.[24]

Gabriela Mistral, a Chilean poetess of continental fame, expressed in vigorous terms a typical attitude: "Hatred of the *yanqui*? He is conquering us, overwhelming us, through our own fault,
because of our torrid languor, our Indian fatalism. . . . Let us hate
that in ourselves which renders us vulnerable to his spike of steel
and gold, his will and his wealth."[25]

In fact, part of the reaction against *yanqui* misbehavior was
really a distressing re-examination on the part of Spanish American
*pensadores* of their own human condition, a search for their true
roots and for a definition of their national identities. The anti-
imperialist campaign was only one phase of a broader attempt
to find their correct way through the labyrinth of modern values.

To a certain extent, the fear of the *yanqui* peril was related to
that widespread tempest, primarily European in origin, in which
racial superiority or inferiority were earnestly debated as if they
were realities. The ideas of Gobineau, Chamberlain, et al. were,
as we have seen, not unknown to certain Spanish American intellectuals who sometimes associated their quarrel with the Colossus
of the North with the facile, deterministic theories of the racists.
Thus the quarrel became a battle in a hypothetical and transcendental war between the Anglo-Saxon or Nordic race and the Latin
race (whatever those terms may mean). A few were pessimistic

24. Ugarte, in Englekirk et al., p. 661; Vargas Vila, *passim*; see also
Enrique José Varona, "El imperialismo yankee en Cuba."
25. Mistral, in *Inter-America* (1922), 6:21.

about the outcome, but others sounded the clarion call for Latin unity against the racial enemy, sometimes dreaming of an ideal coalition of France, Spain, and Latin America; more frequently, as has been noted, they advocated a union of the Latin American republics. Both Vargas Vila and Blanco-Fombona thought they discerned collusion among Great Britain, the United States, and Germany to subdue the Latin race.[26] Vasconcelos was also at times obsessed with the now antiquated social ideology of race struggle and customarily located his early anti-*yanqui* oratory in that context. In view of the complexity of racial mixture in Latin America, conversion of the anti-imperialist crusade into a clear-cut confrontation of Nordics and Latins naturally caused some confusion in the minds of the more realistic crusaders.

Up to this point we have been discussing principally the early phases of anti-imperialist sentiment, phases that may be placed roughly between 1890 and 1933. The loudest battle cries of that period stressed the dangers of aggressive absorption of the Spanish American republics into the *yanqui* empire—the actual loss of their political independence, although economic imperialism was by no means overlooked in the fray. After the termination of United States Marine intervention in the Caribbean, the abrogation of the Platt Amendment, and the inauguration of the Good Neighbor Policy during the administrations of Hoover and Franklin Roosevelt, the older type of attack apparently began to look archaic; the newer emphasis was on the evils of foreign economic penetration.

Because of cultural lag, however, and the constant efforts of the Communists (and the Perón people in their time) to keep it alive, one still runs across occasional survivals of the old style of fustian such as that by Ramón Oliveres, an Argentine publicist. Published in 1956, his *El imperialismo yanqui en América* is a remarkably complete collection of arguments expressed in violent language reminiscent of the old warriors of the first two decades of this century. Another curious survival specimen is a compact volume called *Estados Unidos: una mentira*, allegedly written by an Argentine physician, Daniel Ayres, and published in 1956. Coupled with a bilious discussion of social evils in the United States, Ayres exhibited such bits of rhetoric as this: "Yanqui imperialism comports itself like an octopus which grasps and sucks at its prey from afar by its tentacles and suckers. The blood-bathed strug-

26. Vargas Vila, p. 99; Blanco-Fombona, *La americanización del mundo*, p. 24.

gling of its victims can fight off the invisible hooks only at the beginning and for a moment; then they lie down exhausted at its mercy."[27] Dated as such language may seem today, its influence should not be underestimated as a force confirming a venerable stereotype of the United States in the popular Spanish American mind.

Among recent writers, however, that kind of opposition to *yanqui* imperialism has been rare. Some, while granting the former dangers of North American political imperialism, simply denied its existence in present-day United States foreign policy. Gustavo Otero, a Bolivian man of letters, believed that the anti-imperialist uproar began to die down about 1925 and said cheerily, "We are in 1938 and *yanqui* imperialism is only the empire of a shadow or rather the shadow of an empire."[28] According to an Ecuadorian visitor, the United States at the beginning of the century was like a young fellow boastfully flexing his muscles and acting tough; now he sits down with the other republics, treats them as equals, and discusses cooperation in the Alliance for Progress.[29] Another Ecuadorian tried to extenuate North American guilt by pointing to the fact that the Mexican War and other aggressive acts were unpopular and criticized among American citizens themselves.[30] A Venezuelan journalist voiced moderate commendation of United States treatment of the Philippines, leading to their independence.[31] According to a Cuban journalist writing in 1954, North American imperialism and Dollar Diplomacy were phenomena of the past: "The United States has shown unmistakable signs of having recovered from the imperialistic measles." No longer need the territorial ambitions of the United States or its urge for intervention be feared, he said, "For some time no one in Central or South America has had suspicions of Uncle Sam's intentions."[32]

Yet the evidence of many of our witnesses does not entirely bear out the Cuban journalist's optimistic statement. While few of them

27. Ayres, *Estados Unidos: una Mentira*; other relatively recent and virulent attacks on North American imperialism are Isidro Fabela, *Buena y mala vecindad* (Mexico, 1958); Ramírez Nova, *La farsa del panamericanismo* (Buenos Aires, 1955); Oscar Weiss, *Nacionalismo y socialismo en América latina* (Santiago de Chile, 1954); and Juan José Arévalo, *The Shark and the Sardine* (New York, 1960). Future references to Ayres are in the text.
28. Otero, *Estados Unidos en 1941*, pp. 70–74. Future references to this book are in the text.
29. Miguel Macías, manuscript of lecture given at Centro Ecuatoriano-norteamericano, pp. 2–3.
30. Uzcátegui, *Los Estados Unidos*, p. 7. Future references are in the text.
31. Enrique Bernardo Núñez, *Viaje*, p. 169.
32. Nicolás Bravo, *El destino*, p. 50.

used the old clichés after the 1930s, there was nevertheless a steady current of fear of economic imperialism, centered particularly on North American oil, mineral, and fruit investments in Spanish America. Men like Luis Alberto Sánchez and José Vasconcelos in the bright days of the Good Neighbor Policy were almost persuaded that the crisis of *yanqui* imperialism had passed.[33] Censure of American imperialism, however, usually narrowed down now to fulmination against the injustices committed by United States business interests in Latin America, continued to be a persistent note.[34]

A good example of the continuing campaign against economic imperialism was a symposium published in the prestigious *Cuadernos Americanos* (Mexico) in 1947. Six outstanding intellectuals from all of Spanish America, men of the stature of Mariano Picón-Salas and Ezequiel Martínez Estrada, united in denying or strongly doubting that the Good Neighbor Policy would halt the evils of American economic penetration.[35] However, that sentiment is divided on this issue and varies according to countries and social class, as may be surmised from the results of opinion surveys conducted in Costa Rica and Panama. Seventy-nine per cent of a group of Costa Rican elite students agreed that the United Fruit Company was beneficial to their country, and 71 per cent of the Panamanian group thought likewise. Sixty-one per cent of the Costa Ricans did not believe that North American corporations should be barred from their country, and 64 per cent of the Panamanians were of the same opinion. Eighty-five per cent of the Costa Ricans and 69 per cent of the Panamanians would like to work for an American company.[36]

It is possible that the sentiments expressed in 1954 by Alberto Zum Felde, a respected Uruguayan literary critic, were in some respects representative of a sizeable body of educated opinion: "The imperialist phenomenon," he declared, "persists in deeds, although in a much less aggressive form than before, smoothed down, hidden under gloves and the speeches of Good Neighbor diplomacy." This change he attributed to an evolution in the nature of capitalism and the fact that American businessmen and

33. Sánchez, *Un sudamericano*, pp. 354–61; Vasconcelos, *Hispanoamérica frente a los nacionalismos*, p. 87.
34. See Arango, *Estados Unidos*, pp. 157–70; Beals and Humphrey, passim; Merrill, *Gringo*, p. 23; and J. Fernando Juárez y Aragón, *Más allá de mis lentes*, p. 102.
35. "Mesa rodante: imperialismo y buena vecindad."
36. Daniel Goldrich, *Sons of the Establishment*, passim.

politicians had abandoned their fat-cigar and feet-on-desk manner and had "learned how to deal with Spanish Americans with smiling suaveness." The ideal of Pan Americanism, he added, covered up the facts of economic imperialism.[37]

## VIEWS ON OTHER FOREIGN POLICY MATTERS

In the sources for this study we find relatively little comment on American foreign policy in its broadest scope. So great was the preoccupation with political imperialism and economic domination in Latin America that the worldwide responsibilities and policies of their big northern neighbor failed to interest the Spanish American intellectuals to any significant degree. They, of course, were aware in a general way of the key position of the United States in world affairs, and a few questioned in passing our capabilities of properly discharging our responsibilities.[38] One analyst declared, referring to the British Protestant heritage of the United States: "We sincerely believe that the Anglo-Saxon *ethos*, although it favors peace and tranquil coexistence with other nations, is not naturally inclined, as is the Hispanic-American *ethos*, to eucumenical inspiration, to an open collaboration with all peoples in the realization of values which can ennoble and beautify man's life on earth."[39] Perhaps this indifference to the global involvement of the United States is an important explanation of the feeling prevalent among Spanish Americans after World War II that their good neighbor had slighted and snubbed them.

In contrast to many other foreign critics, the sources for this study remark on Americans' fixation about the Communist menace with surprising infrequency. Once in a while one even runs across a word of gratitude for the United States as a protector against Communism.[40] On the other hand, there is evidence that Mexican journalists have been impatient with our "psychosis" about the Communist bogeyman,[41] and several observers expressed some indignation that our policy-makers have confounded Latin American leftists of purely native descent with the international Communist conspiracy.[42]

But these few and random comments on American foreign pol-

37. Zum Felde, *Indice crítico*, pp. 315–16. Future references are in the text.
38. See Dávila, *We of the Americas*, p. 2.
39. Gómez Robledo, *Idea*, p. 109.
40. Bravo, chap. 28; Mañach, in Joseph, *As Others See Us*, p. 334.
41. Merrill, pp. 23, 38–39, 41–42.
42. Pérez Guerrero, *USA*, p. 45; Merrill, pp. 39–40.

icy are trifling in comparison with the anti-imperialist theme and with its relative, the frequent accusation that the United States favors and supports dictatorial, anti-democratic regimes in Latin America. The latter topic became such a well-known commonplace that I can only illustrate it in summary fashion. The old guard anti-imperialists customarily linked the aggressive plots of the United States with Caribbean petty tyrants and charged that the Colossus of the North maintained them in power or deposed them to further its imperialistic designs.[43]

After World War II, the tide of criticism became more general and frequently centered on military aid given to dictators in the name of continental defense. A visitor whose overall attitude toward the United States was friendly and admiring declared that the urge for security "causes the United States to lend military and financial support to countries ruled by inflexible dictatorships that dare to boast of their democracy and occidental culture."[44] A Cuban, suggesting reforms in United States foreign policy toward Latin America, laid down as one of the primary steps the stoppage of all military aid to the southern republics.[45]

Only one of our witnesses expressed full recognition that the United States policy toward the periodically blooming and evanescent tyrannies in Latin America involved a series of delicate diplomatic problems, including our espousal of the doctrine of nonintervention in the affairs of our neighbors to the south. Acknowledging that democratic regimes could not be imposed on other countries by the United States, he nevertheless hoped that a way could be discovered to reconcile nonintervention with the active encouragement of democratic forces and regimes in Latin America.[46] Ironically enough, this commentator was a Cuban.

POLITICAL INSTITUTIONS AND DEMOCRACY

In spite of more than a century of crucial changes in the position of the United States in the world community and in spite of the wave of fear and anti-imperialism which estranged so many Spanish Americans from the United States, the image of North America as the home of democratic institutions and liberty—so cherished

43. For example, Ugarte in "La nueva Roma," pp. 657–61.
44. Pérez Guerrero, p. 45.
45. Pedro Villoldo, *Latin American Resentment*, passim. Representative of the almost unanimous criticism of support for dictators are Arango, pp. 152–56, and Beals and Humphrey, p. 94.
46. Bravo, chap. 29 and pp. 62–69.

by the early patriots of Latin America—persisted in many minds. To be sure the passage of the years tarnished it here and there, but the general ideal picture was still intact, and was present even in the minds of some of the most articulate critics.

From the point of view of a cultural aristocrat, José Enrique Rodó found some of the results of democracy in general, and in the United States in particular, distasteful and harmful to his ideal society. Nevertheless, he did not quibble about the positive virtues of North American political institutions. Referring to the logical development of the principle of liberty among North Americans, his praise is reminiscent of the days of independence: "The mark of their steps will never be erased from the annals of human rights, because they have been the first to bring forth our modern concept of liberty from the uncertainty of experimentation and the realm of Utopian fantasies and to convert it into imperishable bronze and living reality." He singled out specifically the success of the federative system in the United States.[47]

Additional defenders of the American political system were not lacking. A Chilean journalist, stressing faith in human perfectibility and preference for the welfare of the community over that of the individual as hallmarks of democracy in the United States, wrote, "These principles of a selective democracy have been established [in North America] from the very beginning." Another Chilean said of the United States in 1920, "As a democracy this country was not perfect; it had defects; but the ideal was there as the goal which all wished to reach. A remedy is being found for every evil. Nothing is perfect; but comparing this country with others, is not this the most nearly perfect of democracies?"[48]

José Vasconcelos, influential as he was in propagating fear of the *yanqui* peril, declared in 1934, "I recognize that with all its harshness the rule of caste in North America, imbedded in a relatively sincere democracy, in its beginnings gave to a hundred million people one of the most prosperous and happiest epochs to be found in history." Speaking of the functioning of democracy in the United States, he noted, "democracy withstands the havoc which it itself engenders, and avoids letting it take on catastrophic proportions, either by assimilating a new set of ideas or by expelling it."[49]

47. *Ariel*, pp. 79–80. Future references are in the text.
48. Ernesto Montenegro, *Puritania*, p. 232; Tancredo Pinochet, *The Gulf of Misunderstanding*, p. 256.
49. *Hispanoamérica*, pp. 25–26, 43.

During and after World War II, there were numerous admirers of the American democratic system. Manuel Seoane declared in 1942, "Every American citizen is a real institution of liberty. There votes are not bought or elections falsified. Each citizen is jealous of his rights, a lover of peace and progress." Remarking in 1941 on the display of the flag even by radical orators, Enrique Bernardo Núñez mused, "It is lovely to see the use of the national flag as a symbol of the justice and liberty which it represents, this association of civic life with the emblem of its guarantees and of its history, which is daily life itself, making use of its rights, its most genuine tradition."[50]

Alberto Zum Felde, a Uruguayan literary historian whose view of North American civilization has not always been rosy, said, "Certainly there, in the absence of nobility . . . and since the majority of the powerful and ruling classes come from the people, constitutional democratic order has been more firmly implanted than in any other part of the world" (p. 321).

The words of Leopoldo Zea, the Mexican philosopher, were not unusual. Even while attacking Manifest Destiny, economic imperialism, and racial discrimination, he said, "Hispanic America has felt and will always feel admiration for the North America of the freedoms, for the North America of a Washington affirming the rights of man, the country of a Lincoln abolishing slavery, or of a Roosevelt understanding democracy in a worldwide sense."[51]

Among most of the commentators who were favorably disposed toward democratic institutions in the United States, the spirit of toleration and the freedom of speech and press appeared to be a particularly impressive aspect of those institutions. Perhaps this reaction was a reflection of anger against restrictions so often imposed at home by dictatorial regimes. Even during wartime, an Ecuadorian journalist wrote, "Every idea, every proposal, every attitude is listened to with patience by reason of a kind of 'collective consent' that every man may do that which will benefit himself."[52] And a Colombian editor expressed a similar view: "In this environment of freedom of discussion lies the expression of his tolerance, for he freely debates for the purpose of convincing his opponent, but without renouncing the idea of being convinced."[53]

50. Seoane, *El gran vecino*, p. 144 (future references are in the text); Núñez, *Viaje*, p. 134.
51. Zea, *América como conciencia*, p. 143.
52. Jorge Fernández, quoted in Dozer, *Are We Good Neighbors?*, p. 170.
53. Roberto García Peña, quoted ibid.

The freedom with which sidewalk orators expounded their unorthodox views stimulated surprise and pleasure in some visitors. An Argentine educator said, "Everybody considers that other people have the right to lead their lives as they please."[54] Eighteen per cent of a group of Bolivian grantees marked individual freedom of opinion and freedom of the press as their most favorable impression of the United States, and 29 per cent of Mexican grantees surveyed found freedom of speech in their host country better than they had anticipated.[55] A content survey of the Latin American press revealed admiration for the freedom of expression prevailing in the United States, the openness with which congressmen criticize the administration being particularly notable.[56]

Another facet of political life in North America that was frequently underscored was the power of public opinion and the press in formulating government policy. Núñez in 1941 was surprised that even in those perilous days any change in the government's course of action had to be made within the democratic framework, that is, in consideration of public and press opinion. Jorge Mañach, in his description of the virtues of the American political system, wrote, "in general it can be said that, in the domestic field, policy is always in keeping with the public interest as seen by majority opinion within the corresponding electoral sphere. Precisely from that fact originates certain limitations and errors, derived from the quality of that majority and its judgments or prejudices; but this in itself involves fidelity to the sovereignty of public opinion, which is the real and supreme power in the United States."[57] At least one critic, however, believed that the influence of genuine public opinion in political life was being nullified by the overwhelming power of the press and the radio, and that the American public was far too docile in being guided by the mass media.[58]

Rodó was one of the first in this century to emphasize a trend of derogatory comment on North American political life that saw a deterioration of early political virtues. He declared, "Civic valor,

54. Luis Reissig, *Algunas observaciones de un viaje por América*, pp. 28–30.
55. Instituto Boliviano de Encuestas, *A Study of Former Bolivian Grantees in the United States*, p. 31; International Research Associates, "Study," p. 8; 10 per cent found it worse than expected.
56. Wolfe, "Attitudes," chap. 22.
57. Núñez, *Viaje*, p. 135; Mañach, in Joseph, p. 334; see also Bravo, pp. 65–66.
58. Arango, p. 32.

the old virtue of men like Hamilton, is a steel blade that is becoming rustier every day, forgotten in the cobweb of tradition." Venality, mediocrity, and the power of plutocracy have penetrated the body politic and threaten to bring to it the fate suffered by the Roman republic (pp. 96–97). Rodó's disciple, Carlos-Arturo Torres, asserted that contemporary political parties had betrayed their origins: "The old transcendental principles of the halcyon age of American liberty, vibrant with promises and replete with sound doctrine, have been replaced by topical issues, whose very intrinsic vulgarity excludes any possibility of high-mindedness, and over which constantly floats the threat of blackmail or the shadow of corruption and speculation."[59]

Some anti-imperialists took up this decadence-of-democracy theme. Blanco-Fombona, for example, said, "before the first war with Mexico, the United States . . . was without military or imperial ambition, and was the home of civil liberty. A South American admired its people with the same fervor with which he now detests them." And in 1929, an Argentine critic declared, "The United States, governed by an imperialistic plutocracy, has betrayed completely its early ideals."[60]

There were others, nevertheless, who contradicted Rodó and maintained that the political ideals of the Founding Fathers were still being realized in their essence. Gustavo Otero, a Bolivian visitor, claimed that the democratic ideal had not greatly varied since the time of Tocqueville's praise of it, but that it had been modified by trends toward economic welfare and democracy (p. 39). An Ecuadorian visitor said in 1958, "Liberty, democracy, and religion are the signs that mark the birth of this great nation. And these signs have remained unaltered throughout the ages," despite immigration and the fantastic growth of wealth.[61]

The evolutionary character of North American democracy was recognized by a Cuban educator who stated, "The characteristic of this scheme of life called 'democracy' is constant albeit gradual change in concepts of basic institutions with corresponding changes in action programs." Vasconcelos believed in 1937 that the United States, under the New Deal, was getting back to the old democratic tradition and its sober style of life.[62]

59. Torres, *Idola fori*, pp. 95–96.
60. Blanco-Fombona, quoted in M. Chapman, "Yankeephobia," p. 4; Nydia Lamarque, quoted in Inman, *Latin America*, p. 8.
61. Pérez Guerrero, pp. 36–37.
62. Silvio de la Torre, *Educación y filosofía en Norteamérica*, pp. 10–11; Vasconcelos, *¿Qué es la revolución?*, p. 120.

Naturally, there were dissident voices in the general chorus of respect for the functioning of democratic institutions in the United States. As early as 1890, a Chilean statesman candidly labeled the typical North American politician as uncultured, undignified, immoral, and unscrupulous, but skillful in masterminding sordid deals.[63] According to Rodó, the materialistic nature of American civilization has given first place in political life to "the struggle-for-lifer, daring and shrewd, converted by the brutal efficiency of his forcefulness into the supreme personification of natural energy" (p. 97). To a Central American novelist writing in 1927, the politician in the United States was a crafty, Machiavellian promoter of imperialism.[64] Blanco-Fombona, who as an eighteen-year-old had had a tussle with the New York police, did not mince words in his scorn of American political institutions. Recalling that North Americans foster the legend that theirs is a "model republic," he denied it and fumed, "The most corrupt justice in the world is the *yanquis'*. The most deceitful elections in the world are theirs also. Yes, there is equality and there is liberty—the equality of slavery to the policeman, who is the tyrant of North American cities." Mañach, who was of a generation younger than Blanco-Fombona's and a much more moderate commentator, said in 1959, "The democracy of presidents who are almost always exemplary is also, on its lower levels, the democracy of political 'machines' and state and municipal bosses; of vulgar, hand-shaking politicians; and of unscrupulous or fabulously enriched labor leaders."[65] In later years, however, the kind of accusations made by Rodó and Blanco-Fombona seem to be less frequent.

Understandably, in view of their variety and complexity, the details of the political process in the United States occasioned relatively little comment among our witnesses, who preferred to restrict themselves to generalities. In their study of Mexican students in the United States, Beals and Humphrey found that in a general way they admired American political life, but showed little real knowledge of its actual functioning. One suspects that this is generally true of the men whose writings form the principal source of this study.

The characteristics of the two main political parties aroused

63. Carlos Walker Martínez, quoted in F. B. Pike, *Chile and the United States*, p. 167.
64. Quoted in Avila, p. 116.
65. Blanco-Fombona, *La lámpara de Aladino*, p. 421 (see also p. 283); Mañach, in Joseph, p. 337; see also Arciniegas, *En el país*, p. 105, and Quintanilla, *A Latin American Speaks*, p. 53.

some interest. A Guatemalan witness decided that they were in no sense artificial creations but the result of historical social processes, even though there is little difference between them. Although their main activity takes place before elections, he marvels that they continue their organization, win or lose.[66] For a Bolivian observer, the Republican party was conservative and centralist, tending to emphasize authority and the power of the state, while the Democratic party was less dogmatic and more humane in its programs, and had a greater sense of understanding and tolerance (Otero, p. 129). An Argentine educator identified the Republican party as the one "supported by the great industrial enterprises, who are bitter enemies of price-control and believers in free enterprise."[67]

The available evidence indicates that Spanish Americans, or at least their writers and intellectuals, favored the Democratic Party, believing that it is basically more friendly to their own interests.[68] During the New Deal days, Vasconcelos saw the struggle between Republicans and Democrats as a battle between the ruling aristocracy and the organized masses seeking to maintain or achieve liberty and justice.[69] Franklin D. Roosevelt was remembered by many, not only as the great spokesman for the Good Neighbor Policy, but also as the author of the New Deal, which received considerable praise from Spanish Americans.[70]

## HEROES AND HERO WORSHIP

The North American heroes who loomed so large in the nineteenth-century Spanish American mind—Washington and Franklin—lost much of their magnetism in this century. Washington, in the eyes of some intellectuals, seemed a mediocre man, "bereft of the interior flame of genius"; although he still had his eager readers, Franklin, in the minds of Rodó and his school, symbolized all that was shrewd, materialistic, and limiting to the spirit in Caliban's civilization.[71]

On the other hand, Spanish Americans followed their northern neighbors in gradually taking Abraham Lincoln out of the realm

66. Juárez y Aragón, p. 60.
67. Reissig, p. 17.
68. Merrill, pp. 18, 44, 51; Goldrich, *Radical Nationalism*, p. 18.
69. *¿Qué es la revolución?*, p. 120.
70. See Reissig, p. 19; Vasconcelos, *Hispanoamérica*, p. 61; Sánchez, *Un sudamericano*, chap. 13.
71. Torres, p. 200; Englekirk, "Franklin," pp. 356–58.

of human reality and enshrining him in a golden Valhalla. Visiting Spanish Americans customarily came from their pilgrimage to the Lincoln Memorial with some such thoughts in mind as these of Benjamín Subercaseaux: "The look in Lincoln's eyes is profound; it is neither severe nor solemn, nor even grave. It is a look of impressive cordiality, belonging to a blameless country man, who is telling us that things will be that way and no other, and who asks us, 'And what are you doing to make the world better?'" (p. 105). In a like mood a Venezuelan writer said, "Lincoln becomes an obsession. The man of simple features, of large shoes, and modest dress personifies the spirit and ideal of justice."[72] Lincoln symbolized for many of the other Americans some of the virtues of the United States: opportunities for the most humble to rise, generosity, human simplicity, and grass-roots common sense.[73]

For a group of Spanish American intellectuals earlier in this century, Woodrow Wilson almost achieved the status of a hero. His idealism was very attractive to such men as Juan Zorrilla de San Martín of Uruguay, Joaquín V. González of Argentina, and Víctor Andrés Belaúnde of Peru. But the actions of his administration in Mexico and in the Caribbean prevented Wilson from being unanimously honored in the heroes' pantheon. Even so, a Nicaraguan was moved in 1920 to write an eloquent "Ode to Wilson" which said, in part,

> Wilson, my voice is the voice of a Continent;
> It is the voice of the America of Columbus;
> What thy lips proclaim, my America feels,
> My America has heard the beating of thy heart.
>
> Thou sayest that peoples should determine their own
>     destiny . . .
> Oh Apostle of Justice, in the name of God,
> May the road be open for all peoples . . .
> America listens and has heard thy voice.[74]

During his lifetime, Franklin D. Roosevelt was greatly admired and almost worshipped by Spanish Americans. Even in their disillusion of the post-war years, the figure of the debonair president was venerated and there are indications that he may go down in Spanish American historical memory as a hero or near-hero. Cer-

72. Núñez, *Viaje*, p. 19.
73. See Sánchez, *Un sudamericano*, p. 134; Dávila, p. 222; Seoane, p. 54.
74. Antonio Medrano, quoted in Cabrales, pp. 68–70.

tainly the lines in his praise by a Costa Rican poet are a hymn to
a more-than-human being:

> May time be made of immovable rock
> So that his praises may be chiselled there.
> In the caverns of the rock of time
> This name will echo: Roosevelt,
> Like an oath to the waves of the open seas
> So that it may never be forgotten
> On land or sea, or the face of the earth,
> For if there are free men and nations,
> They owe their freedom to this titan of will.[75]

It is too soon to tell whether or not Roosevelt will join Lincoln
as an enduring hero for Spanish Americans. The same may be said
of John F. Kennedy, who was mourned in Spanish America with
an intensity born of hero worship.

### THE AMERICAN ECONOMY

If one is seeking an analysis by a keen foreign observer of the
American economic system, he need not bother with the writings
of our witnesses. With some exceptions, they are not much interested in the actual mechanics of North America's industrial and
business processes or in the evolution of our economy.

The popular conception, which was that of a good many of the
writers, especially early in the century, was the old tried-and-true
stereotype of ruthless capitalism, monopolies or trusts, and oppressed workers. As in so many parts of the world, "capitalism"
was a nasty word to liberal Spanish Americans, with many un-
pleasant connotations. Even young people who studied in the
United States spoke of capitalism as "fat, gross, and greasy";
"the product of dollar-oriented personalities"; "exploitation of the
country by unrestrained robber barons."[76] Capitalism was equated
with Wall Street in popular Spanish American thought, and Luis
Alberto Sánchez sounded an average note when he said, "Wall
Street—a name which causes blind indignation . . . a wall erected
between North and South America. It is the concrete and representative expression of a mentality and a state of mind which must
be beaten down. It is an oath and an anathema." There is evidence

---

75. Roberto Brenes Mesén, quoted ibid.
76. Quoted in "Latin American Attitudes toward U.S. Business," a study
sponsored by the U.S. Information Agency (mimeographed, 1963).

to indicate that the negative image of United States capitalism was formed not only by Marxist propaganda, but also because of the actions of some American companies and native capitalists in Spanish America.[77]

Very few of our witnesses went to the trouble of listing in any considered detail the specific shortcomings of North American capitalism, contenting themselves with standard generalizations. One of the few who did was Luis Quintanilla (Mexico), who criticized in 1943 the uneven distribution of wealth; the concentration of economic control in a small number of corporations; the disappearance of the small, independent farmer; the wretched plight of farm labor, especially migratory workers; widespread unemployment; and the exploitation of Mexican "wet-backs."[78]

Germán Arciniegas painted a dismal and moving picture of the adversities suffered by migratory workers in California. A more recent observer mentioned with grim foreboding the easy credit and installment buying so characteristic of the economy.[79]

Some of the more perceptive observers, however, became vaguely aware of the fact that the classical capitalism of the nineteenth century was so radically changed in the United States in the twentieth century that it hardly resembled the familiar stereotype. Even as early as 1922, a Dominican observer, noting the enormous potentialities of North American wealth for good or for bad, was gratified to see the efforts to control "the dangerous appetite of the trusts," and the tendency to use accumulated wealth for the benefit of mankind in many parts of the world. He also praised American experiments in sharing profits with the workers and the high level of wages.[80] Writing in 1961, a Chilean journalist declared that technology had changed the American economic system so much that even Franklin D. Roosevelt would not recognize it, and that it certainly was not capitalism in the traditional sense. In contrast to totalitarian economies, he continued, the worker in America has maintained his freedom of choice and leads a good life in the midst of a marvelously productive economic structure.[81]

77. *Un sudamericano,* pp. 307–8; Washington, "Hostility," p. 18.
78. Quintanilla, pp. 53–71.
79. Arciniegas, pp. 85–86, 98–99; Luis López de Mesa, *La sociedad contemporánea y otros escritos,* pp. 42–43.
80. Cestero, pp. xvii–xix. Writing in Mexico, Manuel Cestero also remarked on Theodore Roosevelt's trust-busting campaign but believed it to be a long, hard, and perhaps impossible job (*Estados Unidos por dentro*).
81. Nicolás Velasco del Campo, *El país de Kennedy,* p. 17. Bravo presents a similar defense of the American economy, pp. 217–18.

A Costa Rican statesman stressed the fact that many economic functions in the United States had passed from the hands of individual entrepreneurs to large corporations, which earned profits not for a small band of individuals, but for the multitude of shareholders, who were also the consumers of the company's products. He noted the frequent separation of management from ownership and found little difference between such a structure and the autonomous state-owned enterprises so favored in Latin America. He further commended the economic policies of the United States government because it had not tried to mold reality in accordance with a rigid, preconceived theory, but had tackled concrete problems and let general principles emerge from their solutions.[82]

Oddly, considering the common idea that university students and teachers in Latin America are universally inclined to leftist economic fancies, a group of Bolivian grantees expressed a general opinion that the present economic structure of the United States was congruent with its ideals of freedom and independence, and capable of prevailing over the communist system. One of them wrote, "The present capitalistic system has excelled all other types of economy, for one cannot ignore the fact that even the communist economy basically rests on a type of relatively capitalistic economy, notwithstanding efforts made to show things from a different point of view."[83]

A selection of Mexican students, while not as confident of the virtues of the American economy, did change their preconceptions of gringo big business, regarded it with less hostility, admitted the fact of free competition in a society they had regarded as tightly monopolistic, and even granted in some cases that the economy of their big neighbor was directed toward socially useful ends.[84]

The traditional notion that big business practically runs the government in the United States and molds its civilization was still encountered from time to time. Amanda Labarca, a Chilean educator, and Daniel Cosío Villegas, a Mexican economist—both of the older generation—included this old chestnut in their basket of impressions.[85] It probably is not an uncommon part of the popular stereotype among many Spanish Americans.

In summary, to judge from this batch of witnesses, educated

82. Figueres, in Davis, *Social Thought*, pp. 468–71.
83. Instituto Boliviano de Encuestas, pp. 10–11.
84. Beals and Humphrey, pp. 87–88.
85. Labarca, in Joseph, pp. 316–17; Cosío Villegas, ibid., p. 295.

Spanish Americans seem to have had a jumbled concept of the American economic system in which remnants of Marxist clichés were mingled with fragments of more up-to-date information, the whole image being projected against a background of American investments and business activity in their own countries.

## A Classless Society?

The reader will recall the surprise, usually accompanied by approval, with which the nineteenth-century Spanish American visitor regarded the social equality observed in the United States. The visitors of this century registered the same ritual approval, which became something of a convention.

Their view was ordinarily not very penetrating and was often expressed in a more or less oratorical manner. García Calderón, for example, asserted, "Fair play, the identical chances which the Republic offers her citizens, in creating schools, in fostering the advance of self-made men in society, constitute the firmest foundation of the life of a republic. Equity and equality prevail above the eager onrush of her citizens . . . equality in the churches in place of intolerance, equality in schools instead of the privileges created by wealth."[86]

Other observers cited human-interest circumstances to illustrate the absence or fragility of barriers between classes. One remarked that public markets, in contrast to those of his homeland, were patronized by the public at large and not only by fashionable ladies attended by their servants. A Colombian, perhaps remembering the comparative rigidity of his own society, wrote, "This is the first place in the world where the idea of servitude has disappeared, not only in law, but also in reality. In North America a cook or a maid is just as much of a person as the boss or the President of the Republic."[87] Another witness, Subercaseaux, a Chilean, praised the camaraderie of taxi-drivers who, without any trace of subservience, talk with their passengers as friends and equals. The same man remarked on the fact that in Washington's Mayflower Hotel sailors mingled with high society ladies. "Nobody there," he said, "bothers about social rank. If a fellow has money to pay for his drink, he drinks it where he pleases. This is a new experience for us democratic citizens of monarchical republics" (pp. 148, 115–16).

86. García Calderón, p. 307.
87. Reissig, pp. 10–12; López de Mesa, p. 48.

A few of the witnesses picked up a phrase which North Americans themselves like to use—"a classless society." Carlos Dávila, a Chilean diplomat, stated, "Marx's dream of a classless society has come near realization in the United States, not only because of the levelling in living standards, but also because there is no class feeling among the people." There is little differentiation among income groups with regard to the kind of lives they live, he continued, and Marxism has made negligible headway because there is no real proletariat.[88]

A Bolivian writer was more careful and perceptive in his judgment of North American social equality. According to Otero's observations, there definitely were classes in the United States society, in spite of superficial uniformity, and different character types. The important characteristic was the social mobility, the lack of petrified stratification in American society; it was, he noted, like the elevator in a skyscraper, in which individuals are constantly and rapidly going up and down (pp. 113–15).

Perhaps because of his obsession with the importance of racial influence in society, José Vasconcelos as late as 1934 advanced the rather quaint idea that there was an identifiable controlling class in the United States constituted by a New England aristocracy of pure-blooded Anglo-Saxons. He conceded that a few aristocratic southerners of the same social status, plus an odd Irishman or Jew, had infiltrated the inner circle of rulers. He prophesied a "war of castes" in which the rapidly multiplying members of the "low social layers" would be pitted against the Anglo-Saxon master class.[89] As far as the group of witnesses whose testimony we are examining is concerned, Vasconcelos' theory is unrepresentative.

THE PLIGHT OF THE NEGRO AND OTHER MINORITY GROUPS

It goes without saying that the monstrous flaw in this generally roseate picture of human equality in the United States was the social and economic position of the Negro. This flaw loomed large in Spanish American eyes, as in the eyes of most foreigners and many North Americans. In the writings examined there is little informed analysis; for the most part, the attitude is simply one of conventional censure.

88. Dávila, pp. 129–30. Mexican students also believed in the classless society concept (Beals and Humphrey, p. 86). For other generalized statements on social equality, see Pinochet, p. 265; Pérez Guerrero, p. 32; Mañach, in Joseph, p. 332.
89. *Hispanoamérica*, pp. 21–22; *Bolivarismo*, p. 149.

Within the general pattern of rebuke, however, there are several identifiable threads with slight differences of tint. The standard denunciation of lynching, so common among the earlier commentators,[90] almost disappeared in more recent observations. The difference in the Negro's status in the North and in the South of the United States was occasionally noted, but the northern states by no means came out with a clean bill of health.[91] Vehement and frequent was the charge that the posture of the United States regarding democracy and Nazi racial theories was hypocritical when the situation of its Negroes was considered. Rómulo Betancourt, ex-president of Venezuela, declared in 1945 that American racial discrimination showed "implications of totalitarian viciousness and of unconscious Nazi tendencies in some of the American people: a serious deterrent to a sincere understanding between the two Americas."[92]

Now and then a witness tried to produce scraps of evidence showing improvement in race relations in the United States. Franklin D. Roosevelt's efforts to help the Negro were appreciated by several observers, and Mrs. Roosevelt's gesture of inviting Marian Anderson to sing at the Lincoln Memorial, after the singer had been turned away at Constitution Hall, greatly impressed friendly Spanish American visitors.[93] A Peruvian journalist remarked that Negroes participated in political party conventions and that both major parties were committed to the improvement of the Negro's position in American political life and society.[94] At least one observer took note of the Supreme Court's desegregation decision in 1954, but foresaw formidable difficulties in implementing it.[95] Vasconcelos pointed out that American scholars have given industrious and painstaking attention to the problem of the Negro and that, at least in the North, Negroes were given fair opportunities for education and for earning a decent living.[96]

Particularly among the older commentators writing in this century there was a tendency to emphasize the inherent differences between the Negro race and the white. There were those who clung

90. See as examples Blanco-Fombona, *La lámpara de Aladino*, p. 421, and Pinochet, pp. 91–95.

91. Arango, p. 98; Reissig, pp. 15–17.

92. Quoted in Dozer, p. 182; Arango, p. 92; see also Sánchez, *Un sudamericano*, chap. 7, and Beals and Humphrey, p. 87.

93. Uzcátegui, p. 14.

94. Sánchez, *Un sudamericano*, p. 214.

95. Arango, p. 100.

96. *¿Qué es la revolución?*, pp. 225–26.

to the stereotyped idea that the Negro is more sensual, more primitive in his instincts, and more esthetically gifted, and is endowed with moral values differing from those of the white man. This assumption led to several stock conclusions among a group of our witnesses. One of them was that the Negro was not capable of being assimilated into the white man's civilization, and that therefore we were faced with an insoluble dilemma.[97]

Another conclusion was that the Negro loves poetry, song, the dance, and sensual joy more than his puritanical white compatriots and constitutes therefore a peculiarly valuable element in the North American population.[98] Reference, of course, was often made to the originality of American Negro music. A corollary of this interpretation of the black man's nature was encountered in a few of the sources: the Negro woman was so sexually attractive to the white man's lust that considerable miscegenation had taken place.[99] In one exceptionally misinformed statement, an Argentine alleged that 70 per cent of the population of the United States was either Negro or of mixed Negro and white blood.[100]

These somewhat fanciful speculations were very close to being a defense of racial discrimination and segregation in the United States, and several of the commentators turned against the majority and frankly defended or condoned the denial of equal rights to the American Negro. Quite logically in view of their adherence to Le Bon's theories, the racists of the early years of this period approved of the Negro's lowly status in the United States, regarding him as naturally inferior.[101] Gustavo Otero, while he found racial prejudice irritating, declared that Negroes, with the exception of a small elite group, are inherently inferior. Being inferior, he said, they feel no real resentment against their white fellow citizens and are by nature servile and obedient (pp. 28–34). According to Vasconcelos, the Negro, because of his primitive strength, is indifferent to hardships and is content with his rhythmic music and his close contact with the soil.[102] Subercaseaux, although his artist's soul found the primitivism of the Negro attractive, took the

97. Ezequiel Martínez Estrada, *Diferencias y semejanzas entre los países de la América Latina*, p. 12; Reissig, p. 16; Subercaseaux, p. 9.

98. Sánchez, *Un sudamericano*, p. 214; Martínez Estrada, pp. 120–21.

99. Ayres, p. 48; García Calderón, p. 311.

100. Ayres, p. 50. Blanco-Fombona, while he excoriated the treatment of Negroes in the United States, stated that mixed blood is Venezuela's misfortune and advocated European immigration to whiten the mixture (*La lámpara de Aladino*, pp. 421, 498–99).

101. See, for example, Carlos Bunge, *Nuestra América*, p. 136.

102. *¿Qué es la revolución?*, p. 129.

fatalistic view that the Negro can never become a part of North American civilization. While a few, he believed, could benefit from education, the majority are incapable of marching forward. Most of the slaves, said Subercaseaux, came from the worst African breeds and were superstitious, lazy, and unstable. His exoneration of North Americans from the charge of racial prejudice is unparalleled in this study's sources. "Really it is unjust," he said, "to accuse all North Americans of racial prejudice. I have known hundreds of them who defended the Negro and angrily upbraided the unjust treatment of that innocent race" (p. 124). Even though the majority of Spanish American spokesmen deplored the Negro's position in the United States, it is worth remembering that racial problems also exist in Spanish America, especially concerning the Indians, and that a small minority of our witnesses, possibly for that reason, were aware of the complexity of the North American Negro problem.

There are a few scattered references to discrimination toward minority groups other than the Negroes, but relatively speaking they are of little importance. Considering the extent of the unassimilated Indian population in many Spanish American countries, it is strange that we should have found scant comment on the tribulations of the Indian in the United States. It is true that Luis Alberto Sánchez devoted most of a chapter to the history of their virtual extermination, their grievous problems, and the efforts made under the Roosevelt administration to solve these problems.[103] Helen Hunt Jackson's *Ramona*, translated by José Martí and later by others, had some vogue in Spanish America, and the pathetic lot of the Indian suggested in that novel must have aroused in others the same indignation as expressed by Ernesto Montenegro.[104]

Slight attention was paid to antisemitism. Its existence was noted in passing by Luis Alberto Sánchez; Vasconcelos found some justification for fearing the power of the Jews; Otero simply denied that discrimination against the Jews was a serious problem among educated Americans.[105]

Opinion about the treatment of the Mexican minority and the "wet-backs" in the United States was varied. Octavio Paz, a Mexi-

---

103. *Un sudamericano*, chap. 8.
104. Montenegro, p. 124.
105. Sánchez, *Un sudamericano*, pp. 179–80; Vasconcelos, *¿Qué es la revolución?*, p. 119. Ayres saw a Jewish conspiracy in many corners of American life (passim).

can poet, meditated at length about the sad situation of the *pachuco*, the young Mexican-American who is "lost between two worlds," although he makes no particular accusation of ill treatment by the dominant North American population.[106] Vasconcelos and others expressed anger and annoyance about the discrimination against Mexicans, especially in Texas.[107] On the other hand, a survey of Mexican student opinion revealed very little solicitude for the condition of the Mexican worker in the United States, the common belief being that their social origins in Mexico did not warrant better treatment.[108] A study of the attitudes of the Mexicans in the United States themselves showed an ambivalent frame of mind with regard to the Anglo-Americans. The latter were generally regarded as superior and industrious but also as cold.[109] One social scientist familiar with Mexicans of the lower class believed that most "wet-backs" return from the United States with a favorable impression of that country and are responsible for creating among their neighbors a good image of the United States.[110]

It is apparent, then, that in the minds of most Spanish Americans the most serious weakness in the social life of the United States was discrimination against the Negro and that manifestations of our unjust attitude toward other minority groups interested them relatively little. Probably the majority of the witnesses would have substantially agreed with Luis Alberto Sánchez when he said of the Negro problem, "It is not only a question of a feeling of wounded equality or of an ideological concept which has been damaged, but of something worse: the certainty that if this open sore in the body of the North American people is not healed, sooner or later it will open the way for the germs of decay. . . ."[111]

## Assimilation of Immigrants

We have seen that the nineteenth-century Spanish American commentators were fascinated by the variety of ethnic strains which were going into the formation of American society, some of them acclaiming that society as a haven for the world's oppressed and others speculating on the desirability of imitation. Twentieth-cen-

106. Paz, *The Labyrinth of Solitude*, pp. 14–15.
107. See quotations in Dozer, pp. 179–80.
108. Beals and Humphrey, passim.
109. Ozzie Simmons, "The Mutual Images and Expectations of Anglo-Americans and Mexican-Americans," p. 294.
110. Humphrey, "Mexican Image," pp. 116–17.
111. *Un sudamericano*, p. 218.

tury observers were no less intrigued by ethnic amalgamation in North America, but they judged the process with a wider spectrum of attitudes.

At the turn of the century, probably swayed by racist theories then current, some who surveyed the huge waves of immigration to the United States uttered dire forebodings of the dangers to result from this monstrous mingling of "races." Rodó prophesied that as the wave grew in size, the task of assimilating the immigrants into a coherent nation would become more and more difficult if not impossible (p. 105). García Calderón wrote, "The descendants of alien races will constitute the nation of the future. The national heritage is threatened by the invasion of Slavs and Orientals, and the fecundity of the Negroes. . . . Excessive and heterogeneous immigration prevents any final crystallization." Vargas Vila colored his view of the ethnic variety of the American people with his characteristic loathing of the United States: "Thus there is not a *yanqui* race, but only *yanqui* groups in that conglomeration of all races, in that rubbish heap of all the disinherited bums of the globe. . . . It is made up of the dregs of all nationalities and of the lower layer of all criminals; all the nationless beggars and all the unemployed bandits founded the country."[112] The fears of these men are reminiscent of the "Know-Nothing" movements and of subsequent anti-immigrant doctrines in the United States.

As late as 1939, a Colombian poet saw more tragedy than happy assimilation in the diverse ethnic groups of New York City. He contrasted the weary sadness of "Little Italy" with the gaiety and glory of old Italy, and in the Spanish-speaking districts he found bitterly thwarted dreams of success streaked with hopeless tedium. This witness, incidentally, was one of the few to report on the pockets of poverty in the United States.[113]

Such views, however, were not representative of the majority of the commentators, especially the later ones. Most of them regarded immigration and the process of assimilation as a marvelous social phenomenon. Several different themes are evident in the discussion.

Following the Crevecoeur-Zangwill concept of the "melting pot," a considerable group saw the assimilation of diverse ethnic stocks as a force creating a distinctly new nationality, a way of life differing from those of any of its components. According to an Ecuadorian journalist, "The United States has absorbed the experiences

112. García Calderón, p. 310; Vargas Vila, p. 164.
113. A. Ortiz Vargas, *Las torres de Manhattan*, pp. 136 ff.

of all the nationalities of the world and has transformed the conditions of all the immigrants, giving a new rhythm to its customs and systems." Even Vasconcelos, who had several attitudes toward ethnic melding in the United States, once apostrophized the northern republic as "this country which joins together all races like a Babylon, but not to disperse them but to melt them into a new and vigorous kind of culture."[114]

Luis López de Mesa, a Colombian essayist, after referring to North America as the safe haven for the downtrodden of Europe and to their amalgamation in this country, wrote, "American democracy is the happy result. A certain universality distinguishes it, and its character is unique, an expression of a mysterious amalgam and not of any particular race."[115]

Others, without denying the efficacy of the assimilation process, endorsed what the sociologists call the "Anglo-conformity" viewpoint; that is, they believed that the immigrants were incorporated into the predominantly English pattern of civilization and have not essentially changed the Anglo-Saxon nature of American civilization. Not infrequently, the Spanish Americans implied that such a social phenomenon was distasteful to them. Gustavo Otero believed that the core of American nationality was a legacy of British colonial days that continued to dictate a style of living to the heterogeneous population. Immigrants therefore formed concentric circles; if they were recent they were farther from the core; education shoved them slowly toward the dominating English center (pp. 45–51). Subercaseaux likened the United States to a religious congregation in which men of all origins enter and are bound by its steely, inflexible creed; "unfortunately," he concluded, "this creed is English."[116]

A few found in the successful North American fusion of ethnic stocks a refutation of the racial purity theories of the nineteenth century and saw in it a lesson for Spanish American countries. An Ecuadorian educator said, "Perhaps in no other part of the globe have more men of the most diverse ethnic characteristics been interbred and fused together; in only three centuries these men have built a nation with the highest economic, industrial, social, and cultural development, thus utterly confounding the devotees of

114. Jorge Fernández, quoted in Dozer, p. 178; Vasconcelos, ¿Qué es la revolución?, p. 225.
115. López de Mesa, "Una hora ante Norte América," p. 83; see also Arciniegas, p. 73.
116. Subercaseaux, p. 162; Vasconcelos at times adopted the Anglo-conformity interpretation (e.g., Hispanoamérica, pp. 14–15).

pure racism." He continued by hailing the potentialities of mixing Indian and white blood in his own country. In a similar vein, a Chilean journalist declared, "The United States provides for those of us who live south of the Rio Grande a great lesson. They have formed one great nation of fifty different communities, often sacrificing regional or individual egoism, conflicting religious or political ideas, and—most significantly—the theories of racial purity which boil like a cauldron in the Southern states."[117]

At least one commentator, imbued with the enthusiasm of the majority for the miracle of immigrant assimilation in the United States, deplored the legislation which has in the last forty years severely curtailed the stream of immigration. Carlos Dávila labeled that policy as timid and defensive, "not quite in step with a daring nation." By admitting millions of immigrants the nation had gambled for high stakes and had won. In the long run, he concluded, she would lose by limiting the entry of foreigners who want to make their homes here.[118]

## WOMEN AND THE FAMILY IN THE UNITED STATES

The North American woman and her position in the social structure presented a delicate and sometimes baffling problem for the Spanish American analyst of society in the United States. On the one hand, he had been fed for years with a motion-picture version of a beautiful, seductive creature of obviously questionable moral standards, and sometimes had known the reality of young American women who went about without chaperones on "dates," who had been educated cheek by jowl with the other sex, and who were generally full of health and vitality. On the other hand, the serious observer noted that women in the United States worked hard, having no servants, were aggressively independent, frequently engaged in serious social or community work, and were intellectually cultivated. Both images offered striking dissimilarities with the traditional woman of Spanish America.

The fact of women's relative freedom in American society was almost universally recognized by the witnesses. Judgments on the desirability and results of that freedom varied considerably among them, and depended on the observer's background and temperament. A few were unconditional admirers of the *yanqui* woman and her role in the social order. Hard-bitten *apristas* like Manuel

117. Uzcátegui, p. 6; Velasco, p. 31.
118. Dávila, p. 197.

Seoane and Luis Alberto Sánchez found her ideal. Seoane said, "Frank, educated, clear-minded, full of personality, the American woman is the cleanest friend in the world, and her participation in her country's destiny is growing every day" (p. 76). Sánchez, after praising her industrious spirit, her health and beauty, her contribution to literature, and her pleasingly direct sensuality, concluded, "The average North American woman is in fact as good a wife as any in the world, and often a better friend and collaborator. . . . She is full of vitality, lacking prejudices, incapable of shrinking before any difficulty, always ready to give herself to the future."[119]

Others, for varying reasons, feared that the emancipation of the American woman (and they may often have been thinking of their imitative women back home) would lead to disastrous consequences. Particularly among the older generation there were those who believed that women's freedom endangered the family. López de Mesa said, "The passion-slave of man has achieved such independence and domination, such legal protection and liberty of action, that for a long time she will upset the old balance of family relationships." A Dominican critic in the 1920s accused the American woman of failing in her sacred task of properly raising her children and of leaving the job entirely to the school.[120]

Also among the older witnesses the movie stereotype of the immoral flapper was still current, and continued to be to some extent. Blanco-Fombona, with his customary vehemence, declared, "Yanqui women—easy virtue girls—enjoy throughout the world a reputation for loose morals which they have won and deserved."[121] But this stereotype, part of the man-in-the-street concept of United States society, was undermined by some Spanish American visitors. Seoane claimed, contrary to the usual Latin view that American girls are easy prey, that they are typically chaste and virginal (pp. 69–70). But there is little doubt that sex relationships in North American society confused and confounded the visitor, occasionally to his personal embarrassment. In a study of the attitudes of Mexican students in American universities, it was apparent that, however much they theoretically admired the pattern of equality

119. *Un sudamericano*, pp. 163–64; see also Otero, pp. 83–93, for extensive praise of American women.
120. López de Mesa, "Una hora ante Norte América," p. 84; Cestero, p. xxii.
121. *La lámpara de Aladino*, p. 547; for a Mexican journalist's censure of the morals of American women, see Merrill, p. 39.

among the sexes, they believed that American girls abused their freedom and were less concerned with preserving their virginity than Mexican girls.[122]

Since women observers among Spanish American visitors were likely to be in the vanguard of women's rights movements at home, their views of their northern sisters' emancipation were usually very favorable. Amanda Labarca, a Chilean educator, said, for example, "My admiration for the North American woman dates from the first trip [in 1911]. . . . Collectively women there were already a force, and individually they enjoyed a respect due not just to genteel masculine gallantry but to confidence in their own merits. One felt them to be conscious of themselves as liberated personalities and masters of their destinies, free of the prejudices and timidities that still shackled their South American sisters."[123]

Some of the male witnesses were rather playfully concerned about the emergence of a powerful matriarchy in the United States. Chilean journalist Ernesto Montenegro, while expressing modified admiration for the studious, independent, adventuresome female in the United States, wondered ironically if this would be the future land of the Amazons, where man would be free to create and dream while his woman ran the home and the life of the country.[124]

Intimately joined, of course, with the Spanish American's opinion of our women was his view of North American family life. The stereotype, common in the early years of the century, that the American family was becoming unstable and enfeebled by new social pressures was often nurtured by motion pictures and by sensational press reports. Women's freedom to go and come as they chose, the declining birth rate, and the increasing prevalence of divorce inclined men like García Calderón to take a dim view of the future in the United States of an institution which had such traditionally overwhelming importance in the Latin American social pattern.[125]

While echoes of this wholesome fear were later heard among

122. Beals and Humphrey, p. 90.
123. Quoted in Joseph, p. 312.
124. Montenegro, pp. 276–80; for a more serious charge that the American woman "wears the pants in the family," see Cestero, p. v.
125. García Calderón, pp. 309–10. That the stereotype of the disintegrating American family did not disappear is evident in Arango, chap. 5; see Ayres, p. 145, for a particularly vehement condemnation of the nomadic, "trailer" life of Americans and its effect on the family.

Spanish Americans, closer and more recent acquaintance with the
North American family summoned up some less alarming images
of family life in the United States. A number of witnesses showed
awareness that the scandals of Hollywood had distorted the picture of the American family group and particularly the incidence
of divorce. A Chilean journalist rejected the common idea that the
family was disintegrating in the United States and declared,
"united and well-organized families are not only numerous, but
there are in proportion more of them than in any other country in
the world, except in archaic societies." Luis Alberto Sánchez believed that the new American family was adequate for the changing
times and confessed, "to enter a home in this country is like taking
a bath of optimism." There was laughter, dancing, joking, arguing
without bitterness in the American family circle, he said.[126]

Two particular aspects of the typical *yanqui* family caused surprise in the Spanish American mind: the sharing of housework by
all members of the family, and the permissive attitude in raising
children. Both were quite contrary to traditional Spanish American family mores, where servants did the dirty work and parents
laid down the law. Oddly enough, the participation of father and
children in the household chores usually intrigued rather than repelled the visitor. Germán Arciniegas (Colombia) found the family
dish-washing ritual to be amusing, touching, and even romantic.
An Argentine educator, Reissig, considered the custom not only inevitable but beneficial for family morale. As for the free-and-easy
relationship between parents and children, Velasco, a journalist
from Chile, admitted that it was shocking but pointed to the good
results which come out of such a relationship. An Ecuadorian observer said, "They teach the child to be successful and that is what
the child offers his parents. We teach them obedience and respect
without demanding with equal firmness that they do things well.
Perhaps that idea of sending the boys out to sell newspapers is a
good way of taking advantage of opportunities."[127]

Most of the group of Mexican students to whom we have referred changed their attitudes toward the American family quite
radically after their experience in the United States. The majority
found that our family life did not conform to their preconception
of a divorce-ridden, crumbling institution. While they did not ap-
prove of divorce and were still uneasy about women's freedom,

126. Velasco, p. 13; Sánchez, *Un sudamericano*, p. 163.
127. Arciniegas, pp. 56–58; Reissig, p. 13; Velasco, p. 13; Macías, p. 6.

they generally favored the less authoritarian structure of the North American family, especially with regard to child-rearing.[128]

## THE SINS OF JOURNALISM

The American press as a social force almost unanimously received brickbats rather than bouquets from Spanish Americans. Aside from the nefarious influence of the news services in Latin America, which we have noted, newspapers in the United States were charged with various misdemeanors.

Amanda Labarca, ordinarily an equable commentator, grew quite heated when she referred to her experiences with American newsmen: "Alert, vivacious, they caught the scent of everything that could be spiced up as sensational. Every day they interviewed an infinite number of personages and, with the exception of a few truthful and honorable journalists, they would turn their reports into a spicy stew of what they themselves wanted to say or what they imagined would please the palates of their readers." Again with some exceptions, she excoriated American newspapers: "They smell out and play on the passions, the weaknesses, the hates, the prejudices, and even the hopes of the reading public."[129]

The professional anti-imperialist had his own particular axe to grind. In his eyes, American newspapers were simply lackeys of the aggressive imperialists and slanted their news of Latin America accordingly. Blanco-Fombona believed that *yanqui* newspapers, in spite of their pictures and fancy appearance, were ridiculous rags, far inferior to their European and South American counterparts, which had literary quality and substance.[130] Spanish Americans resented the scanty and distorted coverage given to Latin America in the northern newspapers. A recent critic also castigated the press and especially the newspaper chains for imposing a uniform "canned" opinion on the American public, thus narrowing the arena of free and open discussion of national problems.[131]

In the sources for this study, I have come across only one defender of the North American press. A Venezuelan journalist had high praise for the Columbia School of Journalism, and by implication for American journalism in general.[132]

128. Beals and Humphrey, pp. 90–91.
129. Quoted in Joseph, p. 320.
130. *La americanización del mundo*, p. 14; Vargas Vila, pp. 63, 152.
131. Arango, chap. 4.
132. Núñez, *Viaje*, pp. 128–29.

### THE FRONTIER AND AMERICAN SOCIETY

In the writings of a minority of the critics there was some speculation about the role of the West in determining the North American
social pattern. One suspects that some of this interest was derived
from acquaintanceship with the works of Frederick Jackson Turner, as well as from intense exposure to western novels and movies.

To some the frontier spirit imposed itself on the whole of American society and represented the triumph of the utilitarian cult of
energy over the genteel tradition. Referring to the dominance of
the West, Rodó declared, "With it, utilitarianism, empty of any
idealism, a vague cosmopolitanism, and the levelling process of
democracy will reach its final victory" (p. 98). A later commentator, although he admired to a certain extent the dynamism which
allegedly is the legacy of the western spirit in American civilization, also noted that it could be harsh and unscrupulous.[133]

In the minds of others, the advancing western frontier opened
new horizons for North America, broke the spell of Europe, and
created a new democratic spirit.[134] To an Ecuadorian poet the set-
tlement of the West provided a splendid opportunity for American
literature and poetry to send down deeper roots in the native soil.
The result, he claimed, was "a poetry redolent of democracy, native, alive with genuine folk vigor."[135]

### SUMMARY

Reviewing the images presented in this chapter and attempting to
make some meaningful generalizations, one is inevitably impressed
by the fact that few of them are basically different from those current in the nineteenth century. The picture of the United States as
a dangerous imperialist power has been widened in scope and intensity, and has engaged proportionately more attention than in
the preceding century. Fear of political absorption has largely
given way to apprehension of economic and cultural penetration.
The clearly expansionist activities of the United States in the first
years of the twentieth century and the equally obvious economic
domination of so many southern republics in more recent years

133. Mañach, in Joseph, p. 344. Ugarte stressed the violence and brutality
of the West (p. 12).
134. Sánchez, *Un sudamericano*, pp. 138–39; Vasconcelos, *Hispanoamérica*,
p. 92; and Montenegro, pp. 107–8.
135. Carrera Andrade, *Rostros*, p. 47.

have given factual substance to the anti-imperialist criticism. The critical attitude has also been stimulated by the confusion stemming from racist theories and visions of an inevitable Anglo-Saxon struggle with the Latin race, as well as by the proud search for distinctive national identity.

It is noteworthy, however, that so many of our witnesses clearly separated their condemnation of imperialism from their appraisal of American institutions and character. Their images of American internal political, economic, and social processes were not qualitatively different in any important respect from those of their nineteenth-century forefathers. Our democracy, our ideal of social equality, and the working of our economic system generally commanded respect and even admiration, as from Sarmiento, while the problem of the black man's place in American society continued to appear as a festering sore.

# 10

# The Modern Image: Culture in a Materialistic Democracy

One of the favorite sports of Spanish American intellectuals in this century has been to engage in the tournament where North American "culture" or "spiritual" life marked out the field of battle. It has usually been an interesting but puzzling display of prowess—puzzling because the rules of the game have seldom been defined with any clarity. "Culture" and "spirituality," like the objectives of the medieval tourney, are expansive terms, and, as we read the records of these latter-day jousts, we are never entirely certain what the words mean. We will examine those records in an admittedly arbitrary attempt to sort out the meanings.

Very frequently, among the older critics of this period, the discussion took the form of a generalized and abstract opposition of spirituality to materialism. This confrontation—the Ariel-Caliban antithesis of Rodó—became such a commonplace in the earlier years of the century that it is not always possible to discover the specific content of the two emotionally charged antonyms. It should incidentally be noted that *espiritualidad* in Spanish does not refer exclusively or even primarily to religion, as its translation frequently does in English; our discussion of Spanish American attitudes toward religion in the United States will make it fairly clear that this was not one of the crucial ingredients of the spirituality-materialism debate.

In a general way, as we shall see, spirituality was equated with culture as revealed in refined manners and good taste, as well as in artistic accomplishment and appreciation. The age and maturity of a culture—the frame of reference was usually Europe—were sometimes regarded as a guarantee of *espiritualidad*.

But more often than not spirituality, the quality which North American civilization notably lacked, was simply used as a broad catch-all term to cover sundry virtues allegedly not part of the United States way of life. In this vague sense, spirituality included idealism, harmony, lofty moral vision, etc. Let us examine four representative quotations: "one cannot understand a civilization which is not based on foundations of idealism. . . . The greatest virtues of the heart, the human sentiments most worthy of man's respect meet in this country only the indifferent stare of a society which summarizes its values in frivolous ambitions for luxury and wealth"; "But this civilization has not the majesty of a harmonious structure. It is the violent work of a people of various origin"; "There are those in the world who accomplish things, but without moral grandeur; that is how the United States has dominated and still dominates"; "That country, by its customs, its conception of life, its incapacity for the fine arts, and its lack of ideals is the opposite pole of South America."[1]

There is no question about the pervasive influence of Rodó's *Ariel* in such statements and among young people all over Spanish America in the first two decades of this century; even in contemporary writers one runs across unconscious paraphrases of Rodó's indictment of the northern Caliban, whose utilitarian ways were contrasted with the more delicate sentiments of an Ariel with whom Rodó hoped Latin America could identify itself. Luis Alberto Sánchez recalled that his student image of the United States was derived from Rodó, "whose book *Ariel* we knew by heart." Arturo Torres-Ríoseco said that *Ariel* was "the gospel of the Spanish-speaking New World, much as Emerson's *Self Reliance* was the gospel of the Anglo-Saxon to the North."[2]

Although a careful reading of *Ariel* reveals that the author is much more specific than most of his lesser copyists, Rodó is enough of a dealer in abstract generalizations to set the tone for his followers. Here are some typical examples: "that people has been unable to substitute the inspiring idealism of the past with a high and disinterested conception of the future"; "a deep lack of order in all that pertains to the power of the ideal faculties"; "the effective spark is lacking which would kindle the life-giving and restless flame over the abundant wood" (pp. 87–89).

1. Cestero, *Estados Unidos*, p. xii (future references to this book are in the text); García Calderón, *Latin America*, p. 308; Antonio Caso, quoted in Zea, *América como conciencia*, p. 142; Blanco-Fombona, *La evolución política y social de Hispanoamérica*, p. 133.
2. Torres-Ríoseco, *The Epic of Latin American Literature*, p. 116.

In spite of his wordiness and often nebulous abstractions, Rodó presented his case in an orderly, well-reasoned, and equable fashion. But his readers often snatched from *Ariel* only the naked Ariel-Caliban contrast and applied it in a simplified way to relations between the Americas. What was frequently forgotten by that generation in its eagerness to find its own personality in the Ariel symbol was that Rodó, in addition to painting a picture of an imperfect civilization, also paid handsome tribute to the virtues of the United States and prophesied that eventually the work of Caliban could serve the cause of Ariel. He did not hesitate to hail the United States as the first nation to develop real liberty, as the country which dignified the greatness and power of work, as the diligent propagator of popular education, and as a healthy society full of self-confidence and optimism. Emerson was one of his tutelary gods.

In its crudest and most generalized form, the concept of the United States as a purely materialistic civilization opposed to idealism and the finer things of the spirit did not last well among thoughtful Spanish Americans as the century wore on. Even in the early decades and among the stalwart opponents of *yanqui* imperialism, there were prominent writers who doubted the validity of the black-or-white antithesis of Caliban and Ariel. Four years after the publication of *Ariel*, young Pedro Henríquez Ureña (Dominican Republic) wrote, "But above its practical tendencies, that nation holds aloft a high ideal, although it is different from our intellectualized ideal: that of human perfection, which has as its aim moral good and which should be translated in social terms as the dignification of collective life."[3]

Writing ten years after the publication of *Ariel*, Carlos Reyles, an esteemed Uruguayan novelist, made a frontal attack on some aspects of Rodó's idealism. Influenced by Nietzsche and William James, he proclaimed his preference for men and nations who are frankly egoistic and utilitarian. Paradoxically, Reyles said, they turn out to be generous and idealistic, and he cited the United States as an example of his thesis. "The utilitarianism of Caliban is more healthful in difficult situations than the rationalism of Ariel."[4]

Rubén Darío's attitude toward American materialism is an interesting example of evolution from a simplified, conventional con-

3. Quoted in Alfred A. Roggiano, *Pedro Henríquez Ureña y los Estados Unidos*, p. lxxxix.
4. Reyles, *La muerte del cisne*, pp. 181–84, 240–41.

cept to a more involved view. In 1893, Darío, then a young man of twenty-six, visited New York for the first time and saw it starkly as "the gory, the cyclopean, the monstruous capital of the banknote," where Caliban reigned as he did in the whole "empire of matter." "Here Caliban soaks up whiskey as he soaked up wine in Shakespeare's play."[5] Five years later he published an article entitled "The Triumph of Caliban" in which, using the vocabulary of the time, he referred to Americans as "buffaloes with silver teeth"; "red-faced, heavy and gross . . . like animals in their hunt for the dollar."[6] It might be noted in passing that Darío seized on the Caliban image before Rodó.

Darío's visit to the United States exhibit at the World Fair in Paris in 1900 seems to have generated second thoughts about the northern barbarians. He was surprised at the "plethoric vitality" of the painting and sculpture he saw there and concluded, "No, these strong men from the North do not lack the artistic gift. They too can think and dream. . . . Among these millions of Calibans the most marvellous Ariels come forth." He compared the absence or neglect of artists and writers in Spanish America with their more favored status in the United States.[7]

We have seen that his poem "A Roosevelt" (1904) was a bugle-call for the anti-imperialists, but two years later in "Salutación al águila" he urged his brothers to learn "constancy, vigor, and character" from the *yanquis*. During his last visit to New York, shortly before his death, it was not the Caliban image that he summoned up, but the tenderness of the great metropolis, with its happy laughing boys and bright girls.[8]

The American participation in World War I appears to have occasioned a cluster of contradictions or modifications of Rodó's thesis that stressed the civic, philanthropic, and religious idealism of the United States. Gonzalo Zaldumbide, an Ecuadorian and one of the most respected critics of his generation, wrote in his well-known essay on Rodó (1919), "Are not the crude *yanquis* the real idealists? Is not our Latin idealism a kind of sensuality, while theirs is more spiritual in essence?" While Americans may not be

5. Darío, *Los raros*, in *Obras completas*, 2:259.

6. Darío, "El triunfo de Calibán," in *Escritos inéditos de Rubén Darío*, pp. 160–61.

7. Darío, *Peregrinaciones*, in *Obras completas*, 6:57–58. For further praise of American letters, art, and science, see Darío, *La caravana pasa*, p. 208.

8. Darío, "Salutación al águila," in Englekirk et al., *Anthology of Spanish American Literature*, pp. 428–29; Darío, *Poesía: Libros poéticos completos*, pp. 474–76.

adept in the arts, they have a tremendous respect for them, Zaldumbide believed, and he reckoned our sense of civic and social responsibility, religious zeal, and respect for human rights as "day-to-day idealism."[9]

A Uruguayan, Emilio Frugoni, writing in 1918, found in the land of practicality an amazing capacity for flights of fantasy directed toward concrete achievements: "the lyricism of practical action, the idealism of useful accomplishment, not the contemplative dreaming which achieves nothing."[10]

The Peruvian Víctor Andrés Belaúnde wrote in 1920, "the Anglo-Saxon peoples, so little known in South America, have a greater religious and poetic sense of life than we do, in spite of the common idea which fatuously assigns all lyrical and romantic qualities to us." And two years later a famous Uruguayan poet, Juan Zorrilla de San Martín, also an admirer of Wilson, declared, "It is not true that the economic and industrial progress [of the United States] is in inverse proportion to spiritual, moral, and esthetic progress. What happens is precisely the contrary, if we look at it carefully." He refuted Rodó by defining idealism as the Christian spirit and finding that spirit strong in the United States, as exemplified in Woodrow Wilson. The general reputation of the writers cited placed them on the conservative, establishment side. What did more rebellious spirits say? The fact that Manuel Ugarte was a consistent warrior against *yanqui* imperialism did not prevent him from admitting in 1926, "The United States, 'absorbed in money and figures' as the vulgar saying goes, have made world-famous the names of Poe, Whitman, Whistler, William James, Edison, and a hundred others, who have made an original contribution to beauty, thought, and the progress of the world. Unfortunately, we cannot say as much."[11]

Vasconcelos, who was also fearful of the imperialistic aims of the United States, said in 1926, "There has been a good deal of talk about a busy Martha who is prospering in the North, and about a carefree Mary who dreams in the South; but, unfortunately, the symbols are not accurate, because the United States is not only a Martha given to useful activity, but a dreaming and creative Mary." In 1937, this Mexican critic continued his thought: "Many among

9. Zaldumbide, *José Enrique Rodó*, pp. 73–74.
10. Frugoni, "En la otra América," p. 343.
11. Belaúnde, "Crónicas de América," 5:82; Zorrilla de San Martín, *Las Américas*, pp. 32–39; Ugarte, *The Destiny of a Continent*, p. 169.

us hate to confess that the United States is an idealistic people, the most idealistic of our times."[12]

Meanwhile, however, other crusaders against imperialism occasionally attached the materialism vs. spirituality cliché to their economic and political campaigns. In 1925, for example, Alfredo Palacios, using Waldo Frank and other *yanquis* as sources, denounced the utilitarian materialism of Americans, which choked out the more human and cultural impulses. The mission of Spanish Americans, on the other hand, was to be "interpreters of the spirit."[13]

Especially in the 1930s and 1940s, this stereotype lost ground and was often contradicted by observers (perhaps influenced by the Good Neighbor Policy and later by the common battle against Nazism) who came into direct contact with North American life. Among a good many of them the older cliché has been replaced, as we shall see, by a modified and more complex view of spiritual life in the United States.

Luis Alberto Sánchez, who criticized admirers of Wilson—the so-called professors of idealism—like Zorrilla de San Martín and Belaúnde, made his own views reasonably clear in 1942. After seeing and enjoying an exhibit of great masters in New York, he said, "We must agree that, thanks to a tenacious and intense effort, Caliban has become his opposite, Ariel, or—even better—that he is bringing about their coexistence."[14] Manuel Seoane, another anti-imperialistic *aprista* like Sánchez, also wrote in 1942, "Many thought they saw a spiritual antithesis between the United States, representing the vile part of Caliban, and Indo-America, playing the subtle role of Ariel. Now we see that this is an exaggeration. There are many Ariels in the lands of the North and among us some Calibans who would shock Shakespeare himself."[15]

Even in the post-war period, when the aura of general good will faded considerably, commentators continued to question the earlier simplified contrast. The Chilean diplomat Carlos Dávila in 1949 described American culture as a blending of materialism and spiritualism. "The whole basic American principle of checks and balances written into the Constitution was transferred to the American way of life, and, especially, there exists a continual check and

12. Vasconcelos, *¿Qué es la revolución?*, p. 213.
13. Palacios, *Nuestra América y el imperialismo yanqui*, pp. 114, 119.
14. Sánchez, *Balance y liquidación del 900*, chap. 6, and *Un sudamericano en Norteamérica*, p. 264; see also p. 29.
15. Seoane, *El gran vecino*, p. 4; Emilio Uzcátegui expressed similar views (*Los Estados Unidos*, p. 12).

balance between materialism and spirituality; hence the phrase 'practical idealism,' which is probably the best definition of Americanism yet advanced."[16]

The Mexican *pensador* Leopoldo Zea likewise referred to "practical idealists" in a rather intricate statement. According to him, the spiritual vs. materialistic interpretation of the two Americas "errs by assigning to each part of America one quality and denying it to the other. . . . It does not occur [to holders of this view] to conceive that both possess similar capacities, but that the projects peculiar to each people have caused the differences which stand out. . . . In Saxon America men have not been lacking, nor are they lacking now, who are capable of giving spiritual orientation. Nor does Hispanic America lack men who are capable of achieving a strongly material world. What happens is that each one of these Americas has put the accent on that aspect which seems to characterize it because to do so has been suitable for its projects. One can say that in one America, the Saxon part, its men are characterized as 'practical idealists'; and in Hispanic America as 'idealistic practical men' [*prácticos idealistas*], the first group because they pay more attention to the reality where ideas are to be realized, and the second because they insist on battling against reality in order to impose their ideals."[17]

The Argentine novelist Eduardo Mallea dealt with the same general idea with comparable complexity. He referred to the people of the United States as "that people of pragmatists and idealists, of pragmatic idealists or idealistic pragmatists, since their peculiar essence is a certain aim which, rather than utilitarian, is stabilization in their own self-interest, and which consists of not giving Caesar only that which belongs to Caesar, but also a little of what belongs to God, and to God not only what belongs to God, but also a little of what belongs to Caesar."[18]

The old stereotype was still alive in the popular tradition and occasionally turned up in post–World War II literature. Zum Felde, for example, in 1954 noted the enormous changes in the position of the United States since Rodó's time, but concluded that the scales of relative values with reference to culture, as set forth in *Ariel*, have not changed essentially: "The Titan of the North is still there with his virtues and his defects both magnified by the passing of time" (p. 298).

16. Dávila, *We of the Americas*, pp. 124–25.
17. Zea, *América como conciencia*, p. 145.
18. Mallea, *Historia de una pasión argentina*, p. 135.

Generally speaking, however, the more extreme forms of the spirituality vs. materialism argument were attenuated or dissolved in sophisticated verbal diffuseness.

MEDIOCRITY AND THE EGGHEAD

When members of the older generation discussed cultural life in general in the United States, they were very apt to trot out the old European cliché that democracy in the northern Republic was bound to breed mediocrity. This patrician plaint came naturally to the pen of men born in societies where a simulation of the European aristocratic tradition separated the small well-to-do class—usually land-owning—from the ignorant masses. Rodó made the charge of cultural mediocrity a spearhead in his criticism of the northern Caliban. García Calderón's sentiments were representative of those of the *arielistas*: "All these things contribute to the triumph of mediocrity: the multitude of primary schools, the vices of utilitarianism, the cult of the average citizen . . . and the tyranny of opinion noted by Tocqueville . . . this vulgarity which is devoid of traditions and has no leading aristocracy."[19]

A particular facet of the mediocrity theme was the commonly expressed belief that North Americans are suspicious of the superior man and have only scorn for intellectuals. As a student at Harvard, Jorge Mañach recalled, he felt apologetic that he had bookish and artistic interests and concluded, "For the average American . . . the intellectual, the 'egg-head,' is suspect, little better than an unproductive idler—in any case unworthy to become President of the nation." A Salvadoran publicist asserted, "The man in the street has no idea what an 'intellectual' is or ought be, but the word makes him suspicious . . . hence the treatment the intellectual receives. He is contemptuously called an egg-head and is the butt of sneering jests."[20]

Alone among our witnesses, Vasconcelos expressed a dissident view. Perhaps impressed by Roosevelt's "Brain Trust," he wrote in 1937, "The average North American despises his politicians and reveres his intellectuals and his university men. Among these people the sage's opinion carries weight."[21]

19. García Calderón, p. 309; see Blanco-Fombona, *La lámpara de Aladino*, p. 135, and Cosío Villegas, in Joseph, *As Others See Us*, p. 299, for other examples of the cliché.

20. Mañach, in Joseph, p. 335; Luis Alberto Cabrales, quoted in Wolfe, "Attitudes," p. 523; see also Quintanilla, *A Latin American Speaks*, p. 41.

21. *¿Qué es la revolución?*, p. 76; see also pp. 167–68.

The accusation of mediocrity and disdain for the intellectual was not only an integral part of the *yanqui*-materialism concept, but also probably represented a sense of personal indignation on the part of the Spanish American intellectual, who traditionally has been highly respected even by the common man.

## THE BARBARIANS IMPROVE THEIR MANNERS

We will now examine several more specific facets of the criticism of North American culture. In one relatively simple and common sense "culture" meant for the Spanish American critic refined manners, and to the earlier commentators of this century, continuing the common nineteenth-century complaint, North Americans were disagreeably lacking in this element of culture. The conventional stereotype in the common man's mind undoubtedly included the picture of the cold, unmannerly gringo, who did not know how to behave himself like *gente decente*. This simplified view, derived in part from the reality of some Americans abroad and in part from differences in patterns of social customs, may also be found in the critics' literature.

Cestero explained that our "absence of nicety of the spirit, grace, and good manners" was due to faulty home training (p. xxii). Vargas Vila considered North American civilization, as represented in our manners, barbarous. Roughness, violence, brutality were and continued to be attributed to the American character.[22]

Several more recent writers have taken pains to contradict this commonly held view. A Cuban journalist said, "Even in what I would call the external signs of culture, that is in the question of manners, North Americans have no reason to envy other peoples. . . . Their delicacy of manners, their exquisite personal culture, far from being a surface veneer, is the outward manifestation of an inner feeling toward mankind."[23] Even Vasconcelos, in one of his later phases, was impressed by the growing quality of North American social graces. In 1937, he said, "The fruit of so much schooling and higher education becomes manifest in the notable improvement of manners, in the calmness of tone, and in the refinement which is beginning to conquer the haste and crudity of former times." Impressed by a conversation with a South Carolina taxi-driver, Vasconcelos added, "In very few years, they have come to

22. Vargas Vila, p. 71.
23. Bravo, *El destino*, p. 83.

have a kind of spontaneously courteous manner, which is not merely on the surface, as is the case with the European."[24]

## THE FINE ARTS AND THE *Yanquis*

In a wider sense, culture has been identified by our critics with proficiency and eminence in the fine arts. On these grounds, the earlier witnesses were often explicit, and more recent observers have had their doubts about the aptness of the North American for artistic creation and appreciation. Those who wrote around the turn of the century, captained by Rodó, frequently denied that the denizens of the northern republic had any artistic sense at all. Paul Groussac (Argentina), writing in 1897, alleged that the sons of Tubalcain—the North Americans—lack the esthetic taste of the Latin Americans.[25] Rodó was emphatic on this score. "True art," he said, "has only been able to exist in that environment [the United States] as individual rebellion. . . . Bourget in *Outremer* speaks of the heavy, solemn accent with which the word 'art' hums on the lips of those North Americans whom fortune has favored. . . . But they have never conceived of that divine activity to which they refer so emphatically except as a new way of satisfying their intruding restlessness and as a trophy of their vanity. They are ignorant of the disinterested, selective quality of art. They are ignorant in spite of the free-handed way in which individual fortunes are used to stimulate the formation of a delicate sense of beauty; in spite of the splendor of the museums and expositions of which their cities boast; in spite of the mountains of marble and bronze which they have sculptured for the statues in their public parks" (pp. 90–91).

In the same tradition was the opinion of a Dominican writing in 1918. Cestero claimed that the North American was not stimulated to be a poet, an artist, or a musician because none of those callings can be converted into a trust, which is the supreme aspiration of all *yanquis* (p. xxi). Blanco-Fombona, with his characteristic impetuosity, declared that "the country of the pig" hates and likes to humiliate artists. "It cannot produce them, feel sympathy for them, or understand them."[26]

The *yanqui* millionaire's habit of buying old-world art, to which Rodó referred, has caused considerable comment, some derisive

24. *¿Qué es la revolución?*, pp. 120, 128; see also Pinochet, *Gulf*, p. 265.
25. Quoted in Zum Felde, *Índice crítico*, p. 337.
26. *La lámpara de Aladino*, p. 397.

and some approving. Blanco-Fombona lampooned the ignorance and gullibility of these patrons of the arts. Zorrilla de San Martín thought that their zeal was an admirable trait.[27]

A few dissident voices were heard to praise the esthetic sense and abilities of Americans. The Venezuelan journalist Ricardo Becerra, when he visited the Columbian Exposition in 1893, observed that in the midst of their scramble for material wealth, North Americans held their artists and poets in high esteem and rewarded them handsomely. He contrasted them with his countrymen, who regarded artistic inspiration as "a passport to the hospital or the madhouse." And Darío lauded the artistic skill of Sargent, Whistler, Winslow Homer, and John La Farge, after seeing their work in Paris.[28]

Emilio Frugoni, writing in 1918, applied the Caliban epithet to the United States, but prophesied that the fresh, lively interest of Americans in nature, as shown in their painting, and their cult of bodily fitness and beauty, would eventually bring to world art "an invigorating and renovating breeze." He praised the flights of imagination which he already perceived in American sculpture and painting.[29]

Later, Spanish American opinion of the arts in the United States became less categorically scornful and more qualified. One strand of judgment followed the syllogism that since the United States was a young nation, its art therefore was just beginning and was still dependent on Europe. A Colombian observer in 1959, while denying the allegation that North America had no artistic culture, said that this young country was just making its debut in the world's cultural circles, and that one could not expect too much from its endeavors. Writing during World War II, Subercaseaux expressed gratitude that American museums had become the safe depositories of Western culture and stated, "As time goes on and with a change in its present direction, the United States will also follow the value-scale of our West." At about the same time, Luis Alberto Sánchez saw the United States, after achieving material prosperity and comfort, "looking at the European world and trying to change its awe into creative activity, to equal or surpass its masters. . . . It has ardently thrown itself into the task of making a soul for itself, of building a culture."[30]

27. Ibid., p. 454; Zorrilla de San Martín, p. 42.
28. Becerra, "Crónicas yankees," 2:446; Darío, *Peregrinaciones*, p. 58.
29. Frugoni, "En la otra América," p. 342.
30. Arango, *Estados Unidos*, pp. 104–5; see also Merrill, *Gringo*, p. 41;

In more recent years the popularization of music and the plastic arts in the United States and the increase in opportunities for appreciating the arts astonished many observers. After citing the immense popularity of symphony concerts, Quintanilla concluded, "The plain truth is that the people of the United States are essentially artistic. It is time that Latin Americans become aware of it."[31] Some visitors even adopted the vulgar North American habit of parading statistics to show the extent of art appreciation—the number of art galleries and their attendance, the sale of symphonic records, the number of orchestras, etc.[32]

On the other hand, the value of American creative effort in the fine arts was a moot question among Spanish Americans. With regard to music, Blanco-Fombona in 1902 asked rhetorically what North Americans had produced and replied that their best composer was Sousa, a mediocre Hebrew, born in Holland of Portuguese ancestry. Forty years later, an Ecuadorian visitor disagreed with the common notion that North American music is only jazz: "In its refined forms, music has been enriched by valuable American contributions." He cited Edward MacDowell and a few others as evidence. In 1959, Arango admitted that no great American classical composers have appeared, but noted that Gershwin and Roy Harris were respectable creators who drew on folk tradition.[33] To some the Negro contribution to music—jazz, blues, etc.—was original, admirable, and "capable of bringing about revolutionary changes in universal music."[34] Others, like Vasconcelos, associated jazz and its relatives with lack of cultural refinement.[35]

In the field of architecture, as one might predict, remarks on the skyscraper were the platitude. García Calderón referred to "the architectural insolence of the skyscraper"; to Mañach it represented the "stylization of energy." A Mexican critic said that it "is the outstanding contribution of man to architecture of our times.

---

Subercaseaux, *Retorno*, pp. 178–80 (see also p. 93); Sánchez, *Un sudamericano*, pp. 265–66.

31. Quintanilla, p. 43.

32. See, for example, Bravo, pp. 85–86; Arango, pp. 107–8; Roberto Mujica Laínez, "An Argentine's USA," p. 15. In a study of the reactions of a group of Mexican grantees, we find that about a third of them were primarily impressed during their sojourn in the United States by the generally high level of culture and interest in cultural activities; this was an unexpected reaction for most of them (International Research Associates, *Study*).

33. Blanco-Fombona, *La americanización del mundo*, p. 16; Uzcátegui, p. 19; Arango, pp. 113–14.

34. Quintanilla, p. 42; other admirers of Negro music were Sánchez (*Un sudamericano*, chap. 4), and Otero (*Estados Unidos*, p. 33).

35. Vasconcelos, *Bolivarismo y Monroismo*, p. 153.

... The American architect has found beauty in extreme simplicity
of line and smooth geometric surface." A Bolivian art critic declared that the skyscraper speaks in "a new plastic idiom" and
represents "the constant equilibrium of tortured formulas of re-
sistance, of a geometry anguished by the pain of astronomical
numbers."[36]

Except to a few painters and professional art critics, North
American painting seems to have been little known. The Colombian
Jesús Arango noted that "painters also find a fertile field to express
even the most daring manifestations of their inspirations." Otero,
the Bolivian critic, claimed that the plastic arts in the United
States never have become rooted in the native soil and that contemporary painting, as in Europe, shows a tremendous variety of
schools and tendencies. He named a few painters whose work appealed to him. Pedro Henríquez Ureña, well-known humanistic
scholar, wrote with considerable enthusiasm of American paintings as early as 1915. Reviewing the work of Sargent, Homer, Mary
Cassatt and others, he noted the passion for color and the timidity
in subject matter, concluding, "North American painting is full
of vitality." An Argentine physician and amateur painter, writing
in 1956, found North American painting to be decadent, mediocre,
and lagging behind European and Latin American tendencies.[37]

### SPANISH AMERICA DISCOVERS OUR LITERATURE

For several reasons Spanish American attitudes toward the literature of the United States deserve special treatment in viewing the
general cultural picture. At the turn of the twentieth century,
esteem for our literature was at a low ebb. According to Rodó,
there had been a progressive decline in intellectual brilliance and
originality since the early days of the North American republic and
certainly since the heyday of the New England transcendentalists:
"Who have since taken up the heritage of Channing, Emerson, or
Poe?" he asked. "For some time the wings of their books have not
reached heights where it would be universally possible to take note

36. García Calderón, p. 307; Mañach, in Joseph, p. 336; Quintanilla, pp.
42–43; Otero, p. 165; Ortiz Vargas, *Manhattan*, passim. Curiously, I have run
across almost no mention of other architectural creations, although profes-
sionals must have been aware of them.

37. Arango, p. 106; Otero, passim; Henriquez Ureña, in Roggiano, pp. xvii,
54–55; Ayres, *Estados Unidos*, pp. 54–56. Uzcátegui gave general praise to
American artists and mentioned Sargent, Pennell, and Redfield as outstanding (p. 19).

of them." The leveling process of democracy had brought American taste in letters down to the grey mediocrity of journalism (pp. 92–93).

Three years later Blanco-Fombona was even more blunt in his rejection of the worth of North American literature: "When has literature been the best vehicle of North American thought? If one excepts the sentimental pleading of Mrs. Beecher Stowe, which is destitute of any great literary merit, and some poems of Whittier, what matter of general human interest has been treated by literature in the United States?" Longfellow was dismissed as "a delightful English bard," and Poe could have been born anywhere. Making a possible exception of Whitman, he concluded, "I do not believe that there has existed up to the present an American literature."[38]

With the triumph of new art-for-art's-sake poetic trends toward the end of the nineteenth century (known in Spanish America as *modernismo*), Longfellow's considerable popularity, evident earlier in the century, waned rapidly.[39] A Colombian poet, for example, said of his work, "Virtue without wings, tenderness, sadness, but all in miniature. Where is life?"[40] Poe, on the other hand, became a gifted and heroic precursor for the *modernistas*, and to this day he is one of the best-known and most-published North American authors. There is no mystery about his vogue; his melancholy music and his emphasis on the sensuous pleasure of sound have found a congenial climate in Spanish America.

But, echoing Baudelaire, the early worshippers of Poe refused to consider him as representative of the United States. Rubén Darío, in an article on Poe published in 1893, which in effect inaugurated the great vogue of the northern bard in Spanish America, saw the United States as a drunken Caliban who had grown fat and multiplied: "As God willed it, there occasionally comes forth from among these powerful masters a superior being who spreads his wings toward the eternal Miranda of the ideal. Then Caliban moves against them and he is exiled or killed."[41] This conventional estimate of Poe as a lone, misunderstood figure, neglected and abused by the hostile, mercantile environment of his native land, was repeated by Rodó and picked up by countless Spanish American critics of lesser calibre.

38. *La americanización del mundo*, pp. 15–16.
39. Englekirk, "Notes on Longfellow in Spanish America," p. 308. From 1955 to 1962 only one edition of Longfellow's works was published in Spanish, compared to fourteen during the period 1890–1943.
40. Ortiz Vargas, p. 69.
41. *Los raros*, p. 259.

Whitman attracted less attention at the beginning of this century, but in later decades his reputation spread both as an exponent of metrical freedom and as a voice of social democracy. In contrast to Poe, he was recognized as an authentic representative of his country. A prominent Cuban critic, for this reason, rated him a greater poet: "Whitman, much less of an artist than Poe, was nevertheless newer, more original, more genuinely North American, a more exact, direct, and real reflection of the civilization and peculiar mode of being of his country." Vasconcelos wove him even more closely into America's life: "If there had not been a Whitman, an epic singer of the forests, the civilizing and adventuring impulse would not have had the encouragement to consolidate its conquests from Louisiana to California."[42] Whitman has been much translated and his poetry has influenced the work of a number of modern Spanish American poets. An Ecuadorian poet of continental fame, after documenting that influence, said of Whitman, "The shadow of the youthful, vigorous old man continues to grow endlessly, even today. . . . His hymns constitute an epic of democracy."[43] But Whitman was occasionally linked with Poe, both being considered choice spirits rejected by their homeland as eccentric and immoral.[44]

Although, as we have seen, Emerson was known at least by reputation among a tiny elite in Spanish America during the nineteenth century, his stature grew during the earlier decades of this century. After the first appearance of his essays in Spanish in 1900, numerous editions issued both in Spain and Spanish America became available to the reader in the Spanish-speaking republics.[45] Rodó mentioned him with Poe as examples of "fauna chased from their real milieu by the rigors of a geological catastrophe" (p. 90). Rodó has been called a "Latin Emerson," and there is little doubt that his influence on such early twentieth century *pensadores* as Enrique José Varona (Cuba), José Ingenieros (Argentina), García Calderón, and others was considerable. Varona, unreservedly praising Emerson's qualities, identified them with the spirit of his society. Ingenieros greatly admired the self-reliance, non-conformity, and social morality of the Concord sage, and in 1917 published a

42. Enrique Pineyro, quoted in Englekirk, *Poe in Hispanic Literature*, p. 99; Vasconcelos, *¿Qué es la revolución?*, p. 257.

43. Carrera Andrade, *Rostros*, pp. 99–100. Whitman still is not a widely published poet in Spanish, at least in comparison with Poe.

44. For example, Subercaseaux, p. 174.

45. See Englekirk, *Bibliografía de obras norteamericanas en traducción española*, pp. 34–35.

series of lectures on Emerson.[46] Gabriela Mistral said, "I count your Emerson among those who formed my character; he was invigorating like a breeze from pine groves, a torch in the black mines of the human soul." A less inspired Chilean woman expressed an almost religious devotion to Emerson: "My soul was sick from nostalgia, doubt, restlessness, and you have brought me peace. . . . Those whom I loved left me, and you—sweet friend of the lonely—have taught me to find them in solitude." According to John Englekirk, the appreciation of Emerson reached a high point about 1917.[47]

It is sometimes asserted that, aside from Poe, Longfellow, Whitman, and Emerson, Spanish Americans during the first thirty years of this century knew almost nothing about North American literature.[48] While the intellectuals of those years tended to scorn *yanqui* literature in general, there is evidence that the reading public was not unacquainted with North American authors. A survey of Spanish translations published from 1890 to 1929 shows that, in addition to abundant translations of the four authors cited, works of the following writers were on the market: Louisa May Alcott, Edward Bellamy, Mark Twain, James Fenimore Cooper, J. O. Curwood, Bret Harte, Nathaniel Hawthorne, Lafcadio Hearn, Washington Irving, O. Henry, Jack London, Upton Sinclair, Harriet Beecher Stowe, Lew Wallace, Booker T. Washington, John Dewey, and William James. Of these, if we judge by the number of editions, the most popular were Mark Twain, Irving, Alcott, Cooper, Harte, Hawthorne, and Dewey. For the sake of completeness, we should add that Ralph Waldo Trine and Orison Swett Marden, both precursors of Dale Carnegie and Norman Vincent Peale and hardly literary figures, were tremendously popular.[49]

It would be interesting, but probably not very profitable, to speculate about the kind of image of the United States which these books helped to build in the minds of their Spanish American readers. Aside from the idea that the North Americans had a literature of some quality, it is not likely that the works of Poe, Irving, Lafcadio Hearn, or Lew Wallace gave even the vaguest impression of the writer's homeland. Hearn was valued specifically

46. Varona, "Emerson," in *Obras*, 2:287–313; Crawford, *A Century of Latin American Thought*, pp. 135–36, and Englekirk, "Notes on Emerson in Latin America," p. 231.

47. Gabriela Mistral, "Tiene la palabra Gabriela Mistral," p. 322; Teresa Prats, quoted in Englekirk, "Notes on Emerson," p. 231; ibid., p. 230.

48. See Sánchez, *Un sudamericano*, p. 54.

49. This analysis is based on data in Englekirk, *Bibliografía*.

for his exotic Japanese sketches. Mark Twain, who seems to have been very popular, may have produced some concept of the rough-and-ready American frontier and the peculiar brand of American humor. While a few critics, such as the Chilean Ernesto Monte-negro, recognized the bitterness and social criticism which charac-terized Mark Twain's later writing, he remained for most the great North American humorist. Those who read Emerson faithfully doubtless formed an image of an idealistic, forward-looking Amer-ica, and surely some of Whitman's poems must have projected a picture of a confident, expansive nation. Cooper, who along with Irving was regarded mainly as a writer for juveniles, was prob-ably thought of as a novelist of adventure whose plots happened to develop in North America. The stories of Mrs. Alcott and O. Henry, as well as Longfellow's poetry, perhaps gave some impression of the optimistic and sentimental nature of many North Americans. Mrs. Alcott's tales, although labeled at first as children's literature, subsequently impressed some critics as very North American—realistic, democratic, and honest.[50] The reading of Hawthorne's stories and novels may well have reinforced the image, fairly cur-rent, of a puritanical United States.

The books by Bellamy, Upton Sinclair, Mrs. Stowe, and Booker T. Washington, we may be quite sure, revealed to their readers some of the more serious social evils existing in the United States. The first two authors doubtless confirmed an image of an inhuman American capitalism, while the latter two laid bare the problem of the Negro. Jack London's first attraction lay in his exotic adventure tales, such as *White Fang*. In other novels his romantic socialism and defense of dark-skinned natives raised some admiration among critics ill disposed toward the United States. Curwood's brief popu-larity was due purely to the lure of adventure and sentimentality, and it is unlikely that it affected opinions of the United States. Orison Swett Marden and his long series of "inspirational" books undoubtedly contributed to an image of the American as an ener-getic "go-getter" seeking material success. In fact, Rodó specifically mentioned one of his books in this connection (p. 95).

Bret Harte's works enjoyed great and lasting success in Spanish America. First published in 1875, some of his stories seem to have appealed to that sentimental streak so common in the nineteenth century. Later writers and critics saw in his stories a skillful paral-lel in the North to their own efforts to create a national, native lit-

50. See Arnold Chapman, *The Spanish American Reception of United States Fiction, 1920–1940*, p. 167.

erature replete with earthy American language and rugged New World characters.[51]

Luis Alberto Sánchez marked 1929 as the beginning of the period when sophisticated Spanish Americans discovered the diverse values of modern and contemporary North American literature. According to his interpretation, the lecture tour of Waldo Frank through Latin America in that year was responsible for this enlightenment, because he spoke to his audiences about a United States "with a soul, as well as a body, possessed of a lively and alert modern sensibility."[52] Certain it is that Frank made a loving and lasting impression on Spanish American intellectuals, a fact that may puzzle his compatriots, who do not see him as a major writer. The reasons for his popularity in Spanish America, however, are not at all puzzling. Having written several interpretative books about Hispanic lands, he was one of the few North American intellectuals who took the trouble to interest themselves seriously in the intricacies of the Hispanic mind. His own embroidered and delicate manner of thought and expression was congenial to the Spanish American intellectual atmosphere. Furthermore, his condemnation of North American materialism, his revolutionary attitude toward social injustice, and his desire to unite the "liberal" elements of the two Americas struck a responsive chord among the many intellectuals of the South who were at least theoretically interested in social change.[53]

While Sánchez' insistence on the role of Waldo Frank as the exclusive distributor of knowledge about contemporary literature in the United States may be exaggerated, the influence of Frank's lectures and writings cannot be denied. Before his tour, a few curious souls had become conscious of the early blossoms of the twentieth-century renaissance. Pedro Henríquez Ureña in 1915 wrote for a Havana weekly an informative article on poetry in the United States, mentioning Joyce Kilmer, Vachel Lindsay, William Rose Benét, and Edna St. Vincent Millay. The editor's note accompany-

51. Ibid., pp. 14–24.

52. *Un sudamericano*, p. 54.

53. On Waldo Frank's reception by his Spanish American admirers, see *Waldo Frank in America Hispana*; A. Chapman, "Waldo Frank in the Hispanic World"; Gabriela Mistral, "Waldo Frank y nosotros"; and J. Reid, "As the Other Americans See Our Literature." A beautiful example of a South American writer's devotion to Frank is chapter 7 of Eduardo Mallea's *Historia de una pasión argentina*. Zum Felde says of Frank, "In a general way, the educational influence of Waldo Frank in a contemporary intellectual atmosphere of Argentina . . . can only be compared to that exerted by Ortega y Gasset a little before" (*Indice crítico*, pp. 464–65).

ing the article said, "We believe that it is most interesting since it will correct the common and erroneous belief that the present generation in the United States has left no place for dreams in the everlasting bustle of daily business."[54]

In 1927, Henríquez Ureña published a much fuller account of the new literature in the United States in the prestigious *Nosotros* of Buenos Aires. The short-lived *Revista de Avance* of Havana, spurred by Jorge Mañach, a Cuban who knew the United States intimately, included a number of substantial articles about American literature. During the twenties Ernesto Montenegro, a Chilean journalist, had made known the work of Sinclair Lewis, Theodore Dreiser, Willa Cather, and several poets in a series of articles for *La Nación* of Buenos Aires and *El Mercurio* of Chile.[55] But the whole new and turbulent world of twentieth-century American letters did not attract great attention in Spanish America until the decades following 1930. Full-length works by Sherwood Anderson, John Dos Passos, Joseph Hergesheimer, and Waldo Frank himself were first published in Spanish in 1929. Theodore Dreiser, Sinclair Lewis, and Thornton Wilder made their debuts in the Spanish-speaking world in 1930 and 1931. During the years 1934–40 works were published in Spanish for the first time by William Faulkner, Ernest Hemingway, Eugene O'Neill, Elmer Rice, John Steinbeck, George Santayana, Pearl Buck, and Louis Bromfield. Even Thoreau's *Walden*, which had been practically unknown to Spanish America, was translated in 1937.[56]

It was during those years also that Spanish Americans began to realize that Poe and Whitman were not the last of the North American poets and that verse of a highly original and interesting kind was being written in the businessman's paradise. Vachel Lindsay, Carl Sandburg, Archibald MacLeish, Ezra Pound, and others became known at least by reputation, and a few began the difficult task of translating contemporary North American poetry. In 1943 and 1944 four rather comprehensive anthologies of American verse appeared.

Moreover, in the 1930s Spanish Americans began to pay considerable and respectful critical attention to the literature of the United States. A survey of such representative intellectual journals as *Sur, Nosotros, Revista Cubana,* and *Repertorio Americano* revealed a total of seventy-five items concerning North American

54. Roggiano, pp. 128–34; Chapman, *Reception,* p. 9.
55. Chapman, *Reception,* pp. 9–10.
56. Data from Englekirk, *Bibliografía.*

literature published during those years. Some were articles of original criticism dealing with Poe, Waldo Frank, Mark Twain, Eugene O'Neill, and others. There were also critical studies and literary pieces translated from English. While this material betrays a spotty interest in North American letters, it represented a definite change from earlier years when literary criticism was almost exclusively centered on European or Spanish American authors.[57]

A good example of this quickened interest was the publication in Mexico City in 1935 of *Panorama de la literatura norteamericana* by the Cuban José Antonio Ramos. For the first time in the twentieth century Spanish Americans were introduced to a broad survey of our literary life from its beginnings to contemporary times. Obviously a devotee of Parrington, Ramos took pains to present literature in the United States in its social setting. In spite of its overtones of anti-imperialism, the book showed a sympathetic understanding of American life and considerable admiration for our literature. Later, as an interesting but not very successful tour de force, Luis Alberto Sánchez attempted to combine in one volume North American literary history with that of Latin America.[58]

After World War II, the publication of North American literary works in Spanish translation proceeded apace and by 1960 there was hardly a major author whose works were not available to the Spanish American reading public. The tables in Appendixes 4–6 give an account of the variety and relative popularity of North American authors in the Spanish world, at least as measured by the number of different editions and titles of those authors. Somewhat arbitrarily, novelists such as Rex Beach, Zane Grey, Edgar Rice Burroughs, and Erle Stanley Gardner were excluded from the count, in spite of their overwhelming popularity. Whether or not they have less literary merit than the two alltime favorites, Pearl Buck and Louis Bromfield, is a question for the critics to debate. It will be noted that the ten most published twentieth-century authors during the whole period 1890–1962 were, aside from Bromfield and Buck, Jack London, Sinclair Lewis, John Dewey, William Faulkner, John Steinbeck, Upton Sinclair, Waldo Frank, and Ernest Hemingway; of the ten, four (London, Lewis, Sinclair, and Frank) are generally critical of the faults of American society, and some of the works of both Steinbeck and Faulkner can be interpreted as critical.

Of the ten most popular nineteenth-century American authors

57. Reid, "Other Americans," p. 216.
58. Sánchez, *Nueva historia de la literatura americana.*

during the period only one, Harriet Beecher Stowe, presents a clearly unfavorable picture of the United States. Obviously Mark Twain, Louisa May Alcott, Irving, Cooper, and Lew Wallace are in demand largely for their entertainment value and many of their writings are considered as children's books. Poe's amazingly durable fame surely has little to do with the image of American society.

It is clear that this rapidly growing interest in and regard for the literature of the United States had two different and somewhat contradictory effects on the picture of the United States in the mind of Spanish American readers. On the one hand, there is every reason to believe that the cultural stature of North America grew with the recognition that literature of almost world-wide renown had been produced by the Colossus of the North. Even the sharpest critics of the United States hesitated to deny this circumstance. Daniel Ayres, for example, found American literature lacking in the niceties of style, but admitted that it had gained respect and admiration throughout the world (p. 148).

On the other hand, the novels of such critical realists as Sinclair Lewis, Jack London, and particularly Upton Sinclair tended to strengthen many of the unflattering stereotypes of North American life and culture. Vasconcelos cited *Babbitt* to prove that North American culture is mediocre and said, "It is from *yanqui* authors that we learn to pity the individual accustomed from his childhood to the exclusively pragmatic employment of his energy."[59] More recently the Uruguayan literary critic Zum Felde declared that Rodó's disparagement of life in the United States was confirmed by "the best essayists and novelists produced by that nation in this century. The names of Waldo Frank, of Sinclair Lewis, and of John dos Pasos [*sic*] among others bear witness to the disparagement. Their self-criticism is much more severe than the criticism of Rodó" (p. 297).

## MOTION PICTURES

Without any doubt, American literature—or at least certain books— became known to the Spanish American populace at large through the cinema rather than the printed word. Hemingway's *For Whom the Bell Tolls*, for example, was widely admired as a film, and it is probable that its availability stimulated the sale of the book in translation.

59. Vasconcelos, *De Robinson a Odiseo*, p. 14.

As a rule, the sources consulted in this study looked at American films with jaundiced eyes. In a loose sense, "Hollywood" became a synonym decades ago for all that was trivial, trashy, and even immoral in North American life. The most common charge against Hollywood films was that they falsified and caricatured Latin Americans. While one can guess that the actual percentage of Latin American characters in the total film production of the United States was very small indeed, those that appeared outraged the sensitive Spanish American. It is very probable that the perennial westerns, which were a favorite staple in the export market, were in great part responsible for this tempestuous reaction. Their standard plot usually included a Mexican, who was the villain. According to an Argentine critic, whose attitude was fairly typical, Latin Americans were always portrayed in American movies as "greedy, disloyal, cowardly, boasting, lazy, grotesque mulattoes."[60] A Cuban journalist complained that the North American's image of his hemisphere brothers, derived from cinema and television, was heavily adorned with exotic and picturesque elements—a very partial vision.[61] One angry Argentine went so far as to suspect that the movie version of the Latin American was part of a concerted imperialistic conspiracy to discredit our neighbors to the south.[62]

Visitors recognized that the sword cut both ways, that the motion picture image of the United States was also distorted to the extent of making an unfavorable impression abroad. Seoane said, "Do not believe the film language of Hollywood which had falsified Indo-America as a land of rhumba dancers, highway robbers, and lazy good-for-nothings; and has calumniated its own country by presenting us with a picture of gangsters, cowboys, divorcées, and vampires—all of them greedy and in love with money."[63] American citizens themselves, concerned with international understanding, often have become apoplectic about the adverse effect of American films on the picture of their homeland abroad.[64] The familiar mor-

60. Alberto Fournier, quoted in M. Chapman, "Yankeephobia," p. 36.
61. Bravo, pp. 198–99; similar testimony is given by Gabriela Mistral, "La película enemiga," and Cosío Villegas, in Joseph, p. 291; see also Beals et al., *What the South Americans Think of Us*, p. 91.
62. Luis Pascarella, quoted in M. Chapman, "Yankeephobia," p. 39.
63. Seoane, pp. 63–64; see also Sánchez, *Un sudamericano*, p. 19.
64. See, for example, Duggan, *Two Americas*, pp. 251–52. In my opinion, Thomas Palmer takes a more reasoned attitude when he says that while the picture may be distorted, it is not really very harmful—except insofar as it contributes to the "revolution of rising expectations" (*Search for a Latin American Policy*, p. 121).

alistic condemnation of American films was heard with some frequency. A survey of the Mexican press revealed a good deal of
pious comment about the immorality and brutality portrayed in
*yanqui* movies.[65] One commentator even recommended that the
United States government should prohibit the production of films
dealing with crime and vice.[66]

Surely many sophisticated Spanish Americans had opinions about
the artistic merits and demerits of American films, but the particular group of witnesses in this survey has paid relatively little
attention to this subject. An Argentine labeled American films "an
artistic disaster" (Ayres, p. 139). Luis Quintanilla, in his commen-
tary on the artistic quality of pictures made in the U.S.A., rated
American films as superficial and trivial in subject matter, produced only for amusement. They lacked the serious realism of
European productions. "We are sick," he wrote in 1943, "of melo-
drama, baby-talk, and million-dollar super-productions. We know
that life is not always smooth or beautiful; but we know also that
we can always discover beauty in it."[67] It is likely that an analysis
of movie criticism in Spanish America would show that the artistic
value of a considerable number of North American films of the
period was recognized and praised. This was true, for example, in
the case of the cinematic version of *The Grapes of Wrath*.

Like many other foreign critics, Spanish Americans were en-
tranced by Walt Disney's animated cartoons, and these were generally exempted from the curse laid on other American movies.
After an interview with Disney, Seoane called him "the man who
unveiled a new dimension for motion pictures," and referred to
"the magic wand of this Aesop with the sinews of La Fontaine and
the brush strokes of Rabelais" (chap. 13). Otero, praising Disney's
"Fantasia" as a splendid expression of the North American artistic
genius, asserted that its producer had discovered "a new world for
the cinema."[68] Donald Duck and Mickey Mouse may have saved our
artistic reputation in the Spanish American mind. Television, perhaps because it was not considered as an artistic medium, stimulated practically no comment among our witnesses. Almost alone
among them, a Chilean editor stated that television fare in the

65. Merrill, p. 13.
66. Arango, p. 112; it has been a commonplace among Americans who
worry about our image in foreign countries that the government ought to
control and censor exported films.
67. Quintanilla, pp. 48–49.
68. Otero, p. 175; see also Beals et al., p. 82.

United States is so execrable that it could stupify the youth and ruin the artistic and cultural sense of the nation.[69]

## THE PETRIFIED HEART

If our discussion of the worth of North American culture as conceived in the Spanish American mind has seemed rambling and inconclusive, at least part of the blame must be put on the source material itself. Many sentient men from the other America, escaping from the thraldom of the Ariel-Caliban complex, still felt a vague uneasiness and discomfort as they contemplated what they could discern of the North American's inner life, his aspirations, and his spiritual goals. In the statements we have cited there have been numerous symptoms that, in casting aside the simplified concept of the United States as a land of brutal barbarians, without culture or spiritual values, the Spanish American was nevertheless faced with a pattern of values which seemed in some significant way alien, insufficient, and resistant to facile definition.

In the minds of many it was true that religion appeared to flourish in the northern land, although some had reservations about its depth; on closer examination *yanqui* manners did not seem as crude as painted in the legend; the business of appreciating art was brisk, even though the creation of the fine arts was naturally in a rudimentary stage; even North American philosophy might have its respectable value; science, including the search for its purest principles was, of course, highly developed among the busy northerners, as was literature.

And yet something important seemed lacking in this advanced and apparently cultured society. While they agreed that there was a kind of emptiness in that civilization, they tried to identify it in various ways and presented diverse explanations as to its cause.

Jorge Mañach, whose general view of American society was by no means harsh, said, "The emphasis on deeds, rather than on moral substance, tends to leave the latter without support, giving stimulus to a certain disdain for the inner life; and the emptiness of that life is in turn responsible for the many forms of 'escapism' that abound in North America."[70]

In the eyes of an Ecuadorian poet, what was missing was closeness to nature. According to him, "the countryside has been de-

69. Velasco, *Kennedy*, pp. 9, 31. Amanda Labarca shared this view (Joseph, p. 320).
70. In Joseph, p. 336.

voured by those giants of a thousand eyes and countless steel hands." Even cultural life had become urban, as exemplified in contemporary poetry. This situation, he believed, was in contrast to that in Spanish America, where man and the poet were nearer "the soil, organic feelings, and the world of earthy things."[71]

A Colombian poet, in a long poem, *The Towers of Manhattan*, admired the steel miracle of the skyscraper, symbolizing the American spirit, but exclaimed, "How distant is Athens' light grace, her airy caress, her life-giving breath!"[72] This, of course, is distinctly in the Rodó tradition.

Another poet, Octavio Paz, described the American soul as "petrified" and continued, "They believe in hygiene, health, work, and contentment, but perhaps they have never experienced true joy, which is an intoxicating whirlwind. . . . Their vitality becomes a fixed smile that denies old age and death, but that changes life into motionless stone."[73]

The suspicion that deep and true joy is lacking in the American pattern has been a persistent theme. In Darío's early comments on the United States, he noted that "even gaiety is harsh" in New York City. A later observer expressed the idea in epigrammatic form: "Joy is a fruit which North Americans eat when it is green."[74] The Chilean Subercaseaux was explicit on this point: "It seems to us that they have renounced the immense springs of free animal enjoyment possessed by primitive man and which we would not wish to abandon at any price. There we feel like the Polynesian whom the missionary has clothed in a shirt" (p. 142).

Paz expressed the familiar theme that man in the United States has been conquered by his mechanical world: "In the United States man does not feel that he has been torn from the center of creation and suspended between hostile forces. He has built his own world and it is his mirror. But now he cannot recognize himself in his inhuman objects, nor in his fellows. His creations, like those of an inept sorcerer, no longer obey him. He is alone among his works, lost . . . in a wilderness of mirrors."[75]

An Argentine physician diagnosed our malady as follows: "Even their instinct is deformed by their practical, emotionless feeling about things. They are souls without upheavals, giving off a hollow

71. Carrera Andrade, pp. 67–68.
72. Ortiz Vargas, p. 112.
73. Paz, *Labyrinth*, p. 24.
74. Darío, in Mapes, *Escritos*, p. 161; Armando Zegrí, "Cosas que no debería decir."
75. Paz, pp. 20–21.

echo. . . . There are no gardens in their shrewd, mercantile minds" (Ayres, p. 52).

A Venezuelan commentator has said, "In the midst of the greatest industrial development, man trembles with an empty heart." The fruits of industrial advance "do not prevent that mortal dryness which creeps into the human heart. Man needs something above all that; something which does not depend on the most formidable progress."[76]

A Mexican scholar sought to explain by an unusual interpretation the strangeness (*la otredad*) which he and his countrymen felt in the American way of life: The United States' manner of looking at the world is based on "innocence," that is, a refusal to recognize the real existence of evil or sin. He attributed many peculiar aspects of American life to that fundamental viewpoint, which contrasts sharply, he argued, with the Mexican outlook, or indeed with that of most cultures.[77]

In these comments and in many others which tell of the insufficiency which Spanish Americans so often felt in the inner life of North Americans, it is not easy to find a common denominator which would define very precisely just what the lack is. It doubtless involved the apparent lack of emotional and sensual exaltation, which—they believed—had been shut out by utilitarian goals, industrialization, urbanization, and overspecialized lives. At first glance this would seem to be a reaction peculiar to the poet or artist, but it has been common among so many sophisticated observers that it must be considered as a very significant theme.

In some measure, this impression of emptiness in the deeper recesses of the American spirit may have been simply the result of superficial differences in language habits of the two civilizations. In contrast to the vivacity, sharp articulation, variety of pitch, and expressive accompanying gestures characteristic of Spanish American speech, informal talk in the United States tends to be (or seems to be) slurred, monotonous, drawling, and devoid of bodily movements. Whether or not such speech differences are in fact reflections of mental or emotional states or merely fortuitous variations is a question to beguile the linguists.

In a more general sense, it is more likely that the common even though imperfectly expressed sense of insufficiency in the American character corresponded to a very real difference in the value systems of the two cultures. North American self-criticism has fre-

76. Núñez, *Viaje*, pp. 86–87.
77. Jorge Portilla, "La crisis espiritual de los Estados Unidos," p. 72.

quently lamented that the dominant hierarchy of values in this country has too often excluded knowledge and experience which are not perceived by the intellect, but which can come to us through artistic and intuitive channels. Our own critics have not been oblivious to the deformation of spirit said to result from our technological civilization.

## EDUCATION

Just as many Spanish Americans in the nineteenth century were attracted by the development of education in the United States, so their descendants in this century found education a favorite topic of discussion, and it has occupied a prominent place in their overall image of the United States. In contrast to most of the nineteenth-century observers, not all were pleased by what they saw in the efforts of North Americans to educate their youth.

A common view, which was held by Martí and became almost a stereotype, has been that the tone of American education was too prominently pitched toward utilitarian values. As Galo Plaza (Ecuador) said, "Advocates of the Latin American philosophy of education find fault with the United States system for being too pragmatic, materialistic, and utilitarian, without sufficient interest in the appreciation of the higher values of the spirit." He added that such a generalization could hardly stand up under careful analysis.[78] Men like Camilo Henríquez and Sarmiento were impressed precisely by the practical trend of North American education, and the later repugnance toward it was an integral part of the reaction against the materialism of the nineteenth century that was typified in Rodó's writings.

Rodó saw virtue in the North American's obsession with popular education, which had made the school "the strongest pivot of their prosperity and the child's soul the most cultivated among all delicate and precious things." But the growth of education for the common people had led to a "universal semi-culture in which higher cultural values and superior genius languish" (pp. 81, 91–92).

Variations on this theme continued to be heard among Spanish Americans. In 1904, an official of the Chilean Ministry of Education stated that schools in the United States reflected the national character, and that students were encouraged to study only what is practical and useful, to the neglect of theory and beauty. Their

78. Plaza, "Problems of Education in Latin America," p. 161.

souls became atrophied, and only in physical training were North American schools better than those in Chile.[79]

The Mexican philosopher Samuel Ramos lamented that Mexico had adopted in its educational system the North American "instrumental conception of man" according to which "every level of instruction from elementary school through college is arbitrarily governed by principles of technical skill." "North American pedagogy," he continued, "is unconsciously seasoned with a mechanistic concept of society, which is an abbreviation of the cosmic view that imagines the world as a machine."[80]

Among the many criticisms which Vasconcelos directed at North American education, synthesized, as he believed, in Dewey's educational philosophy, was his rejection of the theory that the child should be taught through experimentation only what is useful and needful to him. Vasconcelos believed that he should be shown "a world that escapes necessity," and that "more important than discovering the characteristics and relations of an object, is to know [*conocer*] the sciences and to distinguish the values which enrich the atmosphere surrounding the student."[81]

The particular demon of North American education, according to these critics, was excessive specialization. Technical specialization in education turns out men, said Ramos, who have "pre-existing solutions for a limited number of typical cases," and the technician can handle only those situations.[82] Pointing to the tendency to offer specialized instruction in the secondary schools and to abuse of the "elective" system in universities, Pedro Henríquez Ureña stated, "The attempt to specialize makes education incomplete and superficial."

This generalized critical concept of education in the United States appeared in its most extreme form in Ramos' conclusion: In contrast to a system restricted to the instruction of material techniques, which sacrifices the authentic life of man for a false one and prepares him "to be devoured all the more easily by civilization," true education is "the vigor of life itself, fighting off a civilization which by converting men into foolproof automatons creates the illusion that it has adequately prepared them for life— though without will, or intelligence, or feeling. In short, without a

79. Moisés Vargas, quoted in Pike, *Chile*, p. 166.
80. Ramos, *Profile of Man and Culture in Mexico*, p. 99.
81. *De Robinson a Odiseo*, pp. 18–21; for other condemnations of utilitarian education, see Mañach, in Joseph, p. 333, and Reissig, p. 25.
82. Ramos, p. 100.

soul." Here it becomes apparent that most of these attitudes toward North American education were but an aspect of a broader dissatisfaction with the American character which we have noted elsewhere.

Not all observers, however, saw our education from the battlements of besieged spirituality. There were those in this century, for example, who praised the very practicality of North American schools which others decried. In 1923, a Bolivian professor said that his country had much to learn from the practical methods used in the United States, and specifically recommended for educating Bolivian Indians model farms such as those set up by Booker T. Washington. A Dominican writer, who otherwise had little use for the United States, said in 1918, "The American school, more practical than the French and German schools, tends to form men of character, well-equipped for life's struggle." A Cuban educator wrote at length in 1952 about the North American educational system, and pointed with approval to its close relation to the needs of society, its penchant for experimentation, its emphasis on social development rather than mere factual knowledge, and its forward-looking initiative.[83]

Dozens of other Spanish American educators studied in American universities and observed educational practices in the United States, often concluding that there was much in the North American experience to imitate back home.[84] The result among their countrymen sometimes was a severe reaction against what they considered a kind of cultural imperialism. Spanish American opinion was undoubtedly divided concerning the net value of American educational ideals and their application. That such was the case is indicated by the reaction of a group of Mexican grantees, many of them educators: 38 per cent found North American education better than they had anticipated, but 20 per cent discovered that it was worse than their expectations.[85]

There were a number of specific aspects of the public school system in the United States that stimulated particular comment among the witnesses. Among them were the lack of a centralizing federal education authority (this circumstance was believed to contribute to a healthy diversity); the interminable use of psy-

83. Ignacio Prudencia Bustillo, quoted in Zea, The Latin American Mind, p. 203; Cestero, p. xx; de la Torre, Educación, passim.

84. As an example of the influence of United States pedagogical theory and practice in Spanish America, see Carlos Salazar Romero, Principios y prácticos para la educación secundaria en el Perú.

85. International Research Associates, Study, p. 8.

chological and other testing procedures (which Vasconcelos resented); the interest and contribution of the whole community in the educational process; the cultural activity in the school and the teaching of art; the daring variety in methodology encouraged by Dewey's experimental philosophy and continued by others; and the liberality of school discipline.[86]

North American higher education received special attention from Spanish American observers, partly because visits to universities were often on their routine schedule. To a certain extent, colleges and universities were exempt from some of the conventionalities applied to education in general in the United States.

Starting with the material aspect of the American university, its physical plant usually commanded sincere admiration. The profusion and magnificence of the buildings on some campuses and the spaciousness and beauty of the campus setting aroused wonder and apparently some envy. A Peruvian statesman, after giving an idyllic description of the Harvard campus, exclaimed, "You could not dream of a more appropriate place for research and study!" Arturo Capdevila (Argentina), whose hatred of North American imperialism and the *yanqui* superiority complex was extreme, marveled at the beauty of the Cornell campus: "Spacious, with numerous buildings scattered like a monumental city in the midst of the countryside, in a land of pastoral poetry. . . . What a setting for the development of clear, pure intelligence!" Vasconcelos praised the beauty of the University of Texas and especially the Renaissance serenity of its library building. The Chilean philosopher Enrique Molina lamented that universities in his country lacked the stadiums, gymnasiums, and tennis courts of their North American counterparts.[87] So many Spanish American intellectuals studied or taught in North American colleges and universities that their writings are studded with recollections of particular institutions, usually gilded with nostalgia.

Frequently accompanying their wonder at the physical setting were praiseful remarks on the generosity of private donors who had made possible the construction of so many fine buildings. According to a Bolivian observer, "Millionaires in the United States try to save their souls by saving others from mental poverty. . . .

---

86. Uzcátegui, p. 9; de la Torre, p. 18; Macías, lecture, p. 7; Velasco, p. 13; Otero, p. 142.

87. Belaúnde, "Crónicas," pp. 2–3; Capdevila, *América: nuestras naciones ante los Estados Unidos,* pp. 94–95; Vasconcelos, *¿Qué es la revolución?,* p. 172; Molina, *Por los valores,* p. 35.

This generous mania of the millionaires is really a high sign of culture in this nation."[88] The role of alumni and state legislators in financing higher education was also recognized.[89]

The image of the university student in the United States gave predominant emphasis to his health and love of sports. Luis Alberto Sánchez described the typical student as "healthy, guileless, impressionable, energetic, good-looking, whose worth is often lessened by his perfect primitivism, but in whose capacity for work and confidence there lies real hope." For some witnesses sturdy health did not counterbalance the students' characteristic deficiencies. Subercaseaux complained that they were superficial, overly concerned with practical matters, and lacking real interest in the life of the mind. Sheltered from the real world on their rural campuses, immured in a world of sports and fraternities, they graduated "ignorant of the life of the instinct without which it is impossible to be an artist, to have refined sensitivity, to be, in short, sorrowfully and effectively human."[90]

Belaúnde took a more kindly view: "These young people like sun, fresh air, sports, dancing, and childlike, uproarious fun. They enjoy life and they work. They can feel the solemnity of certain moments and take pleasure in the humor of ordinary life. They can pray and they can laugh. They are strong and happy because they experience the divine emotion of prayer as well as the human pleasure of laughing."[91]

Foreigners have usually been impressed by the free and friendly relationship between student and professor in the American college, and Spanish Americans were not exceptions. Sánchez remarked on the cooperative, informal nature of that relationship, which contrasted with the more rigid situation traditionally prevalent in Spanish America.[92]

With regard to the work and mission of the North American university, Spanish Americans naturally held varying opinions. Among the older critics, the charge of excessive specialization presumably included higher education, and it continued to be voiced.[93] A Bolivian observer (Otero), writing in 1941, noted the tendency in the

88. Otero, p. 148; see also Pérez Guerrero, USA, p. 50; Capdevila, p. 92; Molina, p. 60.
89. Belaúnde, "Crónicas," p. 82; Vasconcelos, ¿Qué es la revolución?, p. 170.
90. Un sudamericano, p. 268 (see also Seoane, p. 79); Subercaseaux, pp. 169–70.
91. "Crónicas," p. 82.
92. Un sudamericano, p. 257.
93. For example, Juan Oropesa, "Imparidad del destino americano," p. 22.

universities toward professional specialization, which he believed was very suitable for the average student, but also pointed to another trend which he described as "cultural, humanistic, disinterested, without any other aim than culture itself." This kind of higher education, in his opinion, was properly being provided for a select elite (p. 155). Enrique Molina, contrasting universities in Europe and Chile with those in the United States, lauded the care and affectionate attention given by the latter to their students; he also envied the number of courses in the liberal arts which were open to the young people.[94]

Luis Alberto Sánchez devoted many pages to the characteristics of the university in the United States. On the negative side, he listed extreme specialization, a certain provincialism, overemphasis on methodology in research, and a concomitant lack of regard for personal judgment and imagination. But his general estimate appears to be favorable; he admired the general respect for the opinions of others and the freedom of speech. He also respected the sincere passion among scholars for hard work on subjects unrelated to immediate needs. In view of the conventional belittling of humanistic culture in the United States, Sánchez' conclusion is somewhat surprising: "the North American university is perhaps the last redoubt of the old humanism and the first of a new humanism created from the age-long experiences of Europe and the unlimited initiative of the North American."[95]

## SCIENCE

Although it may be assumed that both the common and the more sophisticated picture of North American civilization in the Spanish American mind included a bright spot reflecting scientific activity and achievement, there is surprisingly little comment on science in the sources used in this study. It is unexpected and perhaps significant that coverage of United States science in the Spanish American press appeared to be minimal, ranking in percentage of column inches almost at the bottom.[96] A random perusal of more or less technical publications by Spanish American scientists and technicians who worked in the United States suggests, of course, wider and more appreciative interest.

Rodó in 1900 sounded a familiar note when he declared, "They

94. Molina, pp. 55, 59.
95. *Un sudamericano*, pp. 267–68.
96. Wolfe, "Attitudes," chap. 22.

have not incorporated into the scientific store of knowledge a single general law, a single principle, but they have made science a magician with the marvels of their applied science, they have magnified her in the realm of utility, and have given to the world in the form of steam and electric power billions of invisible slaves who multiply a hundred times the power of Aladdin's magic lamp to serve humanity. . . . [The North American] does not bring to science a disinterested yearning for truth, nor has he in any case ever shown any capacity for loving her for her own sake. Research for him is only the antecedent of utilitarian application" (pp. 81, 91).

Blanco-Fombona, who savagely castigated practically all aspects of American life, made a unique exception in the case of science and technology in the United States. In 1902, he said, "In science and the application of science many North Americans have truly reached great heights. Franklin and Edison belong to that group of names of which humanity may be proud. . . . The electrical and mechanical engineers of the United States are the first in the world, and industrial tools, in the invention of which both science and imagination have played their part, reach their greatest perfection there."[97]

More recent observers, while still marveling at the North American genius for applied sciences, were also aware of the contributions to pure science. Subercaseaux asserted in 1943, "Without any doubt, advancement in modern physics, astronomy, and chemistry has in North America the brain center of the world" (pp. 167–68). Referring to the great university laboratories, Seoane was no less affirmative: "With unlimited funds for pure scientific research . . . the Americans have made fundamental discoveries or inventions" (p. 80).

Recurrently, the social uses of science in the United States were mentioned. A Cuban journalist said in 1954, "Never in the world has there been a greater or more intense mobilization of the sciences, never have greater resources been made available to them, and at no time have they been so actively at work in the great universal task of bettering human destiny."[98] Seoane noted the same phenomenon: "The North American's sharply practical sense cannot conceive of science divorced from reality. He places it at the service of his country and himself" (p. 92).

Occasionally advances in medical science commanded particular

97. *La americanización del mundo*, p. 17.
98. Bravo, pp. 86–87; see also Arango, p. 106.

attention. A survey of the Mexican press revealed some interest in cancer research, heart surgery, etc.[99] Much more sweeping was the condemnation of American medical science by a dyspeptic Argentine physician. According to Ayres, our medical education was sloppy, our doctors only interested in working for money, and our much-touted medical discoveries largely mythical (pp. 57–64).

A Bolivian commentator, Otero, reserved particular praise for American chemists: "A silent legion of modest, hard-working men are laboring, bending over in the laboratories and universities— restless, diligent people. . . . Organic and inorganic chemistry are the real tutelary gods of life in the United States" (pp. 124–25).

### PHILOSOPHY

Perhaps even less than North Americans, Spanish American thinkers have not—at least until very recent years—given much attention to technical, systematic philosophy. They have been interested in the basic problems with which philosophy deals, but for the most part have preferred to express their speculations in personal, somewhat rambling essays that are usually more concerned with problems of their society than with the involved details of professionally conceived philosophy.

It is not unnatural, then, that many writers, following a European habit, equated North American philosophy with pragmatism, and construed pragmatism to mean a utilitarian, materialistic outlook on life. The Chilean Emilo Vaisse doubtless had this connotation in mind when he declared that pragmatism destroys all spiritual values,[100] and this tendency to identify pragmatism with utilitarianism or materialism was not uncommon among those who perhaps had heard of Peirce and William James but had not read their works. Even such a sophisticated *pensador* as Jorge Mañach said, "there is no doubt that in its most primary manifestations the pragmatic spirit engenders a nominalism that is indifferent to the great abstractions usually considered fruitful in other nations. . . . It also produces a casuistic practicalism that tends to prevail over 'principles.' This attitude, fortified as it is by an obsession with economic success, encourages a harshly competitive and money-minded social environment that strangles all moral scruples."[101]

99. Merrill, p. 17.
100. Quoted in Pike, p. 166.
101. In Joseph, p. 336.

In the first decades of this century, however, at least some of the works of William James were well enough known to a minority. In fact, during the period 1890–1943, James ranked among the most published North American author in Spanish-speaking countries.[102] A number of the so-called professors of idealism, men who reacted strongly against the materialistic and deterministic forms of positivism, counted James—along with Bergson and other French thinkers—among their mentors. The best known of James' books were his *Talks to Teachers on Psychology and to Students on Some of Life's Ideals* and *The Will to Believe*, both of which could be interpreted as messages of hope in the face of deterministic materialism. Philosophically minded writers like Carlos-Arturo Torres, Enrique Molina, and Antonio Caso found support for their idealism in James' emphasis on the individual, his interest in free will (which he got from Charles Bernard Renouvier, also a Spanish American favorite), and his openness to experience and change. They were particularly impressed by James' belief in the force of ideals and "overbeliefs."[103] Two writers of that generation, Pedro Henríquez Ureña and Carlos Vaz Ferreira, although they did not agree with all of James' conclusions, devoted serious critical studies to his work.[104] Toward the end of the period under discussion, interest in the philosophy of William James subsided, but the testimony of Carlos Dávila in 1949 indicates that at least a few of the older generation still had a more accurate conception of his pragmatism than the conventional one. After referring to the European confusion of pragmatism with a crude philosophy of results and success, Dávila said, "That theory is far different from what was in the mind of Charles Sanders Peirce, its formulator, or William James, its architect. . . . True pragmatism means, above all, openness, a readiness to accept evolutionary processes, without reference to some preconceived dogma." It is not to be identified, he continued, with Spencerian positivism, and is typically North American.[105]

John Dewey has been consistently one of the widest read of the serious North American authors. During most of this century, his writings ranked high in the lists of translated publications. He was better known, however, as an educational theoretician than as a

102. According to a survey of translation lists; see Appendixes 4–6.

103. See, for example, Molina, p. 48, and Frugoni, p. 342.

104. Henríquez Ureña devoted a section of his *Horas de estudio* to James, and Vaz Ferreira's lectures on James were published in 1908. See Zum Felde, pp. 545–46.

105. Dávila, p. 124.

general philosopher.[106] His philosophy of education was influential among educators, especially in Mexico; the reaction to what were defined as his educational ideals has been treated.

In recent years, more and more professionally trained philosophers have appeared in Spanish America, like Samuel Ramos, Emilio Oribe, and Leopoldo Zea, whose knowledge of contemporary philosophical trends in Europe and the United States has been more specialized than that of their dilettante predecessors. While these thinkers noted that existentialism, in which sophisticated Spanish Americans are much interested, had made little headway in the United States, they were entirely willing to grant that there was a specifically North American philosophy; they even gave high praise to the development of philosophical studies in the United States.

Zea, for example, wrote, "The United States, in spite of itself, has a philosophy which is its own and with which it has grappled with circumstances, a philosophy which has emerged from its needs. It is a philosophy which from the formal point of view is beholden to many influences, but which from the point of view of its content is useful for its own reality. . . . This imprint, created by North American life itself, has given rise, if not to the formulation of a hundred-percent original philosophy, certainly to the choice or selection of those philosophical trends which are adaptable to the life and manner of being of the North Americans. . . . North America has put all philosophy to work for the ideal to which Ralph Barton Perry has given the name of 'individualism,' a way of life inherent in the North American soul."[107]

The Uruguayan philosopher Emilio Oribe declared, "Anyone who has read recent books and journals must recognize that North American philosophy is clearly superior to that of our countries and has a much greater influence. This superiority is being demonstrated more and more clearly in the development of studies, research, ideas, and theories, and in individuals. North American thought has attained a certain status in the contemporary philosophical world because it can point to great and well-known thinkers who have largely overcome the gulf of the Atlantic and familiarized European universities and journals with the works and teachings of several distinguished philosophers of the later nineteenth century and of our century." Oribe remarked particularly

106. See, however, Angélica Mendoza de Montero, *Líneas fundamentales de la filosofía de John Dewey.*
107. *América como conciencia*, pp. 147–52.

on the existence of a professional philosophic tradition in the United States, the emergence of strong university centers specializing in the discipline, and the close association of North American philosophy with science. If Angélica Mendoza's eulogistic and extensive account of the development of philosophy in the United States is representative,[108] one may believe that respect for North American philosophical endeavor was shared by many of Oribe's colleagues of the younger generation.

## RELIGION

Undoubtedly part of the folk picture of the United States in Spanish America was the belief that this is a Protestant country and basically irreligious or indifferent to religion. Distrust of Protestant missionaries in the Spanish-speaking republics perhaps contributed to this general impression. An anthropologist has noted that the average middle-class Mexican identifies his neighbor to the North entirely with Protestantism, which he suspects is really not Christian, and fears his evangelizing efforts as a threat to Mexico's spiritual civilization.[109] When queried about the amount of interest in religion among North Americans, 93 per cent of a group of Mexican journalists indicated that, in their opinion, there was practically no interest or not much interest.[110]

Consequently, it came as something of a surprise to Spanish American visitors to realize that religion appeared to occupy an important place in the life of the United States. Fifty-four per cent of a sizeable group of Mexican grantees stated that they had been most favorably impressed by the North American concern for religion and found it far greater than they had expected.[111] Individual visitors sometimes recorded similar reactions. A Colombian declared, "The American people are essentially religious. People believe in their religion and attend to their worship properly, faithfully, and with all the respect due to whatever religion they profess." Gabriela Mistral considered that the noblest of her impressions of the United States was "the religious feeling of a great part

108. Oribe, "Some Aspects of Thought in the New World," p. 297; Mendoza, *Panorama de las ideas contemporáneas en los Estados Unidos*, pp. 149–86.
109. Humphrey, *Mexican Image*, pp. 117, 120.
110. Merrill, p. 22.
111. International Research Associates, p. 8; Beals and Humphrey, p. 89, noted the same reaction among other Mexicans who studied in the United States.

of the North American people and, especially, the faith that gives attention to the social aspect, which is not only the norm of an individual's life, but which also strives to be that of collective life. From the Quakers to the Catholic Church, Christianity penetrates the life of the masses and faces up to the social question."[112]

Another facet of their surprise concerned the thriving position occupied in North American society by the Catholic Church, a fact which was in contrast to their preconceptions. Even in 1922, the Uruguayan poet and staunch supporter of the Church Zorrilla de San Martín denied that the United States was primarily a Protestant country and said, "A century of democratic liberty has been enough to enable the Catholic religion, which hardly used to exist there, to occupy the first place among those professed there." He cited statistics from the *Osservatore Romano* to prove his point and added that North American Catholics are good ones.[113] A more recent Colombian observer was in agreement: "Today, with thirty-five million proselytes, Catholicism is a living force within the American mixture, and it is daily gaining more and more converts to its creed." Occasionally, the fact that Catholics occupied high positions in the life of the country was worthy of note.[114]

A number of observers believed that the Catholic Church in the United States had acquired characteristics which differentiated it from the Church in Spanish America. It was not so intolerant, they said, and the communicants' faith was more fervent, the hierarchy more socially conscious.[115] A Chilean litterateur said, "North American Catholicism, because of its long struggle within a Protestant country and obeying atavistic traits of the race, has achieved a moral temper and a sense of human coexistence which is more democratic and fraternal than ours." An *aprista* claimed, "There is less attention paid to formulas and more vital religious feeling. . . . For the first time in twenty years, I feel comfort and pride in being a Catholic." A Bolivian witness believed that United States Catholicism had been a force among North Americans for liberalism and reform, and that nowhere had the social ideals of Pope Leo XIII

112. Arango, p. 63; Gabriela Mistral, "Tiene la palabra Gabriela Mistral," p. 322; see also Becerra, 2:146; Juárez y Aragón, p. 43; Vasconcelos, *¿Qué es la revolución?*, p. 169; Sánchez, *Un sudamericano*, p. 194; Núñez, *Viaje*, p. 114, for similar sentiments.

113. Zorrilla de San Martín, p. 131.

114. Arango, p. 63; see also Beals and Humphrey, p. 89; Seoane, p. 125; Sánchez, *Un sudamericano*, p. 194; and Reissig, p. 31.

115. Uzcátegui, p. 13.

had such full development. The Church, he said, "continues to give dynamic form to the social program of Christian democracy."[116]

Continuing a long Spanish American tradition of admiration for the spirit of religious tolerance in the United States, previously noted as fairly consistent in the nineteenth century, modern visitors were also impressed by manifestations of religious liberty. An Argentine educator said, "Through a healthy religious policy of education for tolerance, the United States has been able to shape its development and bring it to the high point it now can boast." Several remarked on the fact that priests, rabbis, and ministers got along together in a friendly fashion and on occasion cooperated in realizing common ends. Vasconcelos was impressed by the fact that parochial schools, whose buildings he found magnificent, readily cooperated with public schools, and that in the latter prayers were said for the benefit of Catholics and Protestants alike.[117]

The multiplicity and proliferation of Protestant sects and Oriental cults is a North American phenomena which has astounded, amused, and sometimes irritated the Spanish American observer. Remarking that religion in the United States now and then was extravagant, Zorrilla de San Martín said, "That is the land of psychic hyperesthesia, of spirits filled with religious restlessness, of apostles in the open air, of singing theologians. . . . There every brand of foolishness finds its follower and its apostle; from the ancient Buddhas and their prophets to their most recent incarnations from India, all idols have their dervishes and holy men among the Anglo-Americans." However grotesque this may be, he concluded that it was better than indifference to religion. A Colombian intellectual, finding Christian Science, Vedanta, and theosophy faintly ridiculous, mused, "To establish a new religion here is not difficult. A bit of luck, a little faith, someone to start it out, and the rest is simply putting up some walls and fastening on the roof." A Bolivian commentator, observing that Americans themselves were amused by the more eccentric sects, said, "Every day a new religion is invented and an advertising campaign is started, as if it were a matter of a new kind of toothpaste." An anonymous Mexican journalist believed that Americans invented religion in order "to feel themselves with a soul."[118]

116. Subercaseaux, p. 268; Seoane, p. 125; Otero, p. 54.

117. Reissig, p. 31; Uzcátegui, p. 12; Seoane, p. 126; Sánchez, *Un sudamericano*, p. 127; Vasconcelos, *Hispanoamérica frente a los nacionalismos*, p. 89; *¿Qué es la revolución?*, p. 77.

118. Zorrilla de San Martín, pp. 39–40; Arciniegas, pp. 61–66 (see also Palacios, p. 121); Otero, p. 61; Merrill, p. 15.

In writings of the earlier days of the century, one occasionally runs across a negative attitude toward religion in the United States. Blanco-Fombona, the old anti-imperialist warrior, said in 1902, "As in all countries, many persons there use religious ideas for moralizing purposes. This religiosity is an English disease, and the melancholy hypocrisy of religion comes to the *yanquis* from ancestors."[119]

A few analysts made more profound criticisms of religious life in the United States. Rodó, while granting that North American religious feeling had been a bulwark of morality in the rough, utilitarian free-for-all, complained that it was little more than that, that neither saintliness nor heroism would ever arise from it, and that the prudent moral code of Benjamin Franklin left little inspiration for high sacrifice or virtue (pp. 93–95). In the same vein, Frugoni observed that religion in America was superficial, a matter of social morality. Churches were practical organizations which encouraged no deeply mystical feelings. This critical note has reappeared now and then in later writers; the Argentine Julio Navarro Monzó wrote in the 1930s, "If religion is reduced to morality, it abandons its own resources. . . . The majority of North Americans seem to have a horror of metaphysics; they seem to be interested only in the practical . . . in the visible, the tangible, the physical. They confound religion with the church, thanks to their mania for institutions. They judge the efficiency of an ecclesiastical organization by the number of its hospitals and clubs, not by the profundity of the character of its members. A purely moral Christian lacks the most important element of all religion: that is, he lacks awe and wonder."[120]

The very social conscience which Gabriela Mistral so admired in North American religion struck a sour note with at least one recent commentator. Eduardo Squirru, an Argentine intellectual, after declaring that technology and our "puritanical abstract *lares*" were estranging North Americans from nature, wrote, "Religion itself seems to be transformed into something philanthropic and practical that serves very well to solve various social problems."[121]

The only really comprehensive condemnation of North American religious life which I have found was in a very bitter volume by Daniel Ayres, an Argentine. His blast covered the American's insincere, materialistic attitude toward his churches, his weakness

119. *La americanización del mundo*, p. 13.
120. Frugoni, p. 344; Navarro Monzó, quoted in Inman, *Latin America*, p. 422.
121. Squirru, *Américas*, p. 16.

for commercialized spiritualism, his historical persecution of Catholics, and his addiction to Masonic lodges, which the author described as a recent Jewish conspiracy (pp. 65–72).

A goodly number of commentators claimed to discern in contemporary North American life the shaping influence of Puritanism. To some it represented a limiting factor in the national character. To others it was a source of admirable strength. The Argentine novelist Eduardo Mallea has said, "The honor of Puritanism is the daily activity of life itself, and its goal is not the search for a dangerous style of heroic transcendency, but the justification of life before God with savings and circumstance. These are the ancient bonds of the North American soul—savings and circumstance. . . . Those men were bound to their Bibles in a violent and, at the same time, limited way." All they derived from their continual Bible-reading was "not much more than an arid and sometimes inhuman moral code. . . . Neither heroism nor saintliness [echoes of *Ariel*] could come to flower in the roughness of that rocky land."[122]

On the other hand, Jorge Mañach of Cuba, while admitting that "certain limitations of the 'classic' American spirit could be attributed to that discipline," declared, "But I am inclined to ascribe to the influence of Puritanism also some of the noblest and 'tenderest' American qualities," which he enumerated as profound moral sanity, integrity, generosity, and a sense of justice.[123]

In summary, the dominant tone of the witnesses concerning religious life in the United States has been favorable and can perhaps be represented in the remarks of Amanda Labarca, the Chilean educator: "Intimate religiosity—living Christianity, the strict and voluntary observation of Christian doctrine and morality—was very much more interwoven in the existence of those people of New England than in the Catholic peoples of South America. Those with whom I lived . . . observed a more sincerely pure, pious, and Christian conduct than any I had known before."[124]

122. Mallea, p. 138.
123. In Joseph, p. 330; another example of praise of Puritanism is Pérez Guerrero, pp. 32–33.
124. In Joseph, p. 312.

# 11

# Images of the American Character
# in the Twentieth Century

It is not always possible to distinguish clearly between the Spanish American's vision of society or of the collective life of the mind and spirit in the United States and his view of the salient characteristics of the North American as a human being. Obviously, since the individual as described by most observers is a composite abstraction derived from impressions made by many persons, his characteristics are inextricably related to those of his society. Nevertheless, in this chapter I shall try to sort out somewhat arbitrarily those traits which appear more applicable to the citizen of the United States than to his society.

## THE DISDAINFUL *Yanqui*

Without much question the most commonly mentioned attribute of the average North American in Spanish American eyes was his chilly attitude of superiority and disdain toward foreigners, particularly toward Latin Americans. While this observation was perhaps more common early in this century, it was also made by later witnesses.

Among the old opponents of United States imperialism, the disdainful *yanqui* was a stock character. Vargas Vila expressed the idea with his customary violent emphasis: "that immature, bastard, cruel people, insolent and contemptuous toward us, with a monstrous idea of its superiority and an invincible idea of conquest." Ugarte complained, "To the popular mind we were savages, ridiculous phenomena, degenerates. . . ." Blanco-Fombona exclaimed, "That inferiority which they impute to us is, on their part, either ignorance, or vanity, or an excuse for their past, present and future abuses." Mr. Danger in Rómulo Gallegos' novel *Doña Bárbara*, with his blind belief in the superiority of the Anglo-Saxon race, is a fictional incarnation of impudent North American arrogance. In the popular Mexican ballads, the haughty presumptuous gringo has been a common figure.[1]

Anti-imperialists of succeeding generations hardly varied the theme. As a young man, Arturo Capdevila attended an inter-American student congress at Cornell University and was furious at the superior, condescending attitude of the North American delegates: "There was something in those hosts of ours which spoiled their hospitality. . . . Sometimes it seemed to be savagery, provincialism, excessive haste. Other times it appeared to be intolerance, scorn. . . . Progressively we were reduced to a subordinate, colonial retinue, without voice or vote." For another observer the American's certainty that he is always right, his cocksureness, would prevent him from being a real philosopher whose essential quality must be the ability to doubt. Luis Alberto Sánchez, who was not unkind to American society in general, was critical of this trait: "He believes excessively in his own abilities. . . . And, since he is moreover handsome and healthy, lacking an inferiority complex, there develops in him a kind of narcissism, a certain superiority complex." Sánchez believed that the *"yanqui* peril" of this superiority complex, deeply rooted in the American character, was potentially more dangerous than Wall Street imperialism. López de Mesa admired much in American life, but found the northern disdain repugnant: "Drunk with a sense of their own ability, they are overbearing toward foreign things, blind to the values of others, like children who understand nothing outside their egotistical impressions."[2]

Some of the more recent interpreters have qualified their image of the arrogant, disdainful American with second thoughts. A few who were very critical of their own societies suspected that the North American's scorn of Latin America might not be entirely unjustified. Subercaseaux confessed in 1943, "I know the North

1. Vargas Vila, *Bárbaros*, pp. 60–61; Ugarte, *The Destiny of a Continent*, p. 13; Blanco-Fombona, *La lámpara de Aladino*, p. 478; Merle Simmons, "Attitudes," p. 36.

2. Capdevila, *América*, pp. 101–2; Zegrí, *Cosas*, 20:359; Sánchez, *Un sudamericano en Norteamérica*, pp. 172–73, 371; López de Mesa, "Una hora ante Norte América," p. 84. This stereotype is common in the writings of a great many other commentators; see, for example, Mañach, in Joseph, *As Others See Us*, pp. 338–39.

American character well enough to understand that it is natural, logical, and true that we should arouse in him a deeply disagreeable and repugnant reaction." The reason, he said, is that Spanish Americans lack moral values and democratic experience (p. 251). A Chilean journalist in the 1920s was unusually self-critical, saying, "Even our protests and our sarcasm against the pretentions of superiority of the *yanqui* over the Hispanic American reveal the desperate effort of one who is trying to convince himself." If the Spanish American were self-confident, like the Englishman, he continued, he would simply smile at North American boasting.[3]

Once in a while visitors sought to explain or attenuate the apparent boorishness of their northern neighbors. Arango admitted that North Americans abroad show a superior attitude which causes resentment among foreigners, but insisted that the trait was not common in the North American at home. A Chilean visitor remarked, "North American people sometimes appear to be sullen and haughty; this is because they are always busy with their work and the progress of the group." Another Chilean stated, "Anyone who thinks he will find the North American, who lives in such splendor, a vain man would be sadly mistaken. Rarely have I seen people so simple, human, almost provincial." An Ecuadorian declared in 1942, "Sometimes possibly he may feel superior, but he keeps it to himself and never tries to flaunt his real or assumed superiority."[4]

One Cuban visitor in the fifties simply denied categorically the alleged self-conceit of the *yanquis*: "What the Cuban appreciates most in the North American citizen is that he no longer shows any feeling of superiority over us Latins." "The people of North America, in contrast to their English cousins, are not frightened when faced with customs different from theirs. . . . The North American usually reacts in the most understanding and human way." He even claimed that this reaction could be noticed in tourists![5] Such an attitude, it should be emphasized, is almost unexampled in our sources.

If the North American is arrogant and condescending toward Latin America, it must be due to the fact that he is ignorant of the republics to the South. So reasoned many Spanish American analysts, not without a kind of logic, and they went on to conclude

3. Montenegro, *Puritanía*, p. 157.
4. Arango, *Estados Unidos*, p. 88; Velasco, *Kennedy*, p. 7; Subercaseaux, *Retorno*, p. 135; Uzcátegui, *Los Estados Unidos*, p. 14.
5. Bravo, *El destino*, pp. 146, 197–98.

that the *yanqui* is oblivious to and ignorant of all foreign cultures. In a study of the attitudes of Bolivian ex-grantees, it was found that 23 per cent gave as their most unfavorable impression of the United States the prevailing ignorance of and lack of interest in other countries.[6] A Mexican journalist complained that North Americans did not have much of a grasp of world problems and that their interest in the world was too narrow. A Guatemalan journalist urged the North American "not to have that superficial knowledge of us; but to search for the deep roots of our structure as free peoples." Luis Alberto Sánchez said that the North American thought the world began with Alaska and ended at the Rio Grande; even when he traveled in other countries he was only thinking of his homeland.[7]

In view of this widespread idea that Americans were ignorant of foreign and specifically Latin American cultures and conditions, a number of visitors in later decades have been pleasantly amazed at the efforts, mostly on an academic level, which had been made to learn about Latin America. "The people of the U.S. know little about our America, Hispanic America, but they are trying to learn a lot and to give it the affectionate attention which they previously have not given, not because of a lack of interest, but because they did not realize our significance." Surprised at the extent of Latin American studies in Western universities, an Ecuadorian visitor exclaimed, "Can you say that these people have no interest in knowing the problems of Latin America?"[8] During World War II, Seoane was impressed by the number of people in the United States who spoke Spanish and by the university work in Hispanic subjects. Granting certain deficiencies, he continued, "Possibly within a few years the North Americans will know more about us than we ourselves do."[9]

We have mentioned the fact that relations between the United States and Latin America after World War II were chilled by the diversion of United States attention to other areas of the world. The resulting chagrin at our neglect and apparent indifference was reflected in journalistic comment. A survey of a hundred Mexican journalists in 1960 revealed that the North American lack of in-

6. Instituto Boliviano de Encuestas, *Study*, p. 32.

7. Merrill, *Gringo*, p. 36; Juárez y Aragón, *Más allá*, p. 101; Sánchez, *Un sudamericano*, p. 187.

8. Velasco, p. 11; Macías, lecture, p. 4.

9. Seoane, *El gran vecino*, p. 66; see also Núñez, *Viaje*, pp. 21–23. Some observers were scornful of efforts just before and during World War II to publicize Latin America in the United States, considering the efforts faddish.

terest in Latin American problems was a cardinal point of criticism.[10] An editorialist in *El Tiempo* of Bogotá wrote in 1959, "In reality, there is no hostility toward the nation of the North. . . . There is simply the natural resentment produced by the permanent oblivion to which we are assigned while the other four continents get not only money but technical assistance."[11] Such reactions, caused by the vagaries of international politics, were but a variation on the older common theme that the North American was scornfully ignorant of Spanish America.

## HOSPITALITY IN THE UNITED STATES

Alongside of the image of the cold and contemptuous North American a picture developed in more recent years of the hospitable and friendly *yanqui*. This view was held particularly by those who visited the United States with the aid of grants from the American government. For this reason, one might possibly question the validity of the concept, discounting it as a courteous "bread and butter" gesture toward a host. But the fact that it was so widely held and expressed with apparent sincerity, even by visitors who otherwise had fairly critical views of North American society, makes it worthy of attention.

Typical of the official grantee's sentiments are the following quotations: "I discovered an affectionate spirit of eagerness to be of service. . . . People always popped up ready to help the foreigner, especially if he was a South American." "We were received so warmly and treated so much like members of the family that we were enchanted." "The North American people, from the lowest classes to the highest, are hospitable and cordial."[12]

In an opinion survey of Mexican grantees, more of them (37 per cent) mentioned cordiality and hospitality as causing a more favorable impression of the United States than any other single item. Data from Bolivian grantees indicated similar attitudes.[13] In another study of Mexican student opinion, the respondents judged Americans more courteous to strangers than Mexicans were, and were impressed by their great friendliness. A number, however, suspected that the friendliness was superficial and that Americans

10. Merrill, p. 22.
11. Quoted in Wolfe, "Attitudes," p. 516.
12. Seoane, p. 64; Juárez y Aragón, p. 46; Velasco, p. 7; and elsewhere.
13. International Research Associates, *Study*, p. 9; Instituto Boliviano de Encuestas, p. 31.

were in fact difficult to know as "real" friends.[14] The latter reaction, incidentally, was not uncommon among student visitors from many parts of the world.

Among about eighty Mexican journalists who were asked to write opinions about the United States and whose comments were generally unfavorable, the friendly qualities of the man across the border were stressed. One newsman said, "I consider the North American a sociable, friendly person. He possesses faults of ostentation but this seems to me natural for one who lives in so wealthy and powerful a country." Another wrote, "They are very friendly persons with all foreigners, and above all, very hospitable; however, they make great errors also."[15]

There is obviously a contradiction between this picture of the friendly, helpful American and that of the haughty, disdainful *yanqui*. Such contradictions are not unusual in the images formed of foreigners. In this case, the apparent inconsistency may possibly be explained by recalling that the haughtiness of the North American was the older concept often associated with the stereotypes of economic exploitation and the tourist, while the cordiality image was more recent, arising principally from contact with North Americans in their own habitat. A few of the commentators seemed to be aware of the contradiction. Arango pointed to the difference in behavior of the North American abroad and at home. A Bolivian witness advanced an ingenious explanation; the boastfulness of the North American is more instinctive than conscious. "This inborn [*orgánico*] imperialism, is diluted, softened, reduced to dust, and lubricated by personal and social education." One can pardon the North American's superior airs because of "the spirit of refinement and courtesy, and good done for others, and the zeal for cooperation and human fellowship which the *yanqui* constantly reveals."[16]

## THE OPEN-HANDED AMERICAN

Associated at times with the idea that North Americans are friendly and helpful to foreign visitors was the fairly current conviction that they were generous. To some observers this generosity was exemplified in the American willingness to contribute to the collective welfare. A Mexican diplomat has said, "they are generous

14. Beals and Humphrey, *No Frontiers*, p. 89.
15. Merrill, p. 45.
16. Arango, p. 88; Otero, *Estados Unidos*, pp. 106–7.

and kind. They not only have brains, but they also have a heart and a very big one at that. There is no country in the world in which private individuals spontaneously give more of their money to charity and social needs." Another diplomat explained the American's charitable instinct: "It is a sense of social sharing and duty, but it often appears as a passion, which in itself brings enjoyment and reward." A Cuban journalist wrote, "It is true that everyone in the United States battles to improve his own material welfare, but most North Americans do not stint their effort to bring this welfare within the reach of all."[17]

In a few of the sources used in this study American generosity in aiding other nations has been mentioned. Quintanilla declared, "American generosity knows no frontiers." An Ecuadorian witness offered the work of the Peace Corps and the hospital ship "Hope" as examples of the generous American's altruism: "This American is the one we often do not know about," he concluded.[18]

Like most foreigners, Spanish Americans were impressed for many years by the largess of wealthy philanthropic Americans. Among the North American virtues praised by Rodó, philanthropy, however lacking in artistic taste, was included (p. 90). Rodó's contemporary and fellow Uruguayan, Zorrilla de San Martín, was enthusiastic about this aspect of the American character and cited gifts of millionaires to universities, churches, and hospitals, the gift of radium to Mme Curie, and the help in rebuilding the Louvain University library. Seoane declared, "The wealthy feel that a social duty obliges them to return part of their fortunes to the community," and he recorded an extensive list of foundations and their work.[19]

## MONEY AND MATERIALISM

A discussion of North American generosity leads almost inevitably to a consideration of one aspect of the stereotype of materialism in the United States—the role of money in the North American scale of values. Partly because of semantic confusion the debates on this matter among Spanish Americans have been abundant and sometimes hot.

17. Quintanilla, *A Latin American Speaks*, pp. 45–46; Dávila, *We of the Americas*, p. 118; Bravo, p. 83.
18. Quintanilla, p. 47; Macías, p. 8; see also Pérez Guerrero, *USA*, p. 48.
19. Zorrilla de San Martín, *Las Américas*, p. 41 (the gift to Mme Curie impressed others—see Dávila, p. 119); Seoane, pp. 92–93 (see also Núñez, *Viaje*, pp. 90–91).

Although Rodó accused the United States of living by utilitarian values, he was careful to absolve the North American from avarice or stinginess (p. 90). That the North American, in contrast to the French peasant or bourgeois of the stereotype, was not miserly (*tacaño*) became almost a platitude.[20] Another frequently expressed conventionality was the idea that the North American regards money as a means, not as an end in itself.[21]

But in spite of these qualifications, the stereotype was common and familiar that the North American was a lover of money. It was often expressed in a very general or hackneyed way—"a nation of money and things"; "money means everything"; "all Americans aspire to be millionaires"; "you join together the cult of Hercules and the cult of Mammon"; "money will buy friends"; the North American has "an exaggerated feeling about money." In Mexican popular songs the gringo thinks he can do anything with money.[22]

Some observers made a more careful and sophisticated analysis of the American's attitude toward money. Mañach believed that for Americans human dignity or happiness did not consist in having money, but that its possession was "one of the objective conditions conducive to dignity and happiness." To have money was "a sign of energy, efficiency and success." Cosío Villegas, while granting that his northern neighbor did not consider money an end in itself, noted that the North American spent so much time and energy in obtaining money that in effect it had become an end in itself. He also feared that Americans made value judgments in terms of quantity, or amounts of money. The fairly common belief that North Americans tended to judge the worth of a person or thing on a financial or other quantitative basis is probably the best-defined meaning which many Spanish Americans have had in mind when they used the epithet "materialistic."[23]

As is the case in the materialistic-uncultured equation, a number of witnesses tried to dismiss the materialistic-money stereotype as untrue or meaningless. Just after World War I, a Chilean visitor

20. Zorrilla de San Martín, p. 40; Bravo, p. 209; Merrill, p. 46; Quintanilla, p. 47.

21. See Mañach, in Joseph, p. 329; Cosío Villegas, in Joseph, p. 305; Quintanilla, p. 47.

22. Merrill, pp. 37, 15; Cestero, *Estados Unidos*, p. xix; Darío, "A Roosevelt," in Englekirk et al., *Anthology*, pp. 406–7; Instituto Boliviano de Encuestas, p. 32 (11 per cent of the Bolivian grantees agreed with this idea); Merle Simmons, p. 36.

23. Mañach, in Joseph, p. 329; Cosío Villegas, in Joseph, pp. 302, 305; Cestero, p. xii; Sánchez, *Un sudamericano*, p. 147; Zegrí, 19:93; Portilla, "La crisis," p. 72.

discarded his preconceptions of the materialistic American businessman when he realized the latter's idealistic and altruistic contributions to the war effort: "They had carried their idealism to
the point of being incorrigible dreamers, the Don Quixotes of the
world."[24] According to one point of view, North Americans were
only interested in money in order to spend it for a higher standard
of living or a more amusing life.[25] Another trend of opinion saw the
North American as no different from other people in his attitude
toward money. Quintanilla said, "Americans like money—who
does not?" And Ernesto Montenegro was cuttingly frank: "The
millionaire is nothing more, in the last analysis, than the fortunate
and envied incarnation of our own more or less concrete ambitions. Which means that in his materialism we abominate the innate vices of our own nature; we rail against his superior dynamism or against a destiny which decreed his birth in wealth. . . ."[26]

## *Yanqui* ENERGY

On one trite concept of the United States there was practically
unanimous agreement among Spanish Americans, as among most
foreigners—that it was a powerful and unbelievably prosperous
nation. As Blanco-Fombona pointed out, foreigners strove mightily
to discover the secret of such rapid development. Some North
Americans and foreigners are prone to grant a large share of credit
to the fortunate and fortuitous circumstance of living in a rich and
spacious land abounding in natural resources. This explanation,
however, was scarcely ever recorded or stressed in the sources for
this section of our study.

The Spanish American typically attributed the northern success
story in the realm of material achievement to a cluster of characteristics allegedly belonging to the North American as an individual: energy, vigor, health, devotion to work, initiative, will power,
efficiency, optimism, honesty, and the spirit of adventure. Such
terms, or their synonyms, recur over and over in the writings of
critics, friendly and unfriendly. They became something of a conventionality, even among the professional anti-imperialists.

Ugarte confessed that North Americans were "the people with
the most exuberant life and the most extraordinary vigor that I
have ever seen." "The United States were great, powerful, pros-

24. Pinochet, *Gulf*, p. 255.
25. Macías, p. 8; Merrill, p. 46; Bravo, p. 209.
26. Quintanilla, p. 47; Montenegro, p. 21.

perous, astonishingly progressive, supreme masters of energy and creative life, healthy and comfortable." García Calderón, in his anti-*yanqui* phase, was imbued with this truism: "Initiative, self-assertion, self-reliance, audacity, love of adventure, all the forces of the victorious will are united in this Republic of energy. . . . An immense impulse of creation builds cities in the wilderness and founds new plutocracies amidst the whirlpool of the market." Blanco-Fombona, in one of his less acrimonious moods, asserted that Americans do not worry about whether others imitate their ideas and tastes: "They are content to be young, healthy, strong; and youth, health, and strength are evident in them in a natural and unpremeditated way, like the charm of a harmonious statue or like the murmur of the sea."[27]

In fact, some of the anti-imperialists appeared to believe that the aggressive expansionism of the United States was the natural and inevitable outcome of the uncontainable energy and initiative of its inhabitants. Ugarte, although he devoted much of his life to preaching the dangers of the *yanqui* peril, held a deterministic attitude: "From first to last the United States, in the process of expansion, were obeying a necessity of their own safety, like the Romans in their palmy days . . . like all people overflowing with vigor."[28]

Vasconcelos, in the midst of warning about North American imperialism, also urged his readers to take heed of "the circumstances which thrust North American development forward. . . . It is clear that without the vigor of Puritanism, the very abundance [of the country] would have been sterile and there would not have been built up . . . a zone of free and happy life for many millions of men."[29]

While the warriors against materialist imperialism might express admiration for the energy of their *yanqui* opponents, critics like Rodó, whose esthetic sense was wounded by the unbounded energy of North Americans, made that trait one of their main salients of attack. Although Rodó admitted that "that extraordinary show of energy gives a certain character of epic greatness even to struggles of self-interest and material life," he was prin-

27. Ugarte, pp. 9, 11; García Calderón, *Latin America*, pp. 306–7; Blanco-Fombona, *La americanización del mundo*, p. 13.
28. Ugarte, p. 9; Francisco Bulnes expressed much the same thought (Crawford, *Century*, p. 258), as did García Calderón (p. 301).
29. Vasconcelos, *Hispanoamérica frente a los nacionalismos*, p. 94.

cipally concerned with the idea that this passion for utilitarian labor shuts out "any concern for the ideal, any disinterested employment of time, any objective of meditation above the immediate utilitarian end" (pp. 84–86).

Following in the Arielesque tradition, Manuel Gálvez, the Argentine novelist, boasted, "We possess hidden energy. But ours will not be a barbarous and automatic energy, like that which boils incessantly in the United States of North America. Ours is and will be a harmonious energy, a force tempered by Latin elegance, an intelligent impulse." For a more recent observer, Jorge Mañach, the cult of energy, a product of the frontier spirit, led to some remarkable achievements, but "imparts a certain crudeness and even a certain underlying brutality to North American life. Since Americans are bound to a preference for action . . . they concede little or no value to the contemplative life and the spiritual predilections on which it draws."[30] This is pure Rodó published in 1959.

Some commentators suggested the possibility that this mania for work, this habit of incessant activity killed the imagination, left an empty void in the personality, and brought on neuroses.[31] This point has been more fully discussed in our analysis earlier in this book of the images of the cultural and spiritual life of the United States.

## HASTE AND NOISE

Naturally associated with the picture of the energetic American, especially among the earlier generations in this century, was the commonplace that this man was always in a hurry and that he lived in a very noisy world. New York, the visitors' mecca and sometimes the only part of the United States seen, was usually the originating point or the confirmation of this stereotype. It was often a companion to the idea that North Americans were rough and ill mannered.

Darío, addressing Teddy Roosevelt, said in an oft-quoted poem, "You think that life is a house on fire,—that progress is an eruption." Speaking of New York in one of his travel notes, the poet grumbled, "I saw the omnipotence of the millionaire and was astounded at the madness of the vast capital of the bank check.

30. Manuel Gálvez, in Davis, *Social Thought*, p. 425; Mañach, in Joseph, pp. 327–28, 335.
31. For example, Labarca, in Joseph, p. 319.

Every time I have visited that land I have had the same impression. The fast pace of life upsets my nerves . . . the atmosphere of delirium has done harm to the meditations of the spirit."[32] A later writer quipped, "In New York you can't take pride in finding ways of killing time. Time hunts you down and kills you."[33]

More recent visitors have also been disturbed on occasion by the rapidity of the North Americans' daily life, but the older stereotype was challenged. Vasconcelos said in 1937, "New York today is almost a pleasant city. The city of prosperous times was crude and in a hurry; the New York of depression days was starkly sober; present-day New York almost seems like Paris. . . ." Carlos Dávila, writing in 1949, simply denied the idea: "Of the always-in-a-hurry American, proverbial abroad, I have seen very little in my twenty years in this country. The first advice any foreigner is given in the United States is to 'take it easy' and 'watch your step,' which is the American way."[34]

## FACE TO THE FUTURE

Another variation on the theme of vigor and initiative was fairly prominent in the two decades following World War II: that North Americans are in constant and restless evolution and live for the future, considering the present only a stage of experimentation. This concept often went with the conventionality that the United States was a young nation. An Ecuadorian journalist said in 1944, "This North America has not yet run its full course. . . . The North American is always seeking a new formula. . . . He does not really believe in what he has already done, but believes only in what he expects to do."[35]

More recently an Argentine educator made a similar observation: "They are a people who are incessantly working and organizing. They do not believe what they do is definitive, but transitory, and that it is always possible to improve, transform, start a new thing from scratch. I think . . . that if they should see that it were

32. Darío, in Englekirk et al., p. 426; "Viaje a Nicaragua," quoted in Marshall Nunn, "Rubén Darío y los Estados Unidos," pp. 61–62. For other testimony of the same sort, see Ugarte, pp. 10–11; López de Mesa, p. 83; Belaúnde, "Crónicas," pp. 1–2; and Cosío Villegas, "México y Estados Unidos," p. 9.

33. Zegrí, 19:93.

34. See Seoane, p. 121; Sánchez, *Un sudamericano*, p. 186; and Juárez y Aragón, p. 34; Vasconcelos, *¿Qué es la revolución?*, p. 116; Dávila, p. 139. This diplomat lamented that the former bold spirit, drive, and intensity of the American seemed to be dwindling in the post–World War II period.

35. Jorge Fernández, quoted in Dozer, *Are We Good Neighbors?*, p. 186.

possible tomorrow to build a new nation, they would do it."[36] We have seen that education in the United States was a field where the experimental nature of the North American struck the visitor with particular force.

## THE ORGANIZATION MAN

Also part of the complex of traits which the Spanish American specified as explanatory of the progress of the United States as a powerful nation was the organizing ability of its citizens. Some of the more individualistic observers, while they believed it doubtless had value, were mildly exasperated and annoyed by this trait. Germán Arciniegas, a Colombian writer, was chagrined to find that his idol, Walt Disney, was not a person but a corporation. "The American's tendency to 'incorporate himself' is irresistible. The milieu in which he lives demands it. Here nobody is a person, but a member of a club." A Mexican newsman wrote, "Your countrymen proclaim individualism to the world in loud and proud words, and then proceed to join groups, clubs, movements, and generally participate in all forms of collective activity. . . . This is certainly a paradox and one which leaves us in Latin America in clouds of bewilderment."[37]

But, for the most part, the propensity of North Americans for organization or, in the broad sense, for successful collective action was a praiseworthy and enviable trait in the minds of the witnesses. To some it has been the source of our strength. An Ecuadorian has said, "I do not hesitate to assert that this broad, powerful spirit of association and of cooperation is what has done most in the best way for the greatness of the Union." Others saw in it the mortar that had cemented together a nation from diverse elements; Dávila referred to "the countless clubs, lodges, fraternities, and other organizations which in the United States are the connective tissues joining together the far-flung population into an entity imbued with a sentiment of nationhood and aware of a common destiny. . . . The American penchant for 'joining up' has been a potent force in molding and producing the pervasive American type." Another Chilean declared, "North American gregariousness is produced spontaneously, like the grass in their meadows, by the natural need felt by the people to surmount differences so that the

36. Reissig, *Algunas observaciones*, p. 3; see also de la Torre, *Educación*, p. 18; Pinochet, p. 264; and Vasconcelos, *¿Qué es la revolución?*, p. 214.
37. Arciniegas, *En el país*, pp. 56, 77–78; Merrill, p. 40.

solidity of the nation and the personal tranquility of the individual can be maintained."[38] The benefits of the organizational mania could transcend the boundaries of the United States, according to several comments.[39]

In the thinking of many commentators, the organizational genius of the North American was in some way linked with his social discipline, his sense of civic responsibility, and his respect for law and order—qualities which were often recognized and envied. Apparently the line of thought was that through cooperation and organization an orderly kind of society ruled by law and respect for the rights of individuals was built up.[40] This point touches on the debate between conformity and individualism, which will be analyzed in some detail.

## OPTIMISM

An inevitable part of the general concept that North Americans were dynamic and industrious was the often-encountered view that they were optimistic and self-confident.[41] This trait may have seemed particularly noteworthy to the Spanish American intellectual since within his own tradition there has been a marked note of pessimism and even fatalism.

As was so frequently the case, Rodó set the tone for many twentieth-century witnesses when he wrote, "And from the concert of their civilization . . . there arises a dominant note of optimism, of confidence, of faith which swells their hearts and pushes them toward the future with the power of an obstinate and arrogant hope, the note of 'Excelsior' and the 'Psalm of Life.' "[42]

It would be an easy conclusion to attribute the optimistic streak in the American character to his residence in a rich land of many resources, and some have so concluded.[43] But others recognized a more complex relationship. A journalist from Chile put it this way: "The North American people are optimistic because they are rich, and they have gained their wealth because they are optimistic.

38. Uzcátegui, p. 15; Dávila, pp. 171–72; Velasco, p. 15.
39. Bravo, chap. 8; Velasco, p. 15.
40. Arango, p. 89; Pérez Guerrero, p. 52; Otero, p. 42.
41. For examples of general comment, see García Calderón, p. 306; Sánchez, *Un sudamericano*, p. 176; Cosío Villegas, p. 10.
42. Rodó, *Ariel*, p. 83. Longfellow's "Psalm of Life" was known to many nineteenth-century Spanish Americans.
43. Cosío Villegas, in Joseph, p. 302.

They do not ordinarily flinch at obstacles nor think about the pitfalls which may lie in their way. They have blind confidence in their pragmatism, in respect for law, and in work."[44]

At least one perceptive observer did not deny that North Americans may have moments of doubt and tribulation. He said, "This is the country of good humor and the enjoyment of life. Sadness and pessimism, which doubtless are present, are borne by each individual tucked away in some secret cell within him. The national characteristic is optimism and everybody tries to show that he is satisfied and happy."[45]

It has been a commonplace among self-analysts in the United States that the threat of atomic destruction and growing internal dissension have robbed their countrymen of their traditional optimism. Spanish American visitors, on the whole, were chary of agreeing with this new platitude. One witness stated that in spite of that threat and the ever present danger of serious war, "the American people keep a steady heart and wait; . . . they have not been raised for war but for happiness and peace." The Mexican poet Octavio Paz made his own special analysis in 1959: "It is true that this faith in the natural goodness of life, or in its infinite wealth of possibilities cannot be found in recent North American literature, which prefers to depict a much more somber world, but I found it in the actions, the words, and even the faces of almost everyone I met." Since the dangers of nuclear annihilation have become apparent, "The North Americans have lost their optimism, but not their confidence, a confidence based on resignation and obstinacy. The truth is that although many people talk about the danger, secretly no one believes—no one wants to believe—that it is real and immediate."[46]

### THE HONEST AMERICAN

A final strand in the pattern of North American civic virtues has been the personal and public honesty of these strange northerners. The evidence on this point is nearly unanimous. Even among the earlier commentators of the century complete honesty in business deals was noted, although the logic of Vargas Vila's philippic against imperialism demanded a collective villain lacking in good

44. Velasco, p. 10.
45. Otero, pp. 107–8.
46. Reissig, p. 19; Paz, *Labyrinth*, p. 22.

faith: "Never has the United States made a pact with us whose purpose has not been to give itself the barbarous pleasure of violating it."[47]

Typical of more recent comments are the following: "One can trust him; when he says a thing, he does it." "Lying is repugnant to him, as a form of cowardice." Referring to the average college student, "his sense of worth is related to his habit of not lying, which he finds an unnecessary trick since he is strong in body and soul." "If the North American answers 'yes,' it is because he is making a true statement; if he says 'no,' he means it. . . . There is a manly sense of responsibility; in short, there is great moral integrity."[48]

Many visitors were impressed with the relative infrequency of petty thievery in the United States, remarking on the absence of iron grillwork and high walls in homes and the fact that milk and newspapers were left unprotected on the front doorstep.[49] Forty-five per cent of a group of Mexican grantees declared that they had found individual honesty better than they had anticipated, and 50 per cent said it was as they had expected.[50]

In a more qualified form, the idea was prevalent that this moral integrity extended into public and political life. A group of Mexican students were struck by the absence of the *mordida* (bribery) system among government officials, although some suspected that bribery took place only when large sums were involved.[51] Mañach stated, "Illicit influence and unwarranted immunity thrive in the United States only so long as they are not uncovered to public opinion, which is usually very alert and is assisted by a press much more independent than is sometimes supposed."[52]

Possibly finding here a contrast to moral patterns in his own country, Subercaseaux said of North American honesty, "we also admire it, but we believe that wealth and a life without pressing necessities makes honesty easier" (p. 263).

47. Pinochet, p. 266; Vargas Vila, p. 186.
48. Bravo, p. 209; Mañach, in Joseph, p. 330; Sánchez, *Un sudamericano*, p. 173; Subercaseaux, pp. 234, 238.
49. See Reissig, pp. 27–28; Subercaseaux, pp. 233–34; and Mujica Laínez, "An Argentine's USA," p. 16.
50. International Research Associates, p. 8.
51. Beals and Humphrey, p. 85; see also International Research Associates, p. 8.
52. Mañach, in Joseph, p. 333.

## BIG CHILDREN

Possibly related in the Spanish American mind to the traits of honesty and buoyant optimism was the youthful ingenuousness so often attributed to the American character. "Americans are just like big children" seems to have become almost a proverbial expression among sophisticates and ordinary citizens alike.[53] It was accompanied by varied and sometimes conflicting reactions on the part of our Spanish American critics.

Some believed that because of our alleged naïveté we had been taken in and imposed upon by foreigners. A Chilean journalist described us as "a simple people who know so little about so much" and who are bewildered by the torrents of criticism from abroad. Luis Alberto Sánchez sympathized with North Americans when, with their confident ingenuousness, they launched on great enterprises abroad and failed after being deceived.[54]

We have previously noted that a Mexican observer based his whole analysis of America's spiritual crisis on his view of us as "innocent," that is, naïve and unwilling to face the realities of an evil world. As he saw it, the philosophy of pragmatism means essentially that its believers are convinced that all must come out well in the end. American fascination with psychoanalysis is an ingenious attempt to sidestep man's basically sinful nature, as are the sexually permissive implications of such studies as the Kinsey report. The crisis, he claimed, came when the United States had to face up to the baleful realities of the outside world; it then naïvely tried to impose its childish moral views on other countries, hence the strongly anti-Communist strain in our foreign relations. While this construct is a very Latin intellectual tour de force, it reflects faithfully enough a fairly current image.[55]

Other judicious observers warned their countrymen that the naïve manner of the North American may be deceptive. According to one: "The North American people are sharp and smart. But overlaying the sharpness and the ability there is a coat of good faith and simplicity. The result is that at times their reflections and thoughts strike us as superficial [*exabruptos*]."[56]

53. Ibid., p. 330; Sánchez, *Un sudamericano*, p. 318; and Otero, p. 106. Thirty-eight per cent of a group of Bolivian grantees considered North Americans ingenuous (Instituto Boliviano de Encuestas, p. 33).
54. Velasco, p. 9; Sánchez, *Un sudamericano*, p. 318.
55. Portilla, passim.
56. Velasco, p. 30; Sánchez emphasized that North Americans are by no

Sometimes the ingenuousness of the North American was contrasted with the *picardía* of the Latin American. The latter term is not easy to translate, which in itself may be significant. *Picardía* refers to actions or words which may be mildly malicious, devious, clever, deceptive, and often wryly humorous. Reissig remarked, "From the standpoint of Latin *picardía* [the American] can look like a naïve country bumpkin, but there is nothing stupid about him."[57] It is apparent that here we are dealing with a difference in social mores because of which Spanish Americans were likely to view their northern neighbor with a mixture of amused compassion and wariness.

## THE ENJOYMENT OF LIFE

In spite of the general respect for and even envy of the confident dynamism of the North American, the Spanish American often suspected that this energetic, hard-working neighbor did not really enjoy life, or as it is popularly phrased, *"no sabe vivir la vida."*[58] This concept has little to do with sports or amusements. Even the man-in-the-street is well aware of the American's addiction to baseball, football, boxing, etc., especially as a spectator. His daily paper often gives abundant coverage to *yanqui* sports, and in the Caribbean countries, baseball and to some extent basketball have become national pastimes.[59] Visitors sometimes expressed satisfaction about the beneficial results of sports. The Colombian Arango stated, "The people of the United States are gay and very fond of sports, of exercising their bodies and spirits. . . . The inherent advantages of sports are tremendous . . . because they lead to that equilibrium of body and spirit so helpful for the normal development of the individual."[60] The motion picture and television, as we have seen, became in the popular mind almost synonymous with the American way of life; sophisticated commentators were prone to assess their artistic quality or moral effects rather than consider them as simple amusements of the American people.

---

means easy marks in business. This continues a stereotype common in the nineteenth century—that of the sharp Yankee trader (*Un sudamericano*, pp. 181–82).

57. Reissig, p. 5; see also Subercaseaux, p. 257.

58. Bravo, p. 209.

59. See Wolfe, p. 522, for data on American sports in the Latin American press.

60. Arango, pp. 75–77; see also his comment on university sports in the section above on education.

The highbrow critic generally found the North American's diversions infantile and silly. The same Colombian who valued sports in American life so highly painted a grim picture of workers in the United States coming from their mechanized work at factory or office so weary and benumbed that they can only indulge in the most simple and childlike pastimes. Subercaseaux pontificated in a similar vein: "passion and biological or sentimental pleasures have been sublimated in work or in innocent amusements which seem flat and tasteless to us." An Argentine found the happy smile of the American to be deceptive: "In the United States there is no happiness of spirit, but the spasm of pleasure is highly regarded; consequently, the joy of their facial expression is false."[61]

Beyond these generalities, those who judged the North American's capacity for enjoyment to be imperfect were not very explicit in their criticism, and they even contradicted one another on occasion. One line of speculation concerned food. A great many visitors confessed that the typical North American diet seemed tasteless and insufficient to them. An Argentine physician, noticing that an office worker lunched on "a miserable sandwich of black bread, lettuce, and tomato," topped off with a vitamin pill, exclaimed that "a dog would have scorned such a banquet!" Luis Alberto Sánchez believed that, in contrast to the French and Chinese, Americans take no real pleasure in eating. They eat only to nourish themselves, he reported sadly, while South Americans consider sitting down to a meal as one of life's joys, to be savored leisurely and with lively conversation.[62]

Another exploratory path into this field of the North American's pleasure in life led to his attitude toward sex. Here opinions were confused and divided. A Chilean man of the world was firmly convinced that North Americans hate and try to ignore sexual life: "they have succeeded in shoving sensuality from the conscious mind, thus making sex a primitive, savage zone grafted into civilized life, which appears to ignore it. Ogling girls, forbidden fruit, the savor of pleasure, risqué conversation—nothing of that exists here." At the other end of the spectrum of opinion, there were a few who conceived of the North American as obsessed with sex. An Argentine physician, for example, emphasized in the record of

---

61. Ibid., p. 81; Subercaseaux, p. 263; Ayres, *Estados Unidos*, p. 157.

62. Ayres, p. 74 (see also Subercaseaux, pp. 77–79, for a particularly plaintive gastronomic lament); Sánchez, *Un sudamericano*, p. 117. For a dissident opinion holding that Americans relax in restaurants and enjoy their leisure, see Otero, p. 94.

his visit to the United States the pornographic publications, the promiscuous love-making in public parks, prostitution, and the mania for sexual rejuvenation.[63]

Considerably more moderate and subtle was the analysis of Gustavo Otero. According to him, Americans, in spite of their sober discipline, have a passion for living and pleasure; they are in no sense ascetics. "*Yanqui* will power," he said, "is linked with strong sensuality and sexuality." The presence of an official puritanical moral code is in itself proof of a powerful undercurrent of sensuality. The pressure of sex, he believed, is continually evident in American life, even though it often may seem covered with "a thick layer of ice" and sublimated in cultural activities.[64]

The fact that we find ambivalent attitudes toward the sensuality of the North American probably indicates that the observers at least recognized a mode or expression of instinctive passion different from their own. One witness attempted to contrast the external vitality of the northerner with the more deeply embedded and "intimate" sensuality of the Spanish American. Another was of the opinion that the difference lies in the more luxuriantly imaginative and emotional nature of Spanish American sensuality.[65]

A third area in which *yanqui* joie de vivre seemed anemic to his hemispheric neighbors was that of *ocio*, which may be roughly translated as productive leisure. It became almost a cliché that North Americans are unable to enjoy doing nothing. Rodó made this proposition a cardinal point in his attack on the quality of American civilization, and in subsequent years it cropped up from time to time. Germán Arciniegas was mildly irritated, for example, when he found that a neighbor in California was sun-bathing as a duty, not as an opportunity for leisurely meditation. Observers often remarked on the absence of sidewalk café life, so dear to Latin urban dwellers, as an unmistakable sign of the busy American's neglect of the art of thoughtful and enjoyable living. A friendly Ecuadorian summarized the matter quite simply when he lamented that in the United States work cannot be interrupted to savor the beauty of a sunrise or sunset or merely to indulge in an interval of daydreaming.[66]

As a footnote, it may be added that not every witness was a

63. Subercaseaux, pp. 141–42, 214–15 (this witness seems to have been especially preoccupied with sex); Ayres, passim.

64. Otero, pp. 103–4.

65. Reissig, p. 14; Otero, p. 103.

66. Arciniegas, p. 76; Subercaseaux, p. 123, and Arciniegas, p. 77; Pérez Guerrero, p. 48.

worshipper of the *ocio* ideal. An Argentine educator, remarking on the decline of vagabond brotherhood in the United States, said of the loafer, "*Ocio* delights his soul. This business about the creative power of *ocio* is a delusion. *Ocio* does not create anything. The truth is that he is not very fond of work."[67]

Although this somewhat topsy-turvy speculation about our ability to enjoy life may seem trivial or unimportant to the North American reader, it touched in fact on one of the sensitive and significant areas of the Spanish Americans' image of the citizen of the United States. They were apt to magnify the differences between the leisure-time patterns of the two cultures. Vasconcelos said, "there exists a deep, important difference between the peoples of Latin America and the people of Anglo-Saxon America. The difference is so much more important because it is a difference of a spiritual sort. Perhaps it lies in the manner of feeling and in the manner of expressing our feelings of life. It is in the type of our higher desires and in the manner we go about our pleasures that we can best distinguish one from the other."[68]

In the Spanish American mind the inability to enjoy life in a proper fashion was part and parcel of the whole emptiness-of-life theme which we have previously examined.

## ROBOT OR INDIVIDUALIST?

One of the questions about the American character which has puzzled the Spanish American observer most has been whether the average North American was an individualist with a true personality, or whether he was simply a cog in a machine, one of a great flock of identical sheep. The question was of absorbing interest to the observer because his own self-image was that of an indomitable and proud defender of his unique personality. He usually approached the North American phenomenon with preconceptions, especially if he had been an assiduous reader of Ortega y Gasset, one of the revered mentors of the Spanish American intellectual. The ordinary feeling was that since the United States was the country of mass production and mechanization par excellence, its citizens were therefore robots who all acted and looked alike, devoid of any individuality.

And indeed the initial impression of the visitor from the South seemed to confirm his preconception. His first experiences were al-

67. Reissig, p. 12.
68. Gamio and Vasconcelos, *Aspects of Mexican Civilization*, p. 19.

most always on the eastern seaboard where the physical environment would strike him as monotonous; city streets and buildings at first glance lacked variety, chain stores of all kinds offered the same merchandise; food (which he often finds insipid anyway) was monotonously uniform. People seemed to dress alike, talk alike (unintelligibly, he frequently discovered), and even think alike. He may have concluded that advertising, which seemed to be everywhere—on billboards, in the subway, in the mass media—had hypnotized Americans to the point that they obeyed their master with regimented regularity.[69]

As he became more familiar with the American scene and especially if he traveled about the country, his preconceptions commonly began to crumble. He discovered the vast variety of the American landscape and climate. The town of the Middle West was quite different from the eastern city. And, most significant of all, he sometimes realized that *Homo sapiens* in the United States breaks down into a number of varieties and that many Americans could be stubbornly individualistic. He saw that the schools placed great emphasis on the development of a child's individual personality, and that the human dignity spoken of in patriotic documents was translated by the man in the neighborhood bar into profane affirmations of his rights as a citizen and human being.[70]

These circumstances seemed to present to our witnesses an enigma. On the one hand, there was no denying the mechanization of life in *yanqui*-land with the consequent trend toward standardization of living habits. Some witnesses simply clung to this stereotype and issued ominous warnings. One said, "The American is becoming the product of the intensive mechanization which characterized modern industrialization." In the end, the routine of factory production "undermines the worker's spirit, destroying his personality, his individualism, cutting off any initiative in his work."[71]

Others were satisfied to halt in this wasteland under the shelter of the commonplace that North Americans had buried their individuality in collective activity and living. An Argentine, noting the tremendous variation in highly individualized human types in Mexico, wrote, "In contrast we can without exaggeration say we

69. Impressions of this sort are set forth in Arango, pp. 27–29; Mañach, in Joseph, p. 337; Bravo, p. 45; Merrill, p. 15; Otero, p. 110; and in a number of other sources.

70. The diversity of the United States is noted in Seoane, p. 255; de la Torre, p. 2; and Sánchez, *Un sudamericano*, p. 92.

71. Arango, pp. 81–83.

are unable to distinguish one American from another, not because they are machine-made men . . . but because in the United States a man is not trained and developed to become an individual, but to be a member of the community."[72]

But other more inquisitive commentators sought to reconcile the North American's obvious zeal for the cultivation of personal individual talents and his cult of protecting individual rights with his equally obvious eagerness for collective activities. Recognizing the apparent paradox, Luis Alberto Sánchez said, "If anyone in the world has the habit of collective life, it is the American citizen; and at the same time, if anyone has developed a sense of individualism to an excess, it is the American." Another discriminating observer noted that the apparent uniformity obscured a great variety of nonmaterial traits and increased the difficulty of interpreting the United States. The "atomization of personal life peculiar to the Protestant style of living" exists with certain common patterns of behavior which, however elastic, outlaw extreme eccentricity by a "gentleman's agreement."[73]

Some of the more nimble observers believed they had solved the riddle with their discovery that the real aim of the passion for collective action was simply to provide United States citizens with the most favorable conditions for freely developing and exercising their individualism. A Cuban journalist, Nicolás Bravo, was impressed by "the will to individual perfection and the will to collective improvement," the specific aim of collective life being "to enable man to become cultivated, to develop his principle of individualism." Mañach called this arrangement "cooperative social individualism." A Bolivian art critic expressed the same idea: "They naturally value highly the citizen's rights, but they value more the rights and duties of society towards the citizen, the organized group being placed at the service of the individual."[74]

This same witness declared that the anarchic individualism of the Spanish American finds this delicate balance bothersome and uncomfortable, and the Chilean Subercaseaux categorically stated that the Spanish American "would never consent to give up his personal liberty, even though it were held at the cost of collective advantages" (p. 255). However true this may be, we are surely dealing here with another of those deep-seated cultural differences between Spanish and Anglo-America, one which projects in the

72. Reissig, p. 6.
73. Sánchez, *Un sudamericano*, p. 177; Mendoza, *Panorama*, pp. 11–12.
74. Bravo, p. 82; Otero, p. 37.

southern mind an image of the United States that is difficult to clarify and that is composed of a mixed reaction of admiration and impatience.

It would be artistically satisfying to be able to brush off the lint, trim the edges a bit, and display in summary a neatly woven, harmoniously patterned tapestry that would clearly represent the total picture of the *yanqui* in the Spanish American mind, as designed by a group of its articulate representatives. It must be apparent by now that this is not possible.

The image of the North American character as put together by our witnesses has been as a whole blurred, inconsistent, and spotted with internal contradictions. Most images of a foreign national character can be described in this fashion, and it seems natural and inevitable that this should be so. Such concepts are composed of a sloppy mixture of conventional stereotypes, old wives' tales, and sketchy impressions derived from short visits to the United States or from miscellaneous North American acquaintanceships—all colored by emotional comparisons with mores and problems at home.

A few spots in the composite picture are relatively clear and cleanly drawn. There is fairly unanimous agreement that the *yanqui* is energetic and industrious, generous, optimistic, honest, and blessed with a notable ability to organize and join in collective endeavor. For the most part, these qualities are admired and, in some cases, envied.

In the case of other traits there is less of a consensus but more disapproval. The older concept of the haughty American clashes with the idea that he is hospitable and friendly. In any event, his ignorance of the realities of Spanish American life and culture is colossal and lamentable. He is probably materialistic in some undefined way, but nevertheless he is a free spender and does not seem to love money for its own sake. However, even among the more objective analysts there is a lingering fancy that the Spanish Americans prize material goods less than we do.

A number of areas in the composite image present confusing questions rather than clear-cut assertions. Is the North American truly naïve? Does he have any real fun in life? Is he always in a hurry or can he enjoy leisure? Is he an individualist or a pitiable automaton and conformist?

It is doubtless significant that these blurred spots where the Spanish Americans have vacillated in their judgment and were uncertain about the answers are precisely those where the problems of intimate living of the two cultures seem to be most at variance: *picardía* vs. youthful frankness; love of stimulating and vociferous conversation vs. laconic reserve; appreciation of sensual joys and beauty vs. busy preoccupation with the job to be done; an extreme devotion to the individual without great regard for society's demands vs. a complicated melding of individual rights with the collective good. These confrontations are themselves stereotyped generalities, but surely it is around these contrasts, however they are phrased, that Spanish Americans feel uncomfortable, disoriented, and sometimes antagonistic when faced with the North American and his way of life.

# 12

# Summary Reflections

$A$ny generalizations that may be made on the basis of the material in the preceding pages must, of course, be considered in the light of the study's limitations, as outlined in the introduction. Particularly pertinent is the question of how representative of general Spanish American opinion are the observations analyzed in this survey. I repeat my conviction that they are generally typical of the thinking of the educated classes in most of the Spanish American republics. My conviction is reinforced, at least for the modern period, by personal acquaintance with many Spanish Americans during a number of years residence in six of the republics. Much of what has been set forth in the preceding chapters could be closely correlated with oral expressions of the same themes, had a tape-recorder been at hand.

Probably the first general proposition that we may safely make is that expressed interest in the United States and its civilization among Spanish American writers has been constant and uninterrupted from Independence days to 1960. In spite of their intellectual and sometimes emotional allegiance to France, or on occasion to Spain, the northern Union, for various reasons, was a continuous source of fascination. Sometimes the fascination stemmed from a search for models, political or economic; for others it was akin to that experienced by a man observing a dangerous animal or reptile; in still other witnesses simple curiosity in the face of a strange and alien culture was the enticement.

A summary statement by a Mexican philosopher, Leopoldo Zea, may help to explain the persistence of this powerful attraction: "Possibly one cannot find in history an example of how one people can be in the consciousness of another people like that of the United States in the consciousness of the Hispanic American peoples. . . . Sometimes North America symbolizes the finest model of their ideals; at other times she stands as the supreme negation of those ideals, as their betrayal. Among other things, North America has also been for Hispanic America the source of its feeling of inferiority. North America has been the ideal never realized by Hispanic America."[1]

A second generalization is more hazardous but, I believe, tenable: In spite of fluctuating changes in the international scene and the transformation of many aspects of American society, the Spanish American image of the United States has changed in essence relatively little during the years covered in this survey. We have seen that fear of American aggrandizement was not absent even in the years of Spanish American independence; since then the curve of concern has followed fairly closely the ups and downs of American aggressive action. Admiration, if not envy, of American political institutions and processes, perhaps at its height in the early years of the nineteenth century, has abated very little over the years, even though closer observation has qualified it. The image of a nation lacking for the most part in appreciation for the finer nuances of culture as understood by our witnesses has been a constant one, albeit complicated in recent decades by the addition of more intricate considerations. The American character, conceived of as industrious, energetic, and optimistic, has remained largely unchanged in Spanish American eyes. Even our egregious faults have persisted with remarkable stability in the minds of most commentators. We have been and continue to be pathologically conscious of money, arrogant, often ill mannered and bumptious; these traits are said to coexist with an immature naïveté.

Such persistence of an image or a group of images, in spite of apparent changes in actual circumstances, is found to be not uncommon in the process of international image-making. It may be, of course, that a nation's character or style of culture is indeed basically stable and that foreigners' images reflect that fact. In my opinion, it is more likely that the images become part of folk or literary tradition passed on from generation to generation and thus are more or less resistant to drastic modification, even among eye-witnesses and in the face of perceptible changes. In his excellent study of French opinion of the United States in the early nineteenth century, Réné Rémond dwells at length on the relative sta-

1. *América como conciencia*, p. 135.

bility of the images he has described, attributing this phenomenon to the powerful influence of a few preceding commentators. Holding preconceptions derived from them, later witnesses often tend to see images which confirm those preconceptions. Rémond displays as an example of this process Chateaubriand's picture of a virgin, innocent America as a strong image reflected in later pictures.[2]

In the third place, it is apparent that throughout the period of this study, the nature of Spanish American images of the United States was determined in part by the interests and the national problems of Spanish America, and the shifting currents of fashionable thought among its intellectuals. I need recall only a few illustrative examples. During the wars for independence and the early republican days observers were almost exclusively interested in the political structure of the northern republic, since they themselves were engaged in drafting plans for their new states. Their picture of the northern model—a result of wishful thinking among many—was usually rosy and omitted imperfections and existing or latent difficulties. As time went on and the material underdevelopment of their new republics was contrasted with the burgeoning growth in the North, their attention was particularly concentrated on those aspects of American institutions and national character that seemed to explain such prosperity and could perhaps be imitated. This attitude was part and parcel of general intellectual trends toward an empiricism and positivism borrowed from contemporary Europe.

We have seen how racist dogma contributed in various ways to the formation of images of the United States, but probably the most striking example of how intellectual currents influenced the picture of the northern republic has been the potency of the search for national identity so salient in Latin America in the first decades of this century. Not only did the direction of that search postulate a chasm between the two Americas, but it seemed to require an image of the northern colossus as lacking in the refined culture, delicacy, and humanistic concern that—according to theory—was the patrimony of Latin America.

In this connection it is opportune to emphasize the influence of French observers of the United States on many of our commentators, especially in the nineteenth century. Tocqueville, of course, was seen as almost inspired scripture for several generations, as has been noted in parts of this survey. In the first part of the nine-

2. *Les Etats-Unis*, pp. 252–57.

teenth century numerous French writers, both liberal and royalist, made a point in their comments on the United States of decrying the growing money-madness and the materialism, bad manners, and general inability of Americans to appreciate the finer and more exquisite pleasures of proper living.[3] Such travelers as the Comtesse de Merlin, Victor Jacquemont, Félix de Beaujour, and Michel Chevalier, for example, remarked on these flaws in American society, and there is good reason to believe that some Spanish Americans followed their lead.

As a matter of fact, there is persuasive evidence to indicate that the well-known Ariel-Caliban antithesis, the contrasting of a spiritual Latin America and an awkward, materialistic North America, derived ultimately from French sources. In the 1850s, partly at the instigation of Michel Chevalier, France adopted the doctrines of Pan Latinism as part of her foreign policy. This ideology pitted the Anglo-Saxon bloc or "race" (including the United States) against the Latin bloc or "race" (including Latin America). Among the tenets of its adherents, which were disseminated to Spanish America through the *Revista Española de Ambos Mundos* and the *Revue des Races Latines*, was the idea that while Anglo-Saxons may be superior in gross material civilization, the Latin tradition excelled in esthetic achievement and "spiritual" culture. As we saw in chapter six, men like Francisco Bilbao, Juan Manuel Carrasco Albano, and Benjamín Vicuña Mackenna echoed this racial confrontation in terms unmistakably drawn from French propagandists for Pan Latinism, applying it to the two parts of the New World.[4] The defeat of Latin Spain by the northern Cyclops in 1898 awakened again this sense of racial solidarity against the Anglo-Saxon enemy. As one aspect of this awakening Rodó framed his Ariel-Caliban metaphor; he again was deeply influenced by French writers of the nineteenth century.

France's cultural hegemony declined after World War I, and it would seem that a good deal more truly independent thought has characterized attitudes toward the United States in this century.

A final and fairly obvious conclusion is that many if not most of the commentators cited in this study display an ambivalent attitude toward the United States. Here, particularly, they are surely representative of both their educated confreres and the man-in-the-street. In the nineteenth century amazed admiration for the physi-

3. Ibid., pp. 512, 648, 678, 682, 764–65.
4. See John Leddy Phelan, "Pan Latinism, French Intervention in Mexico, and the Genesis of the Idea of Latin America," pp. 279–98.

cal and political progress of the northern Union was usually counterbalanced by dislike and fear of its imperialistic design and its uncouth materialism. In the twentieth century we have noted the frequently puzzled and ambivalent state of mind when Spanish Americans meditated on the American character: Is it materialistic or idealistic? Is it individualistic or sadly merged with the herd? Is it haughty and arrogant or warm and hospitable?

This double viewpoint is evident in the reactions of Justo Sierra, a well-known Mexican statesman, educator, and historian, who visited the United States in 1895. He recorded his impressions in a delightful book, *En tierra yankee*.[5] It is replete with contradictory attitudes toward the civilization he found in the North—all quite honestly and simply set forth. Like so many of his Spanish-speaking contemporaries, Sierra was overwhelmed by his northern neighbors' frantic activity, which, as he said, would be sufficient to light up a quarter of our planet, if transformed into electrical energy. "What a lovely and terrible life is this of the Yankees!" he agreed with Herbert Spencer, who had advised Americans just to sit down quietly for a while. Sierra was, however, an enthusiastic admirer of American universities such as Chicago, presumably a result of this intense energy, and prophesied that they would place the United States among the great creative nations of Western civilization.

Sierra wholeheartedly enjoyed what the United States had to offer in the way of the good life—oysters and fine wines at the Hoffman house, the art of Louis Comfort Tiffany, and the elegance of the women, but he could not put his finger on the reason why "shortly afterwards, it becomes cloying."

He called Washington "the center of the republican transformation of the Christian world," but at the same time he could not forget or forgive American injustice toward his homeland or the deep social divisions within the Union, with its oligarchical concentration of wealth.

As he went home, crossing the Rio Grande, leaving "the country of liberty," he felt paradoxically that he was recovering his freedom: "the intense activity, the enormous work of this people . . . had affected me like hundreds of pounds of steel on my chest." Such pessimistic thoughts, he meditated, were probably the result of reading books about the United States, and he tried to refine his own summary judgment: "I caught a glimpse of a great people . . . and I became convinced that liberty is breathable air." His

5. Sierra, *Obras completas*, 6:3, 78, 82, 118–20, 173, 189, 190.

emotions seemed divided between admiration and incompatibility. At the end of his very readable account he said good-bye to the land of the colossal and anticipated with pleasure the huts and the slow, negligent people of his homeland, sweating in a soft and enervating climate. They have chosen, he thought, life's better part, singing in the sunlight. When all is said and done, that was preferable to the *yanqui* ant-hill.

# Appendixes

To attempt to estimate the nature of these stereotypes from the material available is a risky business. But we can make an attempt, giving fair warning that the result will be a composite, synthetic picture, which can make no pretence of having much validity for any particular group of people in any specific time or place.

Many of the witnesses introduced in this study, as they express their opinions about man and his world in the northern republic, sometimes refer specifically to the common opinion on this or that matter which the writer had formerly shared with his neighbors at home. These remarks provide evidence of some value for this study.[1] North American commentators on the Spanish American scene occasionally try to formulate the picture of the United States which, in their opinion, is the prevalent one in Latin or Spanish America. These are data which one must use with caution.[2] The portrayal of the *yanqui* in Spanish American literature, including the Mexican popular ballads, often presents a conventionalized view of the North American which may be related to the popular

1. Such evidence is found in Luis Alberto Sánchez, *Un sudamericano en Norteamérica*, pp. 30–36, 50, 76, 144; Quintanilla, pp. 39–40; Seoane, p. 64; Arango, p. 80; Pérez Guerrero, pp. 9–12; extensive material of this sort is found in Pinochet, passim.

2. For example: Beals, *What the South Americans Think of Us*, passim; Haring, *South America Looks at the United States*, pp. 134–36; Humphrey, "Mexican Image," pp. 116–17; Radler, *El Gringo*, pp. 22–24 and passim.

image.[3] A few opinion surveys of special groups yield some information useful for our purpose.[4] A content analysis of Latin American newspapers provides more doubtful data.[5] The two general public opinion surveys consulted, restricted to Mexico, give almost no data of value for the purpose at hand.[6] Combining somewhat arbitrarily the evidence available in these sources, we can develop a composite stereotype.

The United States is a great world power which either has imperialistic designs on Latin America, or is ignorant and neglectful of that continent, or both. Its cities are enormous and its way of life highly mechanized. Its standard of living is very high.

As a person, the North American is tall and broad-shouldered, energetic and enterprising, blond, blue-eyed, wealthy and in love with his money, very practical and hard-working. He dresses in eccentric fashions and is fond of whiskey and of smoking a pipe or a fat cigar. He is a Protestant and probably, in reality, irreligious. He is conceited, arrogant, cold, disdainful to Latin Americans, and often rude and unmannerly. He (as well as his civilization) is essentially lacking in culture. The American woman is also tall and inclined to be athletic. She is a platinum blonde, free and even loose in her morals, who either henpecks her husband or divorces him with the greatest of ease.

It is apparent that some parts of this composite picture are derived from generalized notions about American tourists and businessmen; others are the product of the average American motion picture; still others doubtless stem from the daily press or from propaganda from Communist and other sources unfriendly to the United States.

If this is truly a widespread and popular image at the present time, it is somewhat disconcerting to review the results of the few public opinion surveys available. In a survey of the attitudes of 1,125 Mexican adults, 31 per cent believed that the United States was the society which offered the best kind of life for them, and North Americans were the foreign people toward whom the largest group of those interviewed felt most friendly.[7] When a group of Mexican children was asked what other nationality they would

3. See Urist, "Portrait of the Yanqui," and Piper, "El Yanqui."
4. Beals and Humphrey, Merrill, and O. Simmons.
5. Wolfe, "Attitudes."
6. International Public Opinion Research reported in William Buchanan and Hadley Cantril, *How Nations See Each Other*, p. 78; a later survey by the same organization: "A Report on Attitudes, etc.," mimeographed, 2 vols.
7. "A Report on Attitudes," passim.

choose for themselves, if they were not Mexicans, 42 per cent of the boys and 29 per cent of the girls chose United States citizenship.[8] According to the results of interviews among some forty representative Chileans, Americans, along with some Europeans, are highly thought of in Chile.[9] In a questionnaire administered to about twenty-five rural people in Guatemala, North Americans ranked highest as the foreign employers preferred by them, even though the United States was considered very imperialistic by the same group.[10] An opinion survey of seventy-eight Panamanian law students revealed that 25 per cent of the extremely nationalistic segment (vociferous supporters of Fidel Castro) liked North Americans and 48 per cent of a more moderate group liked us.[11]

In relation to the composite image, such results raise puzzling questions which only serve to underscore the hazards involved in getting at the opinion of the "man-in-the-street" about the United States. As a matter of fact, it would appear that in Mexico and perhaps in other countries the popular mind is schizophrenic in its attitude toward the United States.[12] Much evidence points to a widespread dislike of North Americans and their way of life. On the other hand, as Oscar Lewis has made abundantly clear, the rising middle class in Mexico and even some of the lower sectors try to imitate the habits and material life of their neighbors to the North.[13] Mexican folk ballads also reveal this ambivalent attitude. Traditionally they are peppered with animosity toward the gringo, but they also sing of the United States as an idealized, prosperous land of high wages and the good life.[14]

8. Oscar Lewis, "Mexico since Cárdenas," pp. 294–95.
9. Silvert, *The Conflict Society*, p. 235.
10. Ibid., pp. 43–44.
11. Goldrich, *Radical Nationalism*, p. 39.
12. See Robert J. Alexander, *Today's Latin America*, pp. 239–40, who states that this schizophrenic attitude is common among all Latin Americans.
13. Oscar Lewis, *Five Families*, pp. 8–9 and passim.
14. M. Simmons, "Attitudes," pp. 37–38.

## APPENDIX 2: TRANSLATIONS OF IMPORTANT UNITED STATES POLITICAL DOCUMENTS

FEDERAL CONSTITUTION

Caracas (?), 1798 (Juan Picornell; see Robertson, *Relations*, p. 64).*
Bogotá, 1811 (Manuel de Pombo).
Philadelphia, 1811 (in Manuel García de Sena, *La Independencia de la Costa Firme justificada por Thomas Paine* . . .).
Bogotá, 1811 (an explanation in Nariño's *La Bagatela*).
Philadelphia, 1821 (in Vicente Rocafuerte, *Ideas necesarias a todo pueblo que quiere ser libre*).
New York, 1823 (in Rocafuerte, *Ensayo político*).

DECLARATION OF INDEPENDENCE

Bogotá, 1811 (in Pombo, *Constitución de los Estados Unidos de América*).
Philadelphia, 1811 (García de Sena).

VARIOUS STATE CONSTITUTIONS

Philadelphia, 1811 (García de Sena).

ARTICLES OF CONFEDERATION

Bogotá, 1811 (in Pombo, *Constitución*).
Philadelphia, 1811 (García de Sena).
Philadelphia, 1821 (in Rocafuerte, *Ideas necesarias*).
New York, 1823 (in Rocafuerte, *Ensayo político*).

WASHINGTON'S "FAREWELL ADDRESS"

Santiago de Chile, 1812 (in Camilo Henríquez, *Aurora de Chile*).
Buenos Aires, 1813 (Manuel Belgrano).
New York, 1823 (in Rocafuerte, *Ensayo político*).

ADDRESSES OF JOHN QUINCY ADAMS

Santiago de Chile, 1812 (the July 4, 1811, address; in Henríquez, *Aurora de Chile*).
Philadelphia, 1821 (the July 4, 1821, address; in Rocafuerte, *Ideas necesarias*).

THOMAS PAINE

Caracas, 1810 (Juan G. Roscío; *Rights of Man*).
Caracas, 1811 (in *Gaceta de Caracas*, Roscío, excerpts from *Rights of Man*).
Philadelphia, 1811 (García de Sena; *Common Sense*).
Caracas, 1812 (in *Gaceta de Caracas*; García de Sena; extracts from *Common Sense*).
Santiago de Chile, 1812 (in Henríquez, *Aurora de Chile*; various excerpts).
Lima, 1821 (Anselmo Nateice, *Reflecciones políticas escritas bajo el título de Instinto Común*).
Philadelphia, 1821 (Santiago Felipe Puglia, *El derecho del hombre*).

*Name of translator or compiler in parentheses.

## APPENDIX 3: SOME ANTI–UNITED STATES NOVELS

| Author | Nationality | Title | Date | Subject |
|---|---|---|---|---|
| Máximo Soto-Hall | Guatemalan | El Problema | 1899 | Political and cultural absorption |
| Carlos Gagini | Costa Rican | El árbol enfermo | 1920 | Cultural absorption |
| Carlos Gagini | Costa Rican | La caída del águila | 1920 | Political absorption |
| Rafael Arévalo Martínez | Guatemalan | La oficina de paz de Orolandia | 1925 | Political absorption |
| Máximo Soto-Hall | Guatemalan | La sombra de la Casa Blanca | 1927 | Wall Street |
| Juan Antonio Ramos | Cuban | Las impurezas de la realidad | 1929 | Sugar |
| Hernán Robledo | Nicaraguan | Sangre en el trópico | 1931 | Intervention |
| César Vallejo | Peruvian | Tungsteno | 1931 | Mining |
| Andrés Garafulic | Chilean | Carnalavaca | 1932 | Mining |
| Hernán Robledo | Nicaraguan | Los estrangulados | 1933 | Intervention |
| Demetrio Aguilera | Ecuadorian | Canal Zone | 1935 | Panama Canal |
| Teodoro Torres | Mexican | La patria perdida | 1935 | Braceros |
| Ramón Díaz Sánchez | Venezuelan | Mene | 1936 | Oil |
| Roberto Leyton | Bolivian | Los eternos vagabundos | 1939 | Mining |
| Ramón Marrero Aristy | Dominican | Over | 1939 | Sugar |
| Bernardino Mena-Brito | Mexican | Paludismo | 1940 | Chicle |
| Carlos Luis Fallas | Costa Rican | Mamita Yunai | 1941 | United Fruit |
| Antonio J. Arano | Colombian | Oro y miseria | 1942 | Mining |
| José Román Orozco | Nicaraguan | Cosmapa | 1944 | Fruit companies |
| Joaquín Gutiérrez | Costa Rican | Manglar | 1946 | Fruit companies |
| Luis Spota | Mexican | Murieron en mitad del río | 1948 | Braceros |
| Joaquín Gutiérrez | Costa Rican | Puerto Limón | 1950 | Fruit companies |

| Ramón Amaya Amador | Honduran | *Prisión verde* | 1950 | Fruit companies |
|---|---|---|---|---|
| Paca Navas Miralda | Honduran | *Barro* | 1951 | Fruit companies |
| Miguel Angel Asturias | Guatemalan | *Viento fuerte* | 1951 | Fruit companies |
| Alberto Ordónez Arguello | Nicaraguan | *Ebano* | 1954 | Fruit companies |
| Miguel Angel Asturias | Guatemalan | *Papa verde* | 1954 | United Fruit |
| Miguel Angel Asturias | Guatemalan | *Week-end en Guatemala* | 1956 | Fruit companies and intervention |

## APPENDIX 4: SPANISH TRANSLATIONS OF AMERICAN AUTHORS, 1890–1943

| Nineteenth Century | Editions | Titles |
|---|---|---|
| Poe, Edgar Allan | 82 | 1 |
| Clemens, Samuel Langhorne (Mark Twain) | 62 | 15 |
| Irving, Washington | 26 | 6 |
| Emerson, Ralph Waldo | 24 | 6 |
| Alcott, Louisa May | 16 | 5 |
| Longfellow, Henry Wadsworth | 14 | 4 |
| Cooper, James Fenimore | 12 | 6 |
| Harte, Bret | 10 | 6 |
| Hawthorne, Nathaniel | 10 | 3 |
| James, William | 10 | 6 |
| Trine, Ralph Waldo | 9 | 8 |
| Stowe, Harriet Beecher | 9 | 1 |
| Wallace, Lew | 8 | 1 |
| Bellamy, Edward | 7 | 1 |
| Whitman, Walt | 6 | 4 |
| Thoreau, Henry David | 3 | 1 |
| Melville, Herman | 2 | 2 |

| Twentieth Century | Editions | Titles |
|---|---|---|
| Sinclair, Upton | 22 | 17 |
| Frank, Waldo | 21 | 14 |
| Dewey, John | 16 | 8 |
| Lewis, Sinclair | 13 | 9 |
| Steinbeck, John | 12 | 6 |
| O'Neill, Eugene | 11 | 10 |
| Bromfield, Louis | 9 | 8 |
| Dos Passos, John | 8 | 5 |
| Buck, Pearl | 8 | 5 |
| London, Jack | 8 | 4 |
| Dreiser, Theodore | 6 | 5 |
| Anderson, Sherwood | 5 | 4 |
| Caldwell, Erskine | 5 | 4 |

| | | |
|---|---|---|
| Hearn, Lafcadio | 4 | 4 |
| Santayana, George | 4 | 4 |
| Hemingway, Ernest | 4 | 3 |
| Faulkner, William | 4 | 3 |
| Porter, W. S. (O. Henry) | 3 | 3 |
| Wilder, Thornton | 3 | 2 |
| Rice, Elmer | 3 | 2 |
| Erskine, John | 3 | 2 |
| Hergesheimer, Joseph | 2 | 2 |
| Saroyan, William | 2 | 2 |
| Wright, Richard | 2 | 1 |
| Washington, Booker T. | 2 | 1 |

SOURCE: Englekirk, *Bibliografía.*

## APPENDIX 5: SPANISH TRANSLATIONS OF AMERICAN AUTHORS, 1944–54

| Nineteenth Century | Editions | Titles |
|---|---|---|
| Clemens, Samuel Langhorne | 66 | 24 |
| Alcott, Louisa May | 35 | 7 |
| Poe, Edgar Allan | 28 | 2+ |
| Cooper, James Fenimore | 24 | 9 |
| Hawthorne, Nathaniel | 10 | 7 |
| Stowe, Harriet Beecher | 10 | 1 |
| Irving, Washington | 17 | 5 |
| Emerson, Ralph Waldo | 9 | 2 |
| Melville, Herman | 8 | 4 |
| James, Henry | 8 | 7 |
| Whitman, Walt | 7 | 5 |
| Wallace, Lew | 7 | 1 |
| Harte, Bret | 6 | 5 |
| Thoreau, Henry David | 3 | 2 |
| Longfellow, Henry Wadsworth | 1 | 1 |

| Twentieth Century | Editions | Titles |
|---|---|---|
| Bromfield, Louis | 41 | 25 |
| Buck, Pearl | 40 | 27 |
| London, Jack | 39 | 25 |
| Lewis, Sinclair | 18 | 14 |
| Steinbeck, John | 15 | 12 |
| Faulkner, William | 14 | 13 |
| Sinclair, Upton | 13 | 12 |
| Dewey, John | 10 | 10 |
| Hemingway, Ernest | 10 | 8 |
| Saroyan, William | 10 | 10 |
| Marquand, John P. | 9 | 9 |
| Dreiser, Theodore | 8 | 8 |
| Erskine, John | 8 | 8 |
| Frank, Waldo | 8 | 7 |

| | | |
|---|---|---|
| Caldwell, Erskine | 7 | 7 |
| Dos Passos, John | 7 | 6 |
| Anderson, Sherwood | 7 | 6 |
| James, William | 6 | 5 |
| Rawlings, Marjorie Kinnan | 6 | 3 |
| O'Neill, Eugene | 5 | 5 |
| Wilder, Thornton | 5 | 4 |
| Rice, Elmer | 4 | 6 |
| Santayana, George | 4 | 4 |
| Prokosch, Frederic | 4 | 4 |
| Hearn, Lafcadio | 4 | 3 |
| Wright, Richard | 4 | 3 |
| Farrell, James | 3 | 3 |
| Fitzgerald, Scott | 3 | 2 |
| Porter, W. S. (O. Henry) | 3 | 2 |
| Miller, Arthur | 3 | 2 |
| Fast, Howard | 2 | 2 |
| Williams, Tennessee | 1 | 3 |
| Capote, Truman | 1 | 1 |
| Cather, Willa | 1 | 1 |
| Jones, James | 1 | 1 |
| Lafarge, Oliver | 1 | 1 |
| Mailer, Norman | 1 | 1 |
| Richter, Conrad | 1 | 1 |
| Styron, William | 1 | 1 |
| Warren, Robert Penn | 1 | 1 |
| Wharton, Edith | 1 | 1 |
| Wolfe, Thomas | 1 | 1 |

SOURCE: Library of Congress, *Provisional Bibliography.*

## APPENDIX 6: SPANISH TRANSLATIONS OF AMERICAN AUTHORS, 1955–62

| Nineteenth Century | Editions | Titles |
|---|---|---|
| Alcott, Louisa May | 49 | 13 |
| Clemens, Samuel Langhorne | 32 | 9 |
| Poe, Edgar Allan (*Tales*) | 14 | 1 |
| Wallace, Lew (*Ben Hur*) | 10 | 1 |
| Irving, Washington | 8 | 2 |
| Melville, Herman (*Moby Dick*) | 7 | 1 |
| Stowe, Harriet Beecher (*Uncle Tom's Cabin*) | 7 | 1 |
| Cooper, James Fenimore | 6 | 4 |
| Whitman, Walt | 4 | 1 |
| Hawthorne, Nathaniel | 3 | 2 |
| Emerson, Ralph Waldo | 2 | 2 |
| Thoreau, Henry David | 2 | 2 |
| James, Henry | 1 | 7 |
| Longfellow, Henry Wadsworth | 1 | 1 |

| Twentieth Century | Editions | Titles |
|---|---|---|
| Buck, Pearl | 49 | 24 |
| Bromfield, Louis | 33 | 17 |
| Faulkner, William | 26 | 13 |
| Lewis, Sinclair | 15 | 12 |
| Hemingway, Ernest | 15 | 8 |
| Marquand, John P. | 12 | 10 |
| Steinbeck, John | 12 | 9 |
| London, Jack | 12 | 8 |
| Saroyan, William | 10 | 10 |
| Dewey, John | 9 | 9 |
| Dos Passos, John | 9 | 9 |
| Fast, Howard | 7 | 7 |
| Caldwell, Erskine | 6 | 6 |
| Frank, Waldo | 6 | 6 |
| Williams, Tennessee | 6 | 5 |
| O'Neill, Eugene | 4 | 12 |
| Miller, Arthur | 4 | 5 |
| Shaw, Irwin | 4 | 4 |
| Santayana, George | 4 | 4 |
| Gallico, Paul | 4 | 4 |
| Hersey, John | 4 | 3 |
| Cozzens, James Gould | 4 | 3 |
| Wilder, Thornton | 4 | 3 |
| Jones, James | 3 | 3 |
| Miller, Henry | 3 | 3 |
| Wright, Richard | 3 | 3 |
| Dreiser, Theodore (*An American Tragedy*) | 3 | 1 |
| Algren, Nelson | 2 | 2 |
| Basso, Hamilton | 2 | 2 |
| Cather, Willa | 2 | 2 |
| McCullers, Carson | 2 | 2 |
| Mailer, Norman | 2 | 2 |
| Nabokov, Vladimir | 2 | 2 |
| O'Hara, John | 2 | 2 |
| Sinclair, Upton | 2 | 2 |
| Warren, Robert Penn | 2 | 2 |
| Welty, Eudora | 2 | 1 |
| Richter, Conrad | 2 | 1 |

SOURCE: Library of Congress, *Translations.*

## APPENDIX 7: LIST OF AUTHORS WHOSE WORKS PROVIDED SOURCE MATERIAL

*Alberdi, Juan Bautista (1801–84), Argentine statesman and writer
Ancízar, Manuel (1820–?), Colombian statesman and writer
*Arango Cano, Jesús (twentieth century), Colombian writer

*Principal source.

Arango y Parreño, Francisco de (1769–1839), Cuban public man

*Arciniegas, Germán (1900– ), Colombian essayist and diplomat

*Ayres, Daniel (twentieth century), Argentine physician and writer

Becerra, Ricardo (1836–1905), Venezuelan writer

*Belaúnde, Víctor Andrés (1883–1906), Peruvian diplomat and writer

Belgrano, Manuel (1770–1820), Argentine general and hero

*Bilbao, Francisco (1823–63), Chilean politician and writer

*Blanco-Fombona, Rufino (1874–1944), Venezuelan novelist, essayist, and diplomat

Blest Gana, Alberto (1830–1920), Chilean novelist and diplomat

*Bolívar, Simón (1783–1830), Venezuelan hero and statesman

*Bravo, Nicolás (twentieth century), Cuban journalist and radio commentator

Brenes Mesén, Roberto (1874–1947), Costa Rican poet and educator

Cabrera, Raimundo (1852–1923), Cuban politician and journalist

Caldas, Francisco José (1741–1816), Colombian scientist, writer, and patriot

*Camacho Roldán, Salvador (1827–1900), Colombian economist and statesman

Campino, Joaquín (early nineteenth century), Chilean diplomat

*Cané, Miguel (1851–1905), Argentine writer and diplomat

*Capdevila, Arturo (1889– ), Argentine writer

Caro, José Eusebio (1817–53), Colombian poet, journalist, and public official

Carrasco Albano, Juan Manuel (1834–73), Chilean statesman and writer

Carrera Andrade, Jorge (1902– ), Ecuadorian poet and diplomat

Cestero, Tulio Manuel (1878–1955), Dominican writer

Colmo, Alfredo (1878– ), Argentine literary critic

*Cosío Villegas, Daniel (1900– ), Mexican economist and essayist

D'Amico, Carlos (nineteenth century), Argentine writer

*Darío, Rubén (1867–1916), Nicaraguan poet, journalist, and diplomat

*Dávila, Carlos (1884– ), Chilean diplomat

Echeverría, Esteban (1805–51), Argentine poet and political writer

Fernández, Jorge (1912–63), Ecuadorian journalist and educator

Figueres Ferrer, José (1906– ), Costa Rican statesman

Frugoni, Emilio (1881– ), Uruguayan literary critic

Gallegos, Gerardo (1906– ), Ecuadorian writer

Gálvez, Manuel (1882–1962), Argentine novelist, essayist, and biographer

Gamio, Manuel (1883– ), Mexican archeologist and sociologist

*García Calderón, Francisco (1883–1953), Peruvian diplomat and publicist

*Godoy Alcayaga, Lucila [Gabriela Mistral] (1889–1957), Chilean poetess, educator, and diplomat

Gómez, Antonio (early nineteenth century), Venezuelan scholar

*Gómez Robledo, Antonio (1908– ), Mexican writer

González, Joaquín Víctor (1863–1923), Argentine statesman, educator, and author

González Vigil, Francisco de Paula (1792–1875), Peruvian churchman and writer

*Gutiérrez de Lara, José Bernardo (1774–1841), Mexican patriot

Haya de la Torre, Raúl (1895–), Peruvian revolutionary and writer

Henríquez, Camilo (1769–1825), Chilean churchman and patriot

*Henríquez Ureña, Pedro (1884–1946), Dominican literary critic and educator

*Heredia, José María (1803–39), Cuban poet and patriot

Ingenieros, José (1877–1925), Argentine criminologist, psychologist, and writer

*Juárez y Aragón, J. Fernando (twentieth century), Guatemalan lawyer and journalist

Labarca, Amanda (1886–1975), Chilean educator

*Lastarria, José Victorino (1817–88), Chilean professor, legislator, and writer

López de Mesa, Luis (1888–1967), Colombian physician and social critic

Lugones, Leopoldo (1874–1938), Argentine poet and historian

Macías, Miguel (twentieth century), Ecuadorian politician

Mallea, Eduardo (1901–), Argentine novelist and essayist

*Mañach, Jorge (1898–1962), Cuban essayist and educator

*Martí, José (1853–95), Cuban patriot, poet, and journalist

Martínez, Fray Melchor (early nineteenth century), Chilean churchman and historian

Martínez Estrada, Ezequiel (1895–), Argentine essayist and poet

Mendoza de Montero, Angélica (twentieth century), Argentine writer

*Milla, José (1822–82), Guatemalan historian and novelist

*Miranda, Francisco de (1756–1816), Venezuelan patriot

Mistral, Gabriela. See Godoy Alcayaga, Lucila

Molina, Enrique (1871–1964), Chilean philosopher and writer

Montalvo, Juan (1832–89), Ecuadorian essayist and politician

Monte y Aponte, Domingo del (1804–54), Cuban writer and educator

Monteagudo, Bernardo (1785–1825), Argentine writer and patriot

*Montenegro, Ernesto (1885–1967), Chilean literary critic and journalist

Moreno, Mariano (1778–1811), Argentine patriot

Nariño, Antonio (1765–1823), Colombian scholar and patriot

*Núñez, Enrique Bernardo (1895–), Venezuelan journalist and litterateur

O'Gorman, Edmundo (1906–), Mexican historian

*Oliveres, Ramón (twentieth century), Argentine publicist

Oribe, Emilio (1893–), Uruguayan philosopher and teacher

Ortiz Vargas, A. (twentieth century), Colombian poet

*Otero, Gustavo Adolfo (1896–), Bolivian art critic and writer

Palacios, Alfredo (1879–1965), Argentine publicist

*Paz, Octavio (1914–), Mexican poet, essayist, and diplomat

Pazos, Vicente (1779–1851?), Bolivian patriot

*Pereyra, Carlos (1871–1942), Mexican historian

*Pérez Guerrero, Alfredo (1901–), Ecuadorian statesman and educator

Pérez Rosales, Vicente (1807–86), Chilean writer

Pinochet, Tancredo (1879–), Chilean writer

Plaza Lasso, Galo (1906–), Ecuadorian statesman and educator

Pombo, Miguel de (1779–1816), Colombian patriot

*Pombo, Rafael (1833–1912), Colombian poet, diplomat, and editor

Portilla, Jorge (twentieth century), Mexican scholar

Prieto, Guillermo (1818–97), Mexican poet and politician

Quesada, Ernesto (1858–?), Argentine writer, diplomat, and educator

*Quesada, Vicente [Domingo de Pantoja] (1830–1913), Argentine journalist and diplomat

Quintana, Juan Nepomuceno (early nineteenth century), Venezuelan scholar

*Quintanilla, Luis (1900–), Mexican diplomat and writer

Ramos, Samuel (1897–1957), Mexican philosopher and educator

*Reissig, Luis (1897–), Argentine educator and writer

Restrepo, José Manuel (1781–1863), Colombian statesman

Reyles, Carlos (1868–1938), Uruguayan novelist

Reynal, Rafael (nineteenth century), Mexican political figure

*Rocafuerte, Vicente (1783–1847), Ecuadorian patriot and statesman

*Rodó, José Enrique (1872–1917), Uruguayan essayist and politician

Rodríguez, Simón (1771–1854), Colombian educator and writer

*Salas, Manuel de (1754–1841), Chilean patriot, educator, and scientist

Samper, José María (1828–88), Colombian author, diplomat, and statesman

*Sánchez, Luis Alberto (1900–), Peruvian literary critic and professor

Santos Chocano, José (1875–1934), Peruvian poet

*Sarmiento, Domingo Faustino (1811–88), Argentine educator, writer, statesman, and diplomat

*Seoane, Manuel (1900–), Peruvian politician and journalist

Sierra, Justo (1848–1912), Mexican educator

*Subercaseaux, Benjamín (1902–), Chilean writer

Tablada, Juan José (1871–1945), Mexican poet and journalist

Torre Grovas, Silvio de la (twentieth century), Cuban educator

Torres, Carlos-Arturo (1867–1912), Colombian writer

Torres, Manuel (1768–1822), Colombian patriot and diplomat

*Ugarte, Manuel (1878–1951), Argentine journalist, lecturer, and novelist

Unánue, Hipólito (1758–1833), Peruvian scientist, physician, and writer

*Uzcátegui, Emilio (1899–), Ecuadorian educator and writer

Valero, Fernando (nineteenth century), Guatemalan diplomat and writer

Varela, José Pedro (1848–79), Uruguayan educator and politician

Vargas H., Jorge (nineteenth century), Colombian writer

*Vargas Vila, José María (1860–1933), Colombian poet and novelist

Varona, Enrique José (1849–1933), Cuban educator, literary critic, and statesman

*Vasconcelos, José (1881–1959), Mexican educator, writer, and politician

Velasco del Campo, Nicolás (1918–), Chilean journalist and editor

*Vicuña Mackenna, Benjamín (1831–86), Chilean statesman and writer

Vidaurre, Manuel Lorenzo de (1773–1841), Peruvian scientist, physician, and writer

Villarán, Manuel Vicente (1873–1958), Peruvian educator and writer

Villoldo, Pedro (twentieth century), Cuban politician and writer

Zaldumbide, Gonzalo (1885–), Ecuadorian literary critic and diplomat

*Zea, Leopoldo (1912–), Mexican essayist and professor

Zegrí, Armando (twentieth century), Chilean journalist

Zorrilla de San Martín, Juan (1855–1931), Uruguayan poet, journalist, politician, and diplomat

Zozaya, Manuel (nineteenth century), Mexican diplomat

*Zum Felde, Alberto (1888–), Uruguayan literary critic and historian

# Bibliography

Abeledo, Amaranto. "Sarmiento en los Estados Unidos." *Revista de Educación* 2 (new ser., March 1957):421–36.

Adams, H. B. *Jared Sparks*. 2 vols. Boston, 1893. Includes letters written to Sparks from Spanish Americans.

Adams, Mildred, ed. *Latin America: Evolution or Explosion?* New York: Dodd, Mead, 1963.

Aguirre Elorriaga, Manuel. *El Abate de Pradt y la emancipación hispanoamericana*. Paris, 1941.

Aikman, Duncan. *The All-American Front*. Garden City: Doubleday, Doran, 1941.

Alberdi, Juan Bautista. In *Obras selectas*, vol. 2, *Memorias e impresiones de viaje*. Buenos Aires: Librería de la Facultad, J. Roldán, 1920.

———. *La vida y los trabajos industriales de William Wheelwright*. Paris, 1876.

Alcedo y Bexarano, Antonio de. *Diccionario geográfico-histórico de las Indias occidentales*. Madrid, 1786–89.

Aldridge, Alfred. "Camilo Henríquez and the Fame of Thomas Paine and Benjamin Franklin in Chile." *Revista Interamericana de Bibliografía* 17 (1967):51–67.

Alexander, Robert J. *Communism in Latin America*. New Brunswick, N.J.: Rutgers University Press, 1957.

———. *Today's Latin America*. Garden City, N.Y.: Doubleday, Doran, 1962.

Allen, David H. "Rubén Darío frente a la creciente influencia de los Estados Unidos." *Revista Iberoamericana* 33 (1967):387–93.

Amunátegui, M. L. *Camilo Henríquez*. 2 vols. Santiago de Chile, 1889.

Arango Cano, Jesús. *Estados Unidos: mito y realidad*. Bogotá, 1959.

Arbena, Joseph L. "The Image of an American Imperialist: Colombian Views of Theodore Roosevelt." *West Georgia Studies in the Social Sciences* 6, no. 1 (June 1967):3–20.

Arciniegas, Germán. *En el país del rascacielos y las zanahorias*. 2 vols. Bogotá: Librería Suramérica, 1945.

Avila, Eneida. "Las compañías bananeras en la novelística centroamericana." *Lotería* (Panama), no. 57, pp. 100–128; no. 58, pp. 75–128; no. 59, pp. 69–128 (1960).

Ayres, Daniel. *Estados Unidos: una mentira*. Buenos Aires: Editorial EFDA, 1956.

Balseiro, José. "Rubén Darío and the United States." In *The Americans Look at Each Other*, by José Balseiro, pp. 59–80. Coral Gables: University of Miami Press, 1969.

Basadre, Jorge. "Conocimiento de desconocimiento de los Estados Unidos en la América latina." In *Conocimiento y desconocimiento de América*, pp. 39–55. Washington: Pan American Union, 1958.

Beals, Carleton. *The Coming Struggle for Latin America.* Philadelphia: J. B. Lippincott, 1939.

Beals, Carleton, et al. *What the South Americans Think of Us: A Symposium.* New York: R. M. McBride, 1945.

Beals, R. L. "The Mexican Student Views the United States." *Annals of the American Academy of Political and Social Science* 295 (September 1954): 108–15.

Beals, R. L., and Humphrey, N. D. *No Frontier to Learning.* Minneapolis: University of Minnesota Press, 1957. A study of the attitudes of Mexican students in the United States.

Becerra, Ricardo. "Crónicas yankees." *El Cojo Ilustrado* (1893–94), 2:272–73, 318, 320, 374–76, 388–89, 446, 448; 3:22–23, 62–63, 104–6, 146–48, 226–28, 270–72.

Belaúnde, Víctor Andrés. *Bolivar and the Political Thought of the Spanish American Revolution.* Baltimore: The Johns Hopkins Press, 1938.

———. "Crónicas de América." *Mercurio Peruano* (1920), 5:1–17, 78–90, 147–49, 225–34, 331–35, 431–38; 6:1–5, 81–85.

———. *La realidad nacional.* Paris: Editorial "Le Livre libre," 1931.

Bemis, Samuel Flagg. *The Latin American Policy of the United States.* New York: Harcourt, Brace, 1943.

Bernardete, M. J., ed. *Waldo Frank in America Hispana.* New York: Instituto de las Españas, 1930.

Bernstein, Harry. *Making an Inter-American Mind.* Gainesville: University of Florida Press, 1961.

———. *Origins of Inter-American Interest: 1700–1812*, Philadelphia: University of Pennsylvania Press, 1945. This and the preceding volume contain valuable and well-documented material on the history of cultural relations between the Americas.

———. "Las primeras relaciones entre New England y el mundo hispánico: 1700–1815." *Revista Hispánica Moderna* 5 (1935):1–17.

———. "A Provincial Library in Colonial Mexico, 1802." *Hispanic American Historical Review* 26 (1946):162–83.

Bilbao, Francisco. *La América en peligro; Evangelio americano; La sociabilidad chilena*, edited by L. A. Sánchez. Santiago de Chile: Nascimento, 1941.

Blanco-Fombona, Rufino. *La americanización del mundo.* Amsterdam: Imprimerie Electrique, 1902.

———. *La evolución política y social de Hispanoamérica.* Madrid: B. Rodríguez, 1911.

———. *La lámpara de Aladino.* Madrid: Renacimiento, 1915.

Blest Gana, Alberto. *De Nueva York al Niágara.* Santiago de Chile, 1867.

Bolívar, Simón. *Selected Writings of Bolivar*, edited by Harold A. Bierck. 2 vols. New York: Colonial Press, 1951.

Bornholdt, Laura. "The Abbé de Pradt and the Monroe Doctrine." *Hispanic American Historical Review* 24(1944):201–21.

———. *Baltimore and Early Pan Americanism: A Study in the Background of the Monroe Doctrine.* Smith College Studies in History, vol. 54. Northampton, Mass., 1949.

Bravo, Nicolás. *El destino humano y las Américas.* Havana: Imprenta Mundial, 1954.

Buchanan, William. "How Others See Us." *Annals of the American Academy of Political and Social Science* 295 (1954):1–11.

Buchanan, William, and Cantril, Hadley. *How Nations See Each Other.* Urbana: University of Illinois Press, 1954.

Bunkley, Allison W. *The Life of Sarmiento.* Princeton: Princeton University Press, 1952.

Burkhardt, F. "Inter-American Scholarly Communication in the Humanities and Social Sciences." *American Political Science Review* 54(1960):835–39.

Burr, R. N., and Hussey, Roland. *Documents on Inter-American Cooperation.* 2 vols. Philadelphia: University of Pennsylvania Press, 1955.

Cabrales, Luis Alberto. *Política de Estados Unidos y poesía de Hispanoamérica.* Managua: Ministerio de Educación Pública, 1958.

Cabrera, Raimundo. "Chicago." *Revista Cubana* 18(November 1893):397–405.

Caillet-Bois, Ricardo. *Ensayo sobre el Río de la Plata y la revolución francesa.* Buenos Aires: Imprenta de la Universidad, 1929.

Camacho Roldán, Salvador. *Notas de viaje.* Bogotá, 1890.

Cané, Miguel. *En viaje, 1881–1882.* Buenos Aires: Biblioteca de "La Nación," 1907.

Capdevila, Arturo. *América: Nuestras naciones ante los Estados Unidos.* Buenos Aires: M. Gleizer, 1926.

Cardot, Carlos F., ed. *La libertad de cultos. Polémica suscitada por William Burke,* vol. 12, *Biblioteca.* Caracas: Academia Nacional de Historia, 1959.

Caro, José Eusebio. *Epistolario.* Bogotá: Ministerio de Educación Nacional, 1953.

Carrera Andrade, Jorge. *Rostros y climas.* Paris: Edition de la Maison de l'Amérique Latine, 1948.

Cestero, Tulio Manuel. *Estados Unidos por dentro.* Mexico: Botas, 1918.

Chandler, C. L. *Inter-American Acquaintances.* Sewanee, Tenn.: The University Press, 1917.

Chapman, Arnold. "Sherwood Anderson and Eduardo Mallea." *Publications of the Modern Language Association of America* 69(1954):34–44.

———. *The Spanish American Reception of United States Fiction, 1920–1940.* Berkeley: University of California Press, 1966.

———. "Waldo Frank in the Hispanic World: The First Phase." *Hispania* 44(1961):626–34.

———. "Waldo Frank in Spanish America." *Hispania* 47(1964):510–21.

Chapman, Mary P. "Yankeephobia: An Analysis of the Anti–United States Bias of Certain South American Intellectuals, 1898–1928." Ph.D. diss., Stanford University, 1950.

Child, Irvin L. "The Background of Public Opinion in Costa Rica." *Public Opinion Quarterly* 7(1943):242–57.

Chinard, Gilbert. "Eighteenth-Century Theories on America as a Human Habitat." *Proceedings American Philosophical Society* 91, no. 1 (1947).

Clark, Allen C. "Doctor and Mrs. William Thornton." *Records of the Columbia Historical Society* 18(1915):144–208.

Clay, Henry. *Works.* Edited by Calvin Colton. 10 vols. New York: G. P. Putnam's Sons, 1904.

Cleven, Andrew N. "Thornton's Outline of a Constitution for United North and South Columbia." *Hispanic American Historical Review* 12(1932):198–215.

Collier, W. M., and Cruz, G. F. *La primera misión de los Estados Unidos de América en Chile.* Santiago de Chile: Imprenta Cervantes, 1926.

Colmo, Alfredo. "La filosofía de Rodó." *Nosotros* 27(1917):181–82.

Commager, Henry Steele. *America in Perspective: The United States through Foreign Eyes.* New York: Random House, 1947. Although this anthology does not include selections by Spanish Americans, it is useful as a basis of comparison.

Corbitt, Roberta. "This Colossal Theater: The United States Interpreted by

282        Bibliography

José Martí." Ph.D. diss., University of Kentucky, 1956 (University Microfilms, Ann Arbor).
Correa, Edmundo. *Sarmiento and the United States*. Gainesville: University of Florida Press, 1961.
Cosío Villegas, Daniel. "México y Estados Unidos." *Cuadernos Americanos* 36 (November–December 1947):7–27.
Crawford, William Rex. *A Century of Latin American Thought*. Cambridge: Harvard University Press, 1945. An excellent survey which provided numerous suggestions for this study.
Crespi, Leo P. "Some Observations on the Concept of Image." *Public Opinion Quarterly* 25(1961):111–18.
Cuevas Cansino, Francisco. *Del Congreso de Panamá a la Conferencia de Caracas, 1826–1954*. Caracas, 1955.
Daniel, Elizabeth Rezner. "Spanish American Travelers in the United States before 1900: A Study in Inter-American Literary Relations." Ph.D. diss., University of North Carolina, 1959. The material presented was of considerable service in the preparation of chapters 4–7 of this study.
Darío, Rubén, *La caravana pasa*. Paris: Garnier, 1919.
———. "Edgar Allan Poe." In *Obras completas*, vol. 2, *Los raros*. Madrid: Editorial "Mundo Latino," 1917–20.
———. *Obras completas*, vol. 6, *Peregrinaciones*. Madrid: Imprenta de G. Hernández y Galo Saez, 1921.
———. *Poesía: Libros poéticos completos*. Mexico: Fondo de Cultura Económica, 1952.
———. "El triunfo de Calibán." In *Escritos inéditos de Rubén Darío*. Edited by E. K. Mapes, pp. 160–62. New York: Instituto de las Españas, 1938.
Dávila, Carlos. *We of the Americas*. Chicago: Ziff-Davis Publishing Co., 1949.
Davis, Harold E. *Latin American Social Thought*. Washington, D.C.: University Press of Washington, 1963. An anthology with intelligent comment.
de Tocqueville, Alexis. *Democracy in America*. Edited by Phillips Bradley. New York, 1958.
Diffie, Bailey W. "Ideology of *Hispanidad*." *Hispanic American Historical Review* 23 (1943):457–82.
Dozer, Donald M. *Are We Good Neighbors?* Gainesville: University of Florida Press, 1959.
Duane, William. "Letters of William Duane." *Proceedings of the Massachusetts Historical Society*, 2d ser. (1907), 20:257–394.
———. *A Visit to Colombia in the Years 1822–1823*. Philadelphia, 1826.
Duggan, Stephen. *The Two Americas: An Interpretation*. New York: Charles Scribner's Sons, 1934.
Dunn, W. E. "The Post-War Attitude of Hispanic America toward the United States." *Hispanic American Historical Review* 3(1920):177–83.
Ellison, Fred P. "Rubén Darío and Brazil." *Hispania* 47(1964):24–35.
Englekirk, John E. *Bibliografía de obras norteamericanas en traducción española*. Mexico, 1944 (Sobretiro de la *Revista Iberamericana*).
———. "El epistolario Pombo-Longfellow." *Thesaurus* (Instituto Caro y Cuervo, Bogotá), vol. 10, nos. 1, 2, 3 (1954).
———. "Franklin en el mundo hispánico." *Revista Iberoamericana* 21 (1957):319–71.
———. "El hispanoamericanismo y la generación de 98." *Revista Iberoamericana* 2 (1938):321–51. Includes some valuable notes on Pan Hispanism.
———. "Notes on Emerson in Latin America." *Publications of the Modern Language Association of America* 76 (1961):227–32.
———. "Notes on Longfellow in Spanish America." *Hispania* 25 (1942):295–308.
———. *Poe in Hispanic Literature*. New York: Instituto de las Españas, 1934.

Englekirk, John E., et al. *An Anthology of Spanish American Literature.* 2d ed. New York: Appleton-Century-Crofts, 1968.

Evans, H. C. *Chile and its Relations with the United States.* Durham, N.C.: Duke University Press, 1927.

Ferris, Nathan L. "The Relation of the United States with South America during the Civil War." *Hispanic American Historical Review* 21 (1941): 51–78.

Figueres Ferrer, José. "Unity and Culture." In *Latin American Social Thought,* by Harold Davis. Washington: University Press of Washington, 1963.

Fosdick, Raymond B. *The Story of the Rockefeller Foundation.* New York: Harper, 1952.

Frugoni, Emilio. "En la otra América." *Nosotros* 28 (1918):332–49.

Fuentes, Carlos. "Party of One." *Holiday,* October 1961, p. 13. On the stereotype of the American tourist.

Furlong, Guillermo. *Historia y bibliografía de las primeras imprentas rioplatenses, 1700–1850.* 3 vols. Buenos Aires: Editorial Guaranía, 1953.

———. "The Influence of Benjamin Franklin in the River Plate Area before 1810." *The Americas* 12 (1956):259.

Galíndez, Jesús. "Anti-American Sentiment in Latin America." *Journal of International Affairs* 9, no. 1 (1955):24–32.

Gallegos, Gerardo. "El destino de América." *América* (Havana) 1 (1939): 33–37.

Gálvez, Manuel. *El solar de la raza.* 2d ed. Buenos Aires: Editorial Tor, 1936.

Gamio, Manuel, and Vasconcelos, José. *Aspects of Mexican Civilization.* Chicago: University of Chicago Press, 1926.

García Calderón, Francisco. *La creación de un continente.* Paris: P. Ollendorf, 1913.

———. *Les démocraties latines de l'Amérique.* Paris: E. Flammarion, 1912.

———. *Latin America: Its Rise and Progress.* New York: Charles Scribner's Sons, 1913.

———. "El panamericanismo, su pasado y su porvenir." *Revue Hispanique* 37 (1916):1–60.

García Samudio, Nicolás. *La independencia de Hispanoamérica.* Mexico: Fondo de Cultura Económica, 1945.

Gerbi, Antonello. *La disputa del Nuevo Mundo: Historia de una polémica, 1750–1900.* Mexico: Fondo de Cultura Económica, 1960. A thorough account of the argument about the inferiority of America.

Gillin, John. "Changing Depths in Latin America." *Journal of Inter-American Studies* 2 (1960):379–89.

———. "Some Signposts for Policy." In *Social Change in Latin America Today,* by Richard N. Adams et al. New York: Council on Foreign Relations, 1960.

Godoy, Alcayaga, Lucila [Gabriela Mistral]. "La película enemiga." *Repertorio Americano* 13 (1932):6–7.

———. "Tiene la palabra Gabriela Mistral." *Repertorio Americano* 8 (1926): 321–23.

———. "Waldo Frank y nosotros." *Repertorio Americano* 25 (1932):257–59.

Goldberg, Isaac. "As Latin Americans See Us." *American Mercury* 3 (1924): 467–73.

———. *Studies in Spanish American Literature.* New York: Brentano's, 1920. Contains an informative discussion of anti–United States sentiment in twentieth-century literature.

Goldrich, Daniel. *Radical Nationalism: The Political Orientation of Panamanian Law Students.* East Lansing: Michigan State University Press, 1962.

————. *Sons of the Establishment: Elite Youth in Panama and Costa Rica.* Chicago: Rand McNally, 1966.

Gómez Robledo, Antonio. *Idea y experiencia de América.* Mexico: Fondo de Cultura Económica, 1958.

González, Joaquín Víctor. "Los Estados Unidos y la América latina." In *Obras,* 10:49–81. Buenos Aires: Imprenta Mercatali, 1936–37.

González, Manuel Pedro. "Intellectual Relations between the United States and Spanish America." In *The Civilization of the Americas,* UCLA Committee on International Relations. Berkeley: University of California Press, 1938.

————. *José Martí: Epic Chronicler of the United States in the Eighties.* Chapel Hill: University of North Carolina Press, 1953.

————. "Two Great Pioneers of Inter-American Cultural Relations." *Hispania* 42 (1959):175–85. José María Heredia and William Cullen Bryant.

Graña, César. "Cultural Nationalism: The Idea of Historical Destiny in Spanish America." *Social Research* (1962–63), 29:395–418, 30:37–52.

Grases, Pedro, and Harkness, Alberto. *Manuel García de Sena y la independencia de Hispanoamérica.* Publicaciones de la Secretaría General de la 10a Conferencia Interamericana; Colección Historia, no. 6. Caracas, 1953.

Griffin, Charles C. *La opinion pública norteamericana y la independencia de Hispanoamérica.* Caracas, 1941.

————. *The United States and the Disruption of the Spanish Empire, 1810–1822.* New York: Columbia University Press, 1937.

Grunwald, Joseph. "Change Does Not Mean the End of Profits." *Challenge* 12, no. 9 (June 1964):34–37.

Guevara, Tristán Enrique. *Las maestras norteamericanas que trajo Sarmiento.* Buenos Aires: Servicio Cultural de los EE.UU., 1954.

Gutiérrez de Lara, José Bernardo. "Diary." *American Historical Review* 34 (1928):55–76, 281–94.

Guyard, M. F. *La littérature comparée.* 4th ed. Paris: Presses Universitaires, 1965. Chap. 8, "L'étranger tel qu'on le voit."

Haring, Clarence R. *South America Looks at the United States.* New York: Macmillan, 1928.

————. "The Two Americas." *Foreign Affairs* 5 (1927):364–79.

Haya de la Torre, Raúl. *El anti-imperialismo y el Apra.* Santiago de Chile: Ediciones Ercilla, 1936.

Helman, Edith F. "Early Interest in Spanish in New England." *Hispania* 29 (1946):339–51.

Henríquez Ureña, Pedro. "La cultura y los peligros de la especialización." *Repertorio Americano* 1 (1920):202–4.

————. *Horas de estudio.* Paris: P. Ollendorf, 1910.

Heredia, José María. "Cartas." *Revista de Cuba* 4 (1878):10–16, 449–55, 614–25; 5 (1879):78–85, 101–8.

————. *Revisiones literarias.* Havana: Ministerio de Educación, 1947.

Hernández de Alba, Guillermo. "Origen de la doctrina panamericana de confederación." *Revista de Historia de América* 22 (1946):376–98.

Holland, Kenneth. "Statistics and Comments on Exchange with the United States." *International Social Science Bulletin* 8 (1956):628–37.

Humboldt, Alexander von. *Ensayo político sobre el Reino de la Nueva España.* 6th Spanish edition. 4 vols. Mexico: Robredo, 1941.

Humphrey, Norman D. "The Mexican Image of Americans." *Annals of the American Academy of Political and Social Science* 295 (1954):116–25.

Ingenieros, José. *Por la unión latino-americana.* Buenos Aires, 1922.

Inman, Samuel Guy. *Latin America: Its Place in World Life.* 2d ed. New York: Committee on Cooperation in Latin America, 1942.

Instituto Boliviano de Encuestas de Opinión Pública. "A Study of Former Bolivian Grantees in the United States." La Paz, 1959. Multilithed.

International Research Associates. "A Study of Reactions to the State Department Exchange Program among Returned Mexican Grantees." Mexico, 1959. Mimeographed.

Johnson, John L. "The Political Role of the Latin American Middle Sectors." *Annals of the American Academy of Political and Social Science* 334 (1961):20–29.

Joseph, Franz M., ed. *As Others See Us: The United States Through Foreign Eyes.* Princeton: Princeton University Press, 1959. Includes articles by Daniel Cosío Villegas, Amanda Labarca, and Jorge Mañach.

Juárez y Aragón, J. Fernando. *Más allá de mis lentes.* Guatemala: Landívar, 1956.

Kilgore, W. J. "The Development of Positivism in Latin America." *Revista Inter-Americana de Bibliografía* 19 (1969):133–45.

Klineberg, Otto. "The Scientific Study of National Stereotypes." *International Social Science Bulletin* 3 (1951):511–12.

———. *Social Psychology.* New York: Holt, 1954. Includes material on the history of the stereotype concept.

———. *Tensions Affecting International Understanding.* Social Science Research Council, *Bulletin,* no. 62. New York, 1950.

Kohn, Hans. *American Nationalism: An Interpretative Essay.* New York: Collier Books, 1961. Contains a discussion of the development of the idea of Manifest Destiny.

Kraus, Michael. *The Atlantic Civilization: Eighteenth-Century Origins.* Ithaca, N.Y.: Cornell University Press, 1949.

Langley, Harold D. "Bolivar as Seen by an American Sailor." *Hispanic American Historical Review* 36 (1956):329–32.

Lastarria, José Victorino. *Obras completas,* vol. 7, *La América,* vol. 8, *Historia constitucional de medio siglo.* Santiago de Chile, 1906–14.

Leavitt, Sturgis E. *Revistas hispanoamericanas: índice bibliográfico, 1843–1935.* Santiago de Chile: Fondo Histórico y Bibliográfico José Toribio Medina, 1960.

Leonard, Irving. "A Frontier Library, 1799." *Hispanic American Historical Review* 23 (1943):21–51.

Lewis, Oscar. *Five Families: Mexican Case Studies in the Culture of Poverty.* New York: Basic Books, 1959.

———. "Mexico since Cárdenas." In *Social Change in Latin America,* by Richard N. Adams et al. New York: Council on Foreign Relations, 1960.

Library of Congress, Hispanic Foundation. *A Provisional Bibliography of United States Books Translated into Spanish.* Washington, 1957.

———. *Spanish and Portuguese Translations of United States Books, 1955–1962.* Washington, 1963.

Lockey, Joseph B. *Orígenes del panamericanismo.* Caracas: Empresa El Cojo, 1927. Translation of *Pan Americanism: Its Beginnings.* New York: Macmillan, 1920.

López de Mesa, Luis. *La sociedad contemporánea y otros escritos.* Bogotá: Editorial Minerva, 1938.

———. "Una hora ante Norte América." *Repertorio Americano* 1 (1919):83–85.

Lugones, Leopoldo. "La América Latina." *Repertorio Americano* 11 (1928): 66–68.

Luiggi, Alice Houston. *65 Valiants.* Gainesville: University of Florida Press, 1965. Translated as *Sesenta y cinco valientes: Sarmiento y las maestras norteamericanas.* Buenos Aires: Editorial Agora, 1959.

McGann, Thomas F. *Argentina, the United States and the Inter-American System, 1880–1914.* Cambridge: Harvard University Press, 1957.

Macgregor, G. F., ed. *Vasconcelos.* Mexico: Ediciones de la Secretaría de Educación Pública, 1942.

Macías, Miguel. "Mi viaje a los Estados Unidos." Manuscript of a lecture given at the Centro Ecuatoriano-norteamericano, Guayaquil, 1946.

Mallea, Eduardo. *Historia de una pasión argentina.* Buenos Aires: Editorial Sudamericana, 1942.

Manning, William R. *Early Diplomatic Relations between the United States and Mexico.* Baltimore: The Johns Hopkins Press, 1916.

Martí, José. *Martí on the U.S.A.* Translated by Luis A. Baralt. Carbondale: Southern Illinois University Press, 1966.

———. *Obras completas.* 74 vols. Havana: Editorial Trópico, 1936–53.

Martin, Percy. *Latin America and the War.* Baltimore: The Johns Hopkins Press, 1925.

Martínez Estrada, Ezequiel. *Diferencias y semejanzas entre los países de la América Latina.* Mexico: Escuela Nacional de Ciencias Políticas y Sociales, 1962.

May, Stacey, and Plaza, Galo. *The United Fruit Company in Latin America.* National Planning Association, *U.S. Business Performance Abroad,* no. 7. New York, 1958.

Mead, Margaret. "The Study of National Character." In *The Policy Sciences,* edited by Daniel Lerner and Harold Lasswell. Stanford, Cal.: Stanford University Press, 1951.

Mendoza de Montero, Angélica. *Líneas fundamentales de la filosofía de John Dewey.* Buenos Aires: Instituto Cultural Argentino Norteamericano, 1940.

———. *Panorama de las ideas contemporáneas en los Estados Unidos.* Mexico: Fondo de Cultura Económica, 1958.

Merrill, John C. *Gringo: The American as Seen by Mexican Journalists.* Gainesville: University of Florida Press, 1963.

"Mesa rodante: Imperialismo y buena vecindad." *Cuadernos Americanos* 6, no. 5 (1947):64–88. A symposium.

Milla, José. *Un viaje al otro mundo, pasando por otras partes, 1871 a 1874.* 3d ed. 3 vols. Guatemala: Tipografía Nacional, 1936.

Miranda, Francisco de. *The Diary of Francisco de Miranda.* Edited by William S. Robertson. New York: Hispanic Society of America, 1928. Spanish text.

———. *Fragments from an Eighteenth-Century Diary: The Travels and Adventures of Don Francisco de Miranda.* Edited by Jordan H. Stabler. Caracas: Tipografía La Nación, 1931. English translation of some parts.

Mistral, Gabriela. See Godoy Alcayaga, Lucila.

Molina, Enrique. *Por los valores espirituales.* Santiago de Chile: Nascimento, 1925.

Monguío, Luis. "Nationalism and Social Discontent in Literature." *Annals of the American Academy of Political and Social Science* 334 (1961):63–73.

Montenegro, Ernesto. *Puritanía, fantasías y crónicas norteamericanas.* Santiago de Chile: Nascimento, 1934.

Monte y Aponte, Domingo del. *Escritos.* 2 vols. Havana: Cultural, 1929. Vol. 2 contains essays on American literature.

Morison, Samuel Eliot. *The Maritime History of Massachusetts, 1783–1860.* Sentry ed. Boston: Houghton Mifflin, 1961.

Moses, Bernard. *The Intellectual Background of the Revolution in South America.* New York: Hispanic Society of America, 1926.

Mujica Laínez, Roberto. "An Argentine's USA." *Americas,* January 1954, p. 15.

Nichols, Madeline. *Sarmiento: A Chronicle of Inter-American Friendship.* Washington, 1940.

Nichols, Roy F. "Trade Relations and the Establishment of United States Consulates in Spanish America." *Hispanic American Historical Review* 13 (1933):289–313.

------. "William Shaler, New England Apostle of National Liberty." *New England Quarterly* 9 (1936):71–96.

Núñez, Enrique Bernardo. *Viaje por el país de las máquinas (Signos del tiempo)*. Caracas: Ediciones Garrido, 1954.

Núñez, Estuardo. *Autores ingleses y norteamericanos en el Perú*. Lima: Ministerio de Educación Pública, 1956.

------. "Franklin en América hispana." *Cuadernos Americanos*, 1956, pp. 155–68.

------. "Hipólito Unánue y la cultura inglesa y norteamericana." *Ipna* (Lima) 28 (1955):23.

------. "El poeta Chocano en Nueva York." *Cuadernos Americanos*, May–June 1954, pp. 292–98.

Nunn, Marshall E. "Rubén Darío y los Estados Unidos." *América* (Havana), February 1939, pp. 61–64.

Nye, Russell B. *The Cultural Life of the New Nation, 1776–1830*. Torchbook ed. New York: Harper and Row, 1963.

O'Gorman, Edmundo. "Carta sobre los norteamericanos." *Cuadernos Americanos*, January–February 1947, pp. 151–57.

Oliveres, Ramón. *El imperialismo yanqui en América*. Buenos Aires, 1952.

Onís, José de. *The United States as Seen by Spanish American Writers*. New York, 1952. A painstaking study with many quotations.

Oribe, Emilio. "Some Aspects of Thought in the New World." In *The Old and the New World: Their Cultural and Moral Relations*. Paris: UNESCO, 1956.

Orjuela, Héctor H. "Rafael Pombo y la poesía anti-yanqui de Hispanoamérica." *Hispania* 45 (1962):27–31.

Oropesa, Juan. "Imparidad del destino americano." *Revista Nacional de Cultura* 7 (1945):22–33.

Ortiz, Fernando. *El engaño de las razas*. Havana: Editorial Páginas, 1946.

Ortiz Vargas, A. *Las torres de Manhattan*. Boston: Chapman and Grimes, 1939.

Otero, Gustavo Adolfo. *Estados Unidos en 1941*. La Paz, 1941.

Otterson, J. E. *Foreign Trade and Shipping*. New York: McGraw-Hill, 1945.

Palacios, Alfredo. *Nuestra América y el imperialismo yanqui*. Buenos Aires: Editorial Palestra, 1961.

Palmer, Thomas W., Jr. *Search for a Latin American Policy*. Gainesville: University of Florida Press, 1957.

Parks, E. Taylor. *Colombia and the United States, 1765–1934*. Durham, N.C.: Duke University Press, 1935.

Paz, Octavio. *The Labyrinth of Solitude*. Translated by Lysander Kemp. New York: Grove Press, 1961.

Pereira Salas, Eugenio. *Las aventuras de don Vicente Pérez Rosales en California*. Santiago de Chile: Imprenta Universitaria, 1949.

------. *Buques norteamericanos en Chile a fines de la era colonial*. Santiago de Chile: Imprenta Universitaria, 1936.

------. *Henry Hill, comerciante, vice-cónsul y misionero*. Santiago de Chile: Imprenta Universitaria, 1940.

------. *Jeremías Robinson, agente norteamericano en Chile, 1818–1823*. Santiago de Chile: Imprenta Universitaria, 1937.

Pereyra, Carlos. *El mito de Monroe*, Madrid: Editorial América, 1914.

Pérez Guerrero, Alfredo. *United States of America: Objective or Beginning?* Quito: Editorial Universitaria, 1958.

Pérez Rosales, Vicente. *Recuerdos del pasado, 1814–1860.* Santiago de Chile: Imprenta Barcelona, 1910.

Perry, Edward. "Anti-American Propaganda in Hispanic America." *Hispanic American Historical Review* 3 (1920):17–40.

Phelan, John Leddy. "Pan Latinism, French Intervention in Mexico, and the Genesis of the Idea of Latin America." In *Conciencia y autenticidad históricas,* edited by Juan A. Ortega, pp. 279–88. Mexico: UNAM, 1968.

Pierson, W. W. "Alberdi's Views on the Monroe Doctrine." *Hispanic American Historical Review* 3 (1920):362–74.

Pike, Frederick B. *Chile and the United States, 1880–1962.* Notre Dame, Ind.: Notre Dame University Press, 1963.

Pinochet, Tancredo. *The Gulf of Misunderstanding.* New York: Boni and Liveright, 1920.

Piper, Anson C. "El yanqui en las novelas de Rómulo Gallegos." *Hispania* 33 (1950):338–41.

Plaza Lasso, Galo. "Problems of Education in Latin America." In *Latin America: Evolution or Explosion?,* edited by Mildred Adams. New York, 1963.

[Poinsett, J. R.]. *Notes on Mexico, Made in the Autumn of 1822 . . . by a Citizen of the United States.* Philadelphia, 1824.

Pombo, Rafael. *Poesías completas.* Madrid: Aguilar, 1957.

Portilla, Jorge. "La crisis espiritual de los Estados Unidos." *Cuadernos Americanos,* September–October 1952, pp. 69–87.

Quesada, Vicente. *Los Estados Unidos y la América del Sur: Los yankees pintados por sí mismos.* Buenos Aires, 1893.

Quintanilla, Luis. *A Latin American Speaks.* New York: Macmillan, 1943.

Raat, William. "Leopoldo Zea and Mexican Positivism." *Hispanic American Historical Review* 48 (1968):1–18.

Radler, D. H. *El Gringo: The Yankee Image in Latin America.* Philadelphia: Chilton Co., 1962. Mostly personal notes.

Ramos, Samuel. *Profile of Man and Culture in Mexico.* Austin: University of Texas Press, 1962.

Rasmussen, Wayne D. "The United States Astronomical Expedition to Chile, 1849–1852." *Hispanic American Historical Review* 34 (1954):103–13.

Reid, John T. "As the Other Americans See Our Literature." *South Atlantic Quarterly* 40 (1941):211–19.

———. "Recent Theories of *Americanismo.*" *Hispania* 23 (1940):67–72.

Reissig, Luis. *Algunas observaciones de un viaje por América.* Buenos Aires, 1947.

Rémond, Réné. *Les Etats-Unis devant l'opinion française, 1815–1852.* 2 vols. Paris: A. Colin, 1962. A very careful study, based on written materials, which provided several valuable suggestions for this survey.

Restrepo, José Manuel. *Autobiografía.* Bogotá: Empresa Nacional de Publicaciones, 1957. Includes *Diario de un viaje de Kingston a Nueva York.*

Reyles, Carlos. "La cultura europea y el rumbo fijo del destino humano." In *Europa-América latina,* Comisión Argentina de Cooperación Intelectual. Buenos Aires, 1937.

———. *La muerte del cisne.* Paris: Ediciones Literarias, 1910.

Reynal, Rafael. *Viaje por los Estados Unidos del Norte, dedicado a los jóvenes mexicanos de ambos secsos.* Cincinnati, 1834.

Rippy, J. Fred. Introduction to Manuel Ugarte, *Destiny of a Continent.* New York, 1925.

———. *Joel R. Poinsett, Versatile American.* Durham, N.C.: Duke University Press, 1935.

———. *Latin America in World Politics.* New York: Knopf, 1928.

———. "Literary Yankeephobia in Hispanic America." *Journal of International Relations* 12 (1922):350–71, 524–38.
———. "Pan Hispanic Propaganda in Hispanic America." *Political Science Quarterly* 37 (1922):389–414.
Robertson, William S. "The First Legations of the United States in Latin America." *Mississippi Valley Historical Review* 2 (1915):193–96.
———. *Hispanic American Relations with the United States.* New York: Oxford University Press, 1923. This excellent study, although old, is still useful.
———. *The Life of Miranda.* 2 vols. Chapel Hill: University of North Carolina Press, 1929.
———. *Rise of the Spanish American Republics.* New York: D. Appleton and Co., 1918.
Robinson, William Davis. *A Cursory View of Spanish America.* Georgetown, D.C., 1815.
Rocafuerte, Vicente. *Colección Rocafuerte.* 16 vols. Quito: Edición del Gobierno del Ecuador, 1947. *Ideas necesarias a todo pueblo que quiere ser libre* in vol. 3; *Cartas de un americano* in vol. 4.
Rodó, José Enrique. *Ariel.* Edited by Alberto Nin Frías and John D. Fitzgerald. New York: Sanborn, 1928.
———. Prólogo to *Idola fori,* by Carlos-Arturo Torres, pp. 11–29. Bogotá: Editorial Minerva, 1935.
Roggiano, Alfred A. *Pedro Henríquez Ureña y los Estados Unidos.* State University of Iowa Studies in Spanish Language and Literature, no. 12. Mexico, 1961.
Rojas Paz, Pablo. *Alberdi, el ciudadano de la soledad.* Buenos Aires: Editorial Losada, 1941.
Romanell, Patrick. *Making of the Mexican Mind.* Lincoln: University of Nebraska Press, 1952.
Romero, José Luis. *Las ideas políticas en Argentina.* Mexico: Fondo de Cultura Económica, 1959.
Rowland, Donald. *History of the Office of the Coordinator of Inter-American Affairs.* Washington, 1947.
Salas, Manuel de. *Escritos de Don Manuel de Salas.* 3 vols. Santiago de Chile: Imprenta Cervantes, 1910–14.
Salazar Romero, Carlos. *Principios y prácticos para la educación secundaria en el Perú.* Lima, 1961.
Samper, José María. Essay in Sociedad de la Unión Americana, *Colección de ensayos y documentos relativos a la unión y confederación de los pueblos hispanoamericanos,* pp. 344–69. Santiago de Chile, 1862.
———. *Historia de una alma.* Bogotá, n.d.
Sanchez, Luis Alberto. *Balance y liquidación del novecientos.* Santiago de Chile: Ercilla, 1941.
———. "A New Interpretation of the History of America." *Hispanic American Historical Review* 23 (1943):441–56.
———. *Nueva historia de la literatura americana.* Buenos Aires: Editorial Americalee, 1944.
———. *Un sudamericano en Norteamérica.* Santiago de Chile: Ercilla, 1942.
Sarmiento, Domingo Faustino. *A Sarmiento Anthology.* Edited by A. W. Bunkley. Princeton: Princeton University Press, 1948.
———. *Facundo o civilización y barbarie.* Buenos Aires: Editorial la Facultad, 1938.
Schmitt, Karl M., and Burks, David D. *Evolution or Chaos: Dynamics of Latin American Government and Politics.* New York: Praeger, 1963.

Schwab, V. F. "El inventario de la bibloteca de Francisco Javier de Luna Pizarro." *Fénix* (Lima), vol. 7 (1950).

Scopes, Wilfred, ed. *The Christian Ministry in Latin America and the Caribbean.* New York and Geneva: The World Council of Churches, 1962.

Seoane, Manuel. *El gran vecino: América en la encrucijada.* 2d ed. Santiago de Chile: Editorial Orbe, 1944.

Shearer, James F. "Pioneer Publishers of Textbooks for Hispanic America: The House of Appleton." *Hispania* 27 (1944):21–28.

Shepherd, William R. "Bolivar and the United States." *Hispanic American Historical Review* 1 (1918):270–89.

Shirley, Elizabeth H. "Fernando Bolivar and the University of Virginia." Pan American Union, *History Series*, no. 1 (1929).

Sierra, Justo. *Obras completas.* Mexico, 1948. Vol. 6 contains notes on his trip to the United States.

Silvert, Kalman H. *The Conflict Society: Reaction and Revolution in Latin America.* New Orleans: Tulane University Press, 1961.

Simmons, Merle E. "Attitudes toward the United States Revealed in Mexican *Corridos.*" *Hispania* 36 (1953):34–42.

Simmons, Ozzie G. "The Mutual Images and Expectations of Anglo-Americans and Mexican-Americans." *Daedalus,* Spring 1961, pp. 286–99.

Stabb, Martin S. *In Quest of Identity: Patterns in the Spanish American Essay of Ideas, 1890–1960.* Chapel Hill: University of North Carolina Press, 1967.

―――. "Martí and the Racists." *Hispania* 40 (1957):434–39.

Stabler, J. H. See Miranda, Francisco de.

Stewart, Watt, and French, William. "The Influence of Horace Mann on the Educational Ideas of Domingo Sarmiento." *Hispanic American Historical Review* 20 (1940):12–31.

Subercaseaux, Benjamín. *Retorno de U.S.A.* Santiago de Chile: Zig-Zag, 1943.

Tablada, Juan José. "Norteamérica rudamente juzgada." *Repertorio Americano* 3 (1921):9–10.

Tannenbaum, Frank. "Toward an Appreciation of Latin America." In *The United States and Latin America.* New York: The American Assembly, 1959.

Thomson, Charles A. *Overseas Information Service of the United States Government.* Washington: The Brookings Institution, 1948.

Thomson, Charles A., and Laves, Walter. *Cultural Relations and United States Foreign Policy.* Bloomington: Indiana University Press, 1963.

Torre Grovas, Silvio de la. *Educación y filosofía en Norteamérica.* Camagüey, Cuba, 1952.

Torres, Carlos-Arturo. *Idola fori.* Bogota: Minerva, 1935.

Torres, Manuel. "The United States in 1850." *Americas,* February 1964, pp. 1–8. Views of José Eusebio Caro.

Torres-Ríoseco, Arturo. *The Epic of Latin American Literature.* Berkeley: University of California Press, 1942.

Ugarte, Manuel. *Destiny of a Continent.* New York: Knopf, 1925.

Unión Panamericana. *Materiales para el estudio de la clase media en la América latina.* Washington: Publicaciones de la Oficina de Ciencias Sociales, Unión Panamericana, 1950.

United States Senate, Committee on Foreign Relations. *Soviet Bloc Latin American Activities and Their Implications for U.S. Foreign Policy.* Washington, 1960.

―――. *United States Business and Labor in Latin America.* Washington, 1960.

Urist, Harold E. "Portrait of the Yanqui." *The International Quarterly* 2, no. 4 (1940):25–30.

Uzcátegui, Emilio. *Los Estados Unidos como los he sentido yo.* Quito: Empresa de Publicidad Dinamia, 1942.

Valero, Fernando. *Bosquejo de los Estados Unidos de Norte América.* Guatemala, 1830.

Vargas H., Jorge. "Cartas importantes." *Papel Periódico Ilustrado* 3 (1884): 338–42.

Vargas Vila, José María. *Ante los bárbaros.* Barcelona: R. Palacios Viso, 1917.

Varona, Enrique José. "Emerson." In Varona, *Obras,* 2:287–313. Havana: Cultural, S.A., 1936–38.

―――. "El imperialismo yankee en Cuba." *Repertorio Americano* 3 (1922): 309–11.

―――. "Ojeada sobre el movimiento intelectual en América." In *Obras,* 2:81–105.

Vasconcelos, José. *Bolivarismo y monroismo: temas iberoamericanos.* Santiago de Chile: Ercilla, 1935.

―――. *Hispanoamérica frente a los nacionalismos agresivos de Europa y Norteamérica.* La Plata, Argentina: Imprenta de la Universidad de Buenos Aires, 1934.

―――. *Indología.* Barcelona: Agencia Mundial de Librería, [1926].

―――. *¿Qué es la revolución?* Mexico: Botas, 1937.

―――. *La raza cósmica.* Paris: Agencia Mundial de Librería, [1925].

―――. *De Robinson a Odiseo.* Mexico: Editorial Constancia, 1952.

Velasco del Campo, Nicolás. *El país de Kennedy.* Santiago de Chile, 1961.

Vicuña Mackenna, Benjamín. *Páginas de mi diario durante tres años de viaje, 1853–1854–1855.* Santiago de Chile, 1856.

Villoldo, Pedro. *Latin American Resentment.* New York: Vantage Press, 1959.

Washington, S. Walter. "A Study of the Causes of Hostility toward the United States in Latin America." Department of State, External Research Paper, no. 126 (Argentina, Chile). Washington, 1956.

Werlin, Joseph S. "Mexican Opinion of Us." *South Atlantic Quarterly* 43 (1944):233–47.

Whitaker, Arthur P., ed. *Latin America and the Enlightenment,* Ithaca, N.Y.: Cornell University Press, 1954.

―――. *The United States and the Independence of Latin America, 1800–1830.* Baltimore: The Johns Hopkins Press, 1941.

―――. *The Western Hemisphere Idea: Its Rise and Decline.* Ithaca, N.Y.: Cornell University Press, 1954.

White, John W. *Our Good Neighbor Hurdle.* Milwaukee: Bruce Publishing Co., 1943.

Wolfe, Wayne. "Attitudes toward the United States as Revealed in the Latin American Press." Ph.D. diss., Indiana University, 1961. Based on a content analysis of twenty-one Latin American newspapers.

Wood, Bryce. *The Making of the Good Neighbor Policy.* New York: Columbia University Press, 1961.

Yepes, J. M. *Del Congreso de Panamá a la Conferencia de Caracas.* 2 vols. Caracas, 1955.

Zaldumbide, Gonzalo, *José Enrique Rodó.* Montevideo: Biblioteca de la Academia Nacional de Letras, 1967.

Zea, Leopoldo. *América como conciencia.* Mexico: Ediciones Cuadernos Americanos, 1953.

―――. *Dos etapas del pensamiento en Hispanoamérica: Del romanticismo al positivismo.* Mexico: Colegio de México, 1949.

―――. *The Latin American Mind.* Norman: University of Oklahoma Press, 1963. Translation of *Dos etapas del pensamiento en Hispanoamérica.* Mexico: Colegio de Mexico, 1949.

———. *El positivismo en México.* Mexico: Colección Studium, 1953.

Zegrí, Armando. "Cosas que no debería decir." *Repertorio Americano* 19 (1929):93; 20 (1930):359.

Zorrilla de San Martín, Juan. *Las Américas.* Montevideo: Editorial Ceibo, 1945.

Zum Felde, Alberto. *Indice crítico de la literatura hispanoamericana: los ensayistas.* Mexico: Editorial Guaranía, 1954.

# Index

293